RIGGED

RIGGED

THE TRUE STORY OF A WALL STREET NOVICE WHO CHANGED THE WORLD OF OIL FOREVER

BEN MEZRICH

BLOOMSBURY

First published in Great Britain 2008

Copyright © 2007 by Ben Mezrich

The moral right of the author has been asserted

No part of this book may be used or reproduced in any manner
whatsoever without written permission from the Publisher
except in the case of brief quotations embodied in
critical articles or reviews

Bloomsbury Publishing Plc
36 Soho Square
London W1D 3QY

Bloomsbury Publishing, London, New York and Berlin

A CIP catalogue record for this book
is available from the British Library

ISBN 978 0 7475 9463 5

10 9 8

Printed in Great Britain by Clays Ltd, St Ives plc

The paper this book is printed on is certified by the © 1996
Forest Stewardship Council A.C. (FSC). It is ancient-forest friendly.
The printer holds FSC chain of custody SGS-COC-2061

FSC
Mixed Sources
Product group from well-managed
forests and other controlled sources
Cert no. SGS-COC-2061
www.fsc.org
© 1996 Forest Stewardship Council

AUTHOR'S NOTE

I never set out to write a book about oil.

The truth is, I've never really seen myself as that kind of writer. My stories—the stories that turn me on enough to get me to dedicate a year of my life to their telling—usually involve brilliant young kids pulling off incredible schemes: wads of cash strapped to backs, Ferraris, and long-legged models and locales so exotic I need the Internet to help me find them on a map.

I usually leave the big geopolitical issues to the kind of writers you normally see published in the *New Yorker* and the *Atlantic Monthly*.

With *Rigged,* I actually stumbled into oil. The story I set out to write was as wild a ride as I'd ever embarked on—involving a brilliant young Ivy League kid with balls of steel who had embarked on an adventure that involved all the elements a method writer like myself lives to chronicle. But the more I researched this Ivy League kid's tale, and the deeper I went into the world he described, the more I realized that there was a much bigger, much more important story to tell.

In real life, the kid's name is John D'Agostino. When I first met

D'Agostino, he was a second-year student at Harvard Business School. His girlfriend introduced me to him, and I was immediately struck by his intensity; in a way, there was something almost frightening about him. He was young, matinee-idol handsome, and polished. He had a grin that was friendly and engaging, but there was also a palpable edge behind his eyes. Maybe it was just me, but I caught a hint of *American Psycho* in him, beneath the polish. Not the part that involved chopping up prostitutes in his bathroom after work, but the smoldering fierceness of a young man powered by pure ambition. Everything about D'Agostino screamed purpose, from his perfect hair, combed so severely that you could see each strand, to the perfect suit, pressed so ruthlessly that you could cut bread with the creases. I knew immediately that D'Agostino was the kind of guy I wrote stories about—but it wasn't until six years later that I found out how right I was. D'Agostino—still with the same girlfriend—had called me out of the blue to invite me to ring the bell at the Mercantile Exchange in Lower Manhattan, where he was already a vice president at the unbelievably young age of twenty-five.

I didn't know anything about the Merc, other than the fact that it was the trading floor that had been featured in the Eddie Murphy movie *Trading Places*. In fact, I didn't even know that it was the place where oil was traded until D'Agostino gave me a tour of the facilities on my way to the bell-ringing ceremony. And it wasn't until I was standing up on a platform in the center of the trading floor, staring out at this crazed mob of Brooklyn-born Italians and Jews, that my mind began to whir and I had that familiar feeling that I was witnessing something that might be worth writing about. Because the Merc wasn't like anything I had ever seen before. *And this was where the price of oil came from? This was part of how that black juice got into my car?*

After ringing the bell, I cornered D'Agostino at the bar on the top floor of the exchange and immediately made my pitch. I wanted to write a story about the Merc, about the crazy young men who made fortunes on that trading floor, then spent those fortunes on fast cars and even faster girls. Etc., etc., etc. But D'Agostino laughed, telling me that the Merc was only the tip of the iceberg. Then his conversation shifted to Dubai—and suddenly I found myself uncovering a whole new story, one that truly blew my mind.

Right then and there, I knew I had the makings of my next book.

The problem was, John D'Agostino didn't want me to write *Rigged*. It wasn't just that the subject matter was controversial, involving the secret workings of a world most people had never even heard of; it was deeper than that, an intensely personal reluctance that had to do with D'Agostino's Italian Brooklyn background and the respect he had for the people who had helped him along the way. D'Agostino was on the inside—and in D'Agostino's world, people on the inside didn't talk to outsiders, especially writers.

Thankfully, I can be pretty persuasive. Eventually I did manage to convince D'Agostino to let me write the book; to appease his fears, I renamed the main character David Russo. Other than obvious public figures, I have not used any real names in telling this story. For the sake of narrative, and to protect the privacy of the individuals in this story, I compressed certain time periods and altered the identity and background of certain individuals so that they would not be recognizable. Characters such as Gallo and Khaled are composites and are not meant to portray particular people.

In the end, after reading the story, D'Agostino agreed to allow his real name in this author's note and in the afterword, which he wrote himself. I know that such an arrangement is unique in a work of nonfiction—but this is indeed a unique book.

Unique for me, as a writer, and hopefully just as unique for you, as a reader.

Ben Mezrich, Boston

PROLOGUE

Oil.

On the Arab street, they have another name for it: "the Black Blood of Allah." A gift, handed down directly from God, endowing the Muslim world with everlasting power over the West.

In the West, oil is no less influential; it is inarguably the most important tradable commodity on earth. Oil is the source of wealth and power, the currency that drives the world economy. Some believe it is also the cause of most wars and acts of terrorism.

In truth, there's a reason men fight wars over oil: at its essence, oil is energy. It powers everything. It is, in itself, *power,* but power with a price—historically, oil has always divided the world into two opposing forces: those who *have,* and those who *need.*

Very soon that historical fact may change. Because very soon oil may also end up bringing the world together in a way that politics, diplomacy, and war never could. . . .

Chapter 1

Three-thirty in the morning, maybe closer to four.

A packed club in the Flatiron District of Manhattan, a place called Gypsy Tea. Trendy as hell, the velvet rope outside lorded over by a doorman with a shaved head and a name nobody could pronounce, and a girl in a leather skirt so short she could have worn it as a wristband. Two couch-strewn floors teeming with pretty people in designer clothes, their New York hip-factor ratified by the fact that it was past three in the morning on a Tuesday and that they'd somehow made it past the door-bitches and their mysterious and uniquely New York vetting practices. The music was dangerously loud, bouncing off the walls in ear-shattering waves, and the champagne was flowing freely, splashing down the sides of crystal flutes and splattering all over the thick faux-leather carpeting.

The VIP area took up most of the back corner of the first floor, separated from the rest of the club by another velvet rope. The bouncers at this rope were wearing headsets and holding clip-boards, but the clipboards were really just for show. If you were going to get into the VIP, the bouncers wouldn't need to find your name on a list. The crowd beyond the rope was young—twenties and thirties—and obviously well-heeled. Bankers in tailored Brooks Brothers mingled with hip-hop execs in Armani and Sean John. Prime Time celebs swirled about like errant weather patterns, trailing wakes of PR flunkies, oversized bodyguards, and harried assistants. And of course, there were girls—there were always girls, models from Ford and Elite and Next, too tall and too thin and too angled, more giraffes than gazelles.

David Russo watched the circus from the safety of a corner banquette, his shoulders tense beneath the thin material of his charcoal-colored Zegna suit. The banquette was lodged behind a black marble table, which struggled beneath a glass metropolis of champagne and vodka bottles, ensconced by overflowing buckets of ice. David had a drink in his hand—something with vodka, he assumed—but he hadn't even taken a sip. Although he was not a stranger to places like this, he was definitely an outsider. At twenty-six, he had never made a hobby of decadence, and at this hour he was usually holed up in his office, preparing for the market's next opening, or home in bed with Serena, his girlfriend of two years. But tonight he hadn't had much of a choice. In less than a week, David's entire life was going to change—and he had to tread carefully. He had to keep up appearances, act as though nothing was out of the ordinary, no matter how far from ordinary things were about to become.

"Fucking awesome, isn't it?"

Michael Vitzioli winked at him from a thickly cushioned couch to his right, then high-fived the two young men sitting across the table from them. Joey Brunetti and Jim Rosa shouted something back, but their voices were lost in the noise of the club. David smiled and nodded, stifling his nervous energy as best he could. He had been watching the three traders decimate bottle after bottle of alcohol for the past few hours, and he was beginning to believe that the night would never end. For the hundredth time, he regretted accepting the invite from Vitzi and his trading partners—but really, David couldn't have turned them down. Over the last six months he had worked hard to win the trust of the traders—no small task, considering how different his background and theirs seemed to be. Even the way the three young men were dressed—Vitzi in a leather jacket and ripped jeans, Brunetti in a denim ensemble that would have given Serena a heart attack, and Rosa in what looked to be an overpriced sweat suit—betrayed the different paths they'd traveled to this chaotic, late-night moment. Even so, the three men had finally grown to accept David as one of their own. And if what David had planned was going to work, he needed to remain in their good graces. *He needed to continue to play the part.*

"Hell of a party," he shouted back to Vitzi. "You're gonna break a record tonight. That waitress nearly fainted when you ordered that twelfth bottle of Cristal."

Vitzi grinned. The excess of the evening was a point of pride to him, especially because he knew that word of the night's spending spree would move across the trading floor faster than he'd been spreading drinks around the VIP room. Vitzi certainly didn't care about the money; he had made five hundred thousand dollars' profit that morning. Half a million wasn't a record for the Merc Exchange, but it was a pretty damn impressive take. Especially considering that just two weeks earlier Vitzi had turned twenty-four.

"Can you fucking believe the girls in here?" Vitzi responded. Then he pointed at Rosa across the table. "Hey, maybe you can bring one of 'em to work with you tomorrow. Even the worst one here would be better than the shit you pulled yesterday."

Rosa's cheeks reddened as David and the others had a laugh at his expense. In truth, David knew that Rosa wasn't really embarrassed by the crack; his escapade of the day before was already fast becoming legend.

Yesterday morning, Rosa's clerk had called in sick just hours before the opening bell. The young trader had needed to find a replacement clerk, anyone at all—he had just needed a body on the floor. So he had brought along the woman who had happened to be in bed with him at the time—a prostitute he'd hired the night before. All morning the nineteen-year-old hooker had strolled up and down the trading floor in transparent, high-heeled shoes, her hair sprayed up to the ceiling.

"And nobody batted a fucking eye," David said out loud, shaking his head. Vitzi and Rosa high-fived again.

A hooker strolling around the trading floor, and nobody had even raised an eyebrow. David had been sequestered in his upstairs office during the entire episode, but he hadn't been surprised when he first heard the story. The New York Mercantile Exchange wasn't Wall Street, and the eight hundred or so traders who worked the Merc floor certainly weren't the regular Wall Street set. They didn't live in houses in the Hamptons or brownstones on Park Avenue. The Merc traders—guys like Vitzi, Rosa, and Brunetti—were mostly young men without college educations, from Italian and Jewish blue-collar backgrounds. *Sons of garbagemen and street cleaners, plumbers and electricians.* When they got rich on the Merc—Vitzi's half a million in an afternoon—they were the first in their families to ever have had access to that kind of wealth, and often they spent it as fast and furiously as they had made it.

If Wall Street was the financial equivalent of Vegas, the Merc was Atlantic City—on crack. At the same time, the Merc was one of the most important financial institutions that had ever been built. Because, unlike Wall Street, the Merc wasn't about stocks or bonds. The Merc was about something much more important. *Much more valuable.*

David felt the nervous energy inside him multiply as he watched Vitzi pour them all another drink, and he quickly took the opportunity to excuse himself. He started off toward the bathrooms, but as soon as he was out of sight of the three traders, he took a sharp right, pushing his way out of the crowded VIP room. A minute later, he had worked his way onto Twenty-first Street.

He moved beyond the velvet rope, strolling as calmly as he could down the sidewalk until he was fairly sure he was out of earshot of the bouncer and the woman in the napkin-sized skirt. Then he took his cell phone out of his pocket.

A brisk breeze pulled at his sleeve as he clicked the phone open. It was the middle of February, and David had left his over-coat back at his office when he joined the three traders for their first drink—fourteen hours ago. Still, the cold didn't bother him. His mind was already someplace else—a place that was always unbearably warm.

He dialed carefully, from memory. If anyone had been close enough to see, they would have been surprised by the number of digits he pressed into the phone. Although the destination of David's call was halfway around the world, that didn't explain all of the numbers he pressed. The first six were part of a code he had been given one week ago by a sixteen-year-old kid who had approached him in a Starbucks near his apartment in Midtown. *Encryption,* the kid had explained, in an accent David hadn't been able to place.

After he finished dialing, David pressed the phone against his ear. There was no ringing, just a series of clicks and a five-second pause. Then a familiar voice.

"It's almost time."

David smiled, despite his nerves. There was something about his friend's voice that always made him feel calm. It had a lilting quality, a mixture of accents that somehow mingled together into a tranquil whole. David immediately imagined his friend's face: the dark caramel skin, the jet black eyes, the ever-present half-smile. Roughly the same age as David, the friend on the other end of the line was more than just his counterpart on the project—he had become almost a brother.

"I'm standing in the middle of it," the friend's voice contin-ued. "Right where it's going to happen."

David closed his eyes and tried to picture it. First the bright-ness. Then the heat—mind-numbing, stifling, utterly debilitating. And then the sand—everywhere, always, shifting and turning like a living creature.

"Bulldozers," David said aloud, imagining them as he said the words. "Cranes. As far as the eye can see."

"The future, David."

"It's really going to be something, isn't it?" David asked. He could feel the nervous energy turning into excitement. He could not believe they were so close to completing what they had been working on for nearly a year. *So close to doing what nobody else had ever done.*

"Our children's children will thank us for it."

David opened his eyes and felt a chill rise through him that had nothing to do with the February breeze. He wasn't going to pretend that he really knew how much what he and his counterpart were about to do would affect the future. He didn't know if his children's children would thank him, or if he'd even ever have children who'd live to see what he'd done.

What David *did* know was that the thing he and his friend two continents away were planning was going to change the world. He also knew that there were people—powerful people—who would do almost anything to see them fail.

"I guess I'll see for myself in a few days," David said quietly.

"Allah willing," the young man responded. Then the line went dead.

Allah willing. Though the voice had remained lilting and calm, the words themselves were like a belt snapping tight. *Allah willing. My God,* David thought to himself, *do I really know what I've gotten myself into?*

He paused for a moment, staring at the phone in his hand.

TWO HUNDRED YARDS away and thirty feet up, a figure crouched low against the roof of a three-story warehouse. The figure was dressed entirely in black, nearly invisible against the backdrop of the predawn sky.

The figure watched through a high-powered telescopic lens as David Russo slid his cell phone into his pocket, took a deep breath, and slipped back into the throbbing club.

Chapter 2

David Russo would always remember the moment when clarity first hit him, mainly because clarity had chosen such an unfortunate, clichéd instance to finally find its way into his life.

David had spent nearly half of his twenty-five years on earth running away from the clichés of his background. Barely one foot out of the thickest Italian ghettos of Brooklyn and Staten Island, he had clawed and kicked his way to become the first kid in the history of his family to attend an elite college. From Williams, he had managed to get a partial-ride scholarship to Oxford; then on to Harvard Business School, where he had graduated near the top of his class. And yet as much as he'd always had an idea of what he was running from, he'd never had any clear vision of where he was trying to go. That was, until thirty seconds ago, when his destiny finally smacked him full in the face—ironically enough, as he was reaching toward a tray of hand-rolled cannolis.

At least the cannolis were being carried past David's table by a waiter in a tuxedo, each twist of sweet-cheese-filled pastry glistening in the soft light of the Waldorf-Astoria main ballroom's massive crystal chandelier. But they were indeed cannolis, and

David was, at that moment, surrounded by more Italian Americans than he'd ever seen in one room in his entire life.

"Just one, David. Not the whole tray."

David blinked at the sound of his girlfriend's voice, realizing suddenly that he had frozen in place, halfway out of his chair, both hands above the waiter's tray. He had no idea how long he had been standing like that; he had momentarily left his body as his attention was captured by something all the way on the other side of the massive, ornate banquet hall. He smiled sheepishly at the waiter, took one of the pastries, and lowered himself back into his chair as his gaze remained pinpointed on the far side of the hall. Even though the enormous room was filled with people, congregating in groups around the three dozen or so tables that pockmarked the lush carpeting, David had a clear line of sight all the way to the edge of the long wooden stage that framed the far side of the hall. There, seated at a table set off from the rest, surrounded on either side by the most recognizable faces of the Italian American community . . .

"That's him," David said simply. And suddenly everything seemed so clear to him. Why he was there—not just at the National Italian American Heritage Institute dinner, but there, in New York, after all those years of running away . . .

"That's who?" Serena interrupted, and David finally broke his gaze and turned to look at her. Even confused, she was beautiful. Cascading brown curls framing her angled, vaguely exotic face. Dark, almond-shaped eyes that hinted at her South American heritage. A black, strapless dress that showed off her porcelain shoulders and the soft glade of skin beneath her long, flawless neck. David had no idea how he'd found a girl like her in Boston, during his final year at HBS, or how he'd convinced her to move to New York with him just five months after they'd met. But however it had worked out, he was glad she was with him at this moment, glad she had accompanied him to the dinner, which at first had seemed like such a chore.

"Anthony Giovanni," David finally responded.

Serena reached for the brochure that had been placed next to the salad plate on the table in front of her. She skimmed past the long-winded title that filled most of the front page—"National Italian American Heritage Institute Dinner to Honor the Italian American Man of the Year"—and skipped straight to the bios. Of course Giovanni's came first, as he was the focus of the evening. Italian American Man of the Year, the reason that the most expensive ballroom in New York had been rented and invites had gone out to every rich or important Italian American in the tristate area—which pretty much meant every powerful Italian American in the country.

David knew that somewhere near the bottom of that same brochure, his own bio was laid out—in small type, two or three sentences jammed right up against the binding, a pair of staples crucifying half the letters of his last name. Along with his bio was some small mention of the scholarship the Heritage Institute had given him to pay for HBS—the reason he had been forced to piece together a tuxedo, dredge up one of his crimson Harvard ties from the back of his closet, and take Serena shopping for the dress neither one of them could really afford. But now it all seemed worthwhile.

"Right, Anthony Giovanni," Serena repeated, obviously not getting the bigger picture. "I guess he's the one getting the award tonight. Do you know him?"

David stared at her. She didn't understand. He turned back toward Giovanni. Now David had to crane his neck to catch a glimpse of the man, as he had almost vanished in a swirl of fawning sycophants. David recognized many of the faces bobbing in and out of his line of sight: Rudy Giuliani, of course. The police commissioner as well. A few heads of banks, a few CEOs—all fawning over Giovanni like he was royalty. And in truth, the man cut a royal figure. Midfifties, more than six feet tall, slick dark hair just barely graying at the edges, chiseled features—hell, he looked like a movie star. And he moved through the crowd around him like a rock star—shaking hands, kissing cheeks, sending ripples of admiration outward in concentric wavelets all the way across the hall.

"I don't *know* him," David said. "I want to *be* him."

David had never been more certain of anything in his life. In twenty years, he wanted to be sitting at that head table, right up against the stage. He wanted to be the man at the center of those waves. He had no idea how he was going to get there—but now at least he had a real flesh-and-blood goal. Before, he had read about Giovanni, even written a paper about him back at Oxford. But now, seeing the man real and alive for the first time, David was having an epiphany.

An epiphany with a side of cannoli, that is. He took a bite of the pastry, making sure the mascarpone didn't run down the lapels of his tux or ruin his tie. Though Serena wouldn't have minded if the entire pastry had ended up on the crimson strip of material; she had only tolerated it because he had bribed her with the dress she was wearing.

"So go over and talk to him," Serena said.

David rolled his eyes at her, exasperated. Seeing the man in the flesh was one thing. You didn't just go up and *talk* to Anthony Giovanni. The guy had more money than God. He was one of the richest Italian Americans in the country. He had made a fortune on Wall Street, then gone on to create a real estate empire. He owned restaurants, golf courses, movie theaters, whole fucking neighborhoods in Brooklyn and Staten Island. Currently, he was chairman of something called the New York Mercantile Exchange, some sort of stock market for energy futures that David had read about in business school. David wasn't exactly sure what the Mercantile Exchange was all about, but if Anthony Giovanni was involved, it had to be something important.

"Yeah, right." David glanced across the table at the other four couples relegated to the Siberia-like seating as far away from the stage as was geographically possible. Rented tuxes, a fair amount of hair spray, economical shoes and purses that reminded David of his aunts and cousins in Staten Island. It seemed like the

Waldorf-Astoria ballroom had boroughs just like the city outside.

"Seriously, David. I'm sure he'd be happy to offer you some advice. Just start off by asking him what he thought of your speech."

David shook his head grimly. He had given a short speech to a small crowd gathered in one of the tearooms of the hotel during the cocktail hour, well before the real dinner had begun, and he certainly would have noticed if Anthony Giovanni had been in the audience. As far as he could tell, Giovanni had only just arrived, considering the swarm of well-wishers that had swamped him over the past few minutes. The truth was, David was actually kind of glad Giovanni hadn't been there at the cocktail party to hear David's take on what it was like being a kid from his background at Oxford and HBS. David had read Giovanni's bio many times before; Giovanni had gone to the Citadel, spent time in the Navy, then returned to New York to build an empire with his bare hands. David had rowed crew, agonized through a couple of Boston winters, and in a few days was about to begin a crappy first-year analyst job at Merrill Lynch. David doubted the man would have seen much potential in him—at least not the sort of potential that turned on guys like Giovanni.

"Why don't I just go up on stage, grab the mike, and do a little karaoke to get his attention? Maybe a little Sinatra to get this started right."

Serena did what she usually did when he started acting like a jackass. She ignored him, instead turning toward one of the other women seated at the table to compliment her on her earrings. The conversation was over it seemed, and David was happy, for the moment, to just watch his idol from afar while finishing his cannoli and, for that matter, going to work on his oversize goblet of red wine.

At least the food was nothing to complain about. A mishmash of Italian delicacies served in no particular order—salads were still on the table, and David was already threatening the buttons of his tux jacket. He'd gone through a selection of focaccias, bruschettas, and prosciutto-wrapped asparagus; two different types of lasagna served as an appetizer; a carbonara that his mother would have flipped for; even a risotto with a fancy name he couldn't pronounce. And they hadn't even gotten to the main course yet. There was something about Italian food that seemed to make you hungrier the more of it you ate; it was no wonder most of David's uncles were clinically obese, and he was thankful that Serena's family staple of beans and rice had kept him from ballooning up in the three months since they'd been back in New York.

Still, he was already searching for the cannoli guy when his attempt at continued gluttony was interrupted by a thick hand on his shoulder. David looked up from his chair, only to see the light from the chandelier nearly blocked out by a massive, thick-necked man in an ill-fitting gray suit. The guy had a crew cut and a nose like a pug, and when he leaned close to David's ear, David had the sudden urge to hide under the table. Then to David's utter shock, the thick-necked guy uttered eight incredible words:

"Mr. Giovanni would like to speak with you."

David's jaw went slack as he stared at the behemoth. He didn't respond until Serena kicked him under the table. She'd obviously overheard.

"Are you sure?" David asked, feeling stupid the minute the question left his lips.

The man added a little pressure to the grip he had on David's shoulder.

"Listen, kid, I don't have all day. Are you coming or not?"

It was like something right out of a *Godfather* movie, but David didn't care, he was out of his chair so fast he nearly over-turned the table in the process. Serena squeezed his hand as he left the safety of the Staten Island table, following the big man on a winding path through the center of the great hall. Well, the giant didn't wind exactly, he waded right through the crowd, people scrambling to get out of his way. But David had to do his best serpentine just to keep up; by the time they reached the special table by the stage, David was nearly out of breath.

Christ, he thought to himself as the giant waved him through the group of mostly men who were still surrounding Giovanni's perch, *these are the most powerful gavones in the country.* Before David could dwell on the thought, he found himself face to face with Giovanni himself. Or more accurately, chest to face, as Giovanni was peering up at him from the comfort of his chair, a half-grin on his lips. David glanced around at the bank presidents, politicos, and CEOs who were watching with a mixture of amusement and irritation in their eyes, and then shrugged. *Fuck it, I'm here, I'm making the most of it.*

David tried to calm his racing heart as he held out his hand. Giovanni looked at the proffered appendage trembling in the air between them, then finally gave it a cursory shake, his grin deepening.

"I caught the tail end of your little speech earlier tonight from out in the hallway. You've got an interesting story, kid."

"Thank you, Mr. Giovanni," David blurted, his face flushed. He couldn't believe he was standing there, talking to one of the most powerful men in the country. He didn't want to fuck up the opportunity with too many words, but at the same time he could feel a million responses rising in his chest. He had never been that good at controlling what came out of his mouth in times of high pressure. But for the moment, he managed to keep it simple. "It's an honor to meet you."

Giovanni cocked his head to the side.

"Oxford. Harvard. Couldn't have gotten any farther away from Brooklyn if you'd hopped a boat to China."

David wasn't sure whether he was supposed to laugh, or whether Giovanni was being serious. David could see that most of the other guests at Giovanni's table were now listening to their conversation. David swallowed back a sudden burst of fear, doing his best not to topple over.

"Boston's not that far," he blurted. "There's a bus from the Port Authority every two hours."

"Hah," Giovanni grunted. The smile didn't change, so David

had no read on what Giovanni thought of his answer. "So what are you doing now?"

David was almost embarrassed to answer truthfully.

"I start with Merrill Lynch on Monday."

"Merrill Lynch? Why the fuck do you want to work there?"

The truth was, Merrill hadn't exactly been David's first choice. Unfortunately, he had graduated from business school in one of the worst years in MBA history. Where two years ago, kids were getting ten or eleven offers months before graduation, David's classmates were lucky to find one or two by the end of the school year. Although 9/11 was already a year old, the tragedy had killed the financial job market; there were signs that things were on the mend, but in the meantime, David had been forced to take the best job he was offered. Now he was looking forward to pushing paper around, compiling statistics, and cold-calling clients for a year or two as he tried to get his foot in the door somewhere else. But at least Merrill paid well. It wasn't the optimal situation, but it was a start.

"I like photocopy machines," David responded. "And making coffee. I'm really good at making coffee."

David knew that he was taking a chance, letting the thoughts come out as words without much interference. But he wanted to make some sort of impression at least, and he seemed to be succeeding. Giovanni was really looking at him now, that smile still firmly fixed on his handsome face.

"What are you afraid of, kid? What really scares you?"

It was an odd question, and David didn't know how he was supposed to answer. He could feel the rest of the table's attention on him, all those super-rich and super-powerful Italians watching him stew. *Well, fuck it,* he thought to himself. *I've been honest so far. No reason to change tack midsail.*

"Bears."

David regretted the answer the minute it left his lips. *Bears? What the fuck did that mean?* But it was too late to take it back. Giovanni's eyes widened a fraction of an inch. Then he crossed his arms against his chest.

"You're a real smart-ass, aren't you?"

David felt the heat rising in his cheeks. The conversation was not going well. Had he already screwed up his chance of getting in good with his idol, just minutes after meeting him? He wished Serena had been nearby to deck him before he'd let it go in this direction. But he was on his own.

"I try to be more smart than ass," he said, in the way of a quick apology, "but sometimes they seem to blend together."

Giovanni was smiling fully now, and David felt some of the pressure release. Maybe honesty had been the right choice all along. Giovanni was a god, to be sure, but he was also an Italian from Brooklyn.

"You got a sharp mouth, kid. When was the last time you got into a real fight?"

It was another strange question, and it kind of reminded David of the more bizarre interviews he'd had after business school, the kind where the guys in suits would try to throw you off by asking about the number of piano tuners in New York or the type of tree you'd like to be. But Giovanni wasn't interviewing him—was he? Maybe Giovanni was kidding—or maybe again he was seeking the truth.

The last real fight he had been in? David immediately flashed back to his first year at Oxford. Even though he had been through the preppy training camp that was Williams, he'd still had much of the street in him. He'd been tapped for the crew team based on his moderately athletic size and sports résumé—he'd lettered in both football and baseball in high school—but he hadn't quite gotten the knack of the Gentile endeavor. Then one sunny afternoon, during a multischool race on the Thames, the Cambridge crew "accidentally" bumped David's Oxford boat. After the two boats reached the finish line, the other members of David's crew had gotten out and were shaking the Cambridge team's hands. Without pause, David had walked right past them, picked out the biggest guy on the Cambridge crew, and decked the guy with a right hook to the jaw. Even though David had nearly gotten kicked out of Oxford for the incident, he had also gained the immediate respect of his crew team. They had felt he was just stupid and bullheaded enough to be their new captain—and nobody had ever "accidentally" bumped the Oxford boat again.

A good story, but David wasn't sure whether it was something you talked about in the Waldorf-Astoria ballroom with guys like Giuliani and a police commissioner listening in. So instead, David once again went with the first thing that popped into his head.

"About two hours ago," he said. "My girlfriend didn't like my tie. She feels that it's enough to have graduated from Harvard; you don't have to wear your résumé on your shirt."

Giovanni raised an eyebrow. "And you wore it anyway?"

David shrugged. "I like my girlfriend. But I worked my ass off to get this tie. It's not often I get invited to events where I get a chance to wear it."

Giovanni looked at David for a second. Then he grinned and reached into his jacket pocket. He handed David an embossed, robin's-egg-blue card: ANTHONY GIOVANNI, CHAIRMAN, NEW YORK MERCANTILE EXCHANGE.

"I like you, kid. I could use a smart-ass like you. See if you can get on my schedule."

David stared at the card, sparks flying through his veins. Was Giovanni offering him a job? Well, not exactly—"see if you can get on my schedule" wasn't quite the way Merrill Lynch had gone about it—but still, it was something, if not an open door maybe a window that wasn't entirely locked. David jammed the card into his pocket, shook the man's hand again, and started back toward his table. Before he'd gotten very far, Giovanni called out to him again.

"Hey, kid, next time listen to your girlfriend. If you showed up on the trading floor of the Merc wearing a tie like that, they'd be fishing you out of the Hudson the next morning."

This time David was pretty sure Giovanni was kidding.

Chapter 3

There was something uniquely soothing about the whir of helicopter blades. The rhythmic, circular disruption of air, each and every turn applying calculable lift, allowing a thing that should not fly instead to float, like a magic carpet in a child's coloring book—a carpet made of steel and Plexiglas and in this case solid gold. Even as the rhythm slowed and the floating, five-ton, bug-eyed carpet came to a gentle rest on the jutting ivory-white helipad, the whirring blades continued their soulful cadence, the long steel appendages cutting slower and slower arcs until all that was left was the beat of the thing itself, the soothing rhythm of a thing that should not be—but, indeed was.

Khaled Abdul-Aziz let the rhythm of the great mechanical carpet wash over him as he half-crouched, half-walked out from under the slowing rotors of Sheik Oman's luxury C-14 helicopter and onto the marble deck of the magnificently opulent yacht. When he was clear of the blades, he rose to his full six-foot-two and quickly surveyed his beautiful surroundings.

The view from the heavily tinted helicopter windows had not done the sheik's yacht justice. The ship was, in a word, fantastic.

Over three hundred feet long from bow to stern, four stories high, with a deck of solid white marble. The helipad behind Khaled was actually only one of two matching pads; the other was barely visible now, a hundred yards away at the other end of the massive ship. In between, Khaled could make out all three topside swimming pools, each almost as pristine and azure as the Mediterranean that surrounded them. Though it was barely ten in the morning, both Jacuzzis were in full use, as was the regulation-size beach-volleyball court, complete with bone-white sand imported directly from a beach in Carmel, California. In fact, the yacht seemed fairly crowded, especially considering that this was not exactly a leisure cruise. But then, the sheik never traveled with less than a small army. The yacht alone kept a full-time staff of forty, and that did not include the sheik's bodyguards, chefs, and attendants. Nor did the number include the beautiful women who always seemed to surround him—his wife, his seven daughters, and the miscellaneous hangers-on. Khaled doubted even the sheik could keep track of them all—or, for that matter, tell them all apart.

Khaled smiled as he saw Ali Agha, the sheik's favorite bodyguard, approach down a red carpet that had been laid out across the middle of the marble deck. Khaled had always liked Agha, probably because he had known the man since his early childhood. Agha had worked for the sheik for more than twenty years now; when Khaled had first met the former Lebanese soldier turned body builder, he had thought he was some sort of giant, like something from a fairy tale. Of course, Khaled had been six at the time, visiting his uncle in his summer palace in the kingdom for the very first time. It was shortly after Khaled's father's death, and he had been in need of fairy tales.

But Agha was no mythical creature—he was flesh and blood. All three hundred pounds of him, at the moment jammed into a dark three-button suit that seemed about to burst at every seam. He was grinning like a madman by the time he reached Khaled at the edge of the helipad, and he held out both hands, pulling Khaled in for a monstrous bear hug.

"Salaam Alekhem," Agha said, choosing the formal greeting, as the two had not seen each other for more than a year now. "Geneva has been good to you, Khaled. You look more like your father every time we meet."

Khaled smiled back. It was a wonderful compliment. His father had been one of the most popular actors in the Arab world, before the cancer had cut him short. His success in film was so great that Khaled had been forced to choose a career path as far from the arts as he could so as not to compete with an image he could only tarnish.

"Alekhem Salaam," Khaled responded. "And you look more like a mountain every day. Is the sheik well?"

"As well as can be considering all of his daughters are on board. I told him to leave half of them behind when we left Monte Carlo, but he never listens."

"To any of us," Khaled agreed.

As they spoke, he let Agha lead him across the polished deck. The breeze was warm and peaceful, even though they were a good mile from shore. But the breeze was always peaceful here, Khaled reminded himself. He had spent so much time in the more landlocked parts of Europe, he had almost forgotten how beautiful the South of France was this time of year. Now that he was finished with his schooling, he was hoping to spend more time in warmer climes. However, he knew that would not be his decision to make. The business school in Geneva had been expensive, and now Khaled had debts to pay. Debts he would gladly pay, considering who his generous benefactor had been.

"He's in the parlor," Agha said, pointing past a pair of bikini-clad blond women sunning themselves on deck chairs. "In case you've forgotten, down the hatch, first door on your left."

Khaled nodded, trying not to stare at the women as he followed Agha's directions. They looked young, barely as old as Khaled himself, and at least twenty-five years younger than the sheik, but that was really par for the course. The sheik had built himself quite a reputation over the years, and it was not unwarranted. There were great benefits to being a secular innovator who also happened to be a high-ranking member of a royal bloodline. Especially a royal bloodline that happened to come from the most oil-rich region in the world.

The girls smiled at Khaled as he navigated past them, but he ignored their entreaties. He wasn't shy, but he was proper; where he was from, women did not dress like that, and it simply wasn't something he was used to. He had had one Western girlfriend during his college years at Cambridge, but she had been from a family almost as religious as his own. Different religion, of course, but she had not challenged his upbringing the way these two near-naked friends of his uncle's might. So instead of responding, he simply bowed at them as he went past, then quickly entered the interior of the yacht by way of the open hatch.

A carpeted stairway led down into a vast, ornate parlor. The carpets were all real fur, the walls thick leather, and there was artwork everywhere. Khaled recognized one Picasso and two Mondrians; his uncle had always been a fan of the post-impressionists. Khaled wasn't sure that the light from the twin Swarovsky crystal chandeliers hanging from the parlor's ceiling was sufficient for the artwork, but he certainly would not have insulted the sheik by bringing the fact to his attention. The sheik took such things very seriously.

Khaled spotted his uncle on the other side of the vast room, seated at a beautiful antique wooden desk by a pair of circular windows. As usual, the sheik was dressed in his white robes, complete with headdress. His square chin was resting on one hand as he leafed through a thick notebook, his lips moving as he worked through some arcane calculations in his head.

He looked up as Khaled crossed toward him, and a huge smile broke across his sun-darkened face. He leapt up from behind the desk, clapping his hands together.

"Khaled. Right on time. I trust the trip from Geneva was no problem?"

Private jet from Geneva to Nice. Private helicopter from Nice down the French coast to Monte Carlo, where a second helicopter had been waiting to take him directly to the yacht. *No problem at all.*

"I would travel half the world by donkey to see you, Uncle."

Khaled embraced the older man, nearly losing himself in the creases of the sheik's robes. When he pulled away, he saw that there were tears in his uncle's eyes. He knew what the older man was thinking: that Khaled's father was there, in Khaled's high caramel cheeks and striking dark eyes. Khaled took a step back, bowing slightly. Though the attention embarrassed him, he would never have complained. He owed the sheik so much. Geneva, Cambridge, before that a year at NYU—he would never have been able to make such a journey without the sheik's money and influence. And now, he knew, he would have to begin to repay that debt. The sheik had brought him to this yacht for a reason—and though Khaled did not yet know the sheik's plan for him, he would follow that plan to the ends of the earth.

The sheik shook the tears away, and without another word reached into the top drawer of his desk and retrieved a leather portfolio, zipped shut on one side. He looked Khaled straight in his dark eyes.

"You know the history of our family, Khaled?"

Khaled nodded.

"Of course, Your Excellency," he responded, using the most formal words he could find. He wasn't sure where his uncle was leading with this, but he knew he had not been brought to the yacht on a whim. His uncle had a plan for him—had always had a plan for him. "A thousand years in the desert—"

"Bedouins, nomads, wandering—and do you know how we survived for so long? Prospered, for so long?"

Khaled looked at the sheik. It was hard to picture the man he had always known like this—resplendent in robes, embraced by the trappings of an unimaginable fortune—as the heir to one of the oldest Bedouin dynasties in the region.

"We kept our eyes open," the sheik continued, answering his own question. "And we saw when the sand was shifting."

He took a heavy breath, then handed the leather portfolio to Khaled.

"The sand is shifting now, my nephew."

Khaled unzipped the portfolio and glanced inside. It was a letter of acceptance, an appointment to a position the sheik had obviously arranged for him. Khaled looked up from the portfolio, eyebrows raised—then nodded. If this was how his uncle felt he could best repay his debt, then he knew where he was headed next.

He embraced the sheik again. Then he headed out of the parlor. The sun hit him full in the face as he rose back onto the deck. The bikinied girls were on their stomachs now, but still they smiled up at him as he passed. Khaled did his best to ignore them; his heart was pounding, and he could feel the tension rising in his chest. *Anticipation.*

The sands were shifting, indeed. And his uncle was sending him directly into the center of that coming sandstorm.

Chapter 4

I'm sorry, David. He's on his way to his son's swim meet. But I'll give him the message that you called, I promise. And thanks again for the flowers. You're such a sweetheart."

David sighed to himself, the phone heavy against his ear. He rubbed his free hand against his bleary eyes.

"No, Harriet, you're the sweet one. I think I've spent more time this week talking to you than my girlfriend. But at least you still take my calls."

The woman on the other end of the line laughed. "Flowers today, chocolates yesterday, a photo of yourself on Wednesday with a box of freshly baked cookies—heck, David, you can call me for the next five years if you want. I just wish I had better news for you. But thank you again, and have a nice day."

David didn't move the phone right away, even as the dial tone lashed out at his eardrum. This was getting ridiculous. *Beyond ridiculous.* How long could Giovanni keep avoiding him? Seven days of phone calls—sometimes five, six times a day—and the furthest he had gotten was Harriet Farelli, Giovanni's pleasant if a bit matronly-sounding secretary. And David had tried everything.

First he'd sent résumés, references, transcripts. Then he'd moved on to the flowers and chocolates, resolved to at least win over Harriet, keeper of the phone, if he couldn't get to Giovanni himself. But now he was beginning to lose hope. Maybe he could get away with bothering Harriet for a few more days, but sooner or later someone at Merrill was going to wonder why he kept making these trips to the shared office attached to the firm's main library. And he certainly couldn't have made these calls from his cubicle up on the eighth floor. Not only didn't he have a door upstairs, he didn't really have walls or even much of a desk either. Just a chair, a computer, and a phone in full view of the thirty-five other first-year Merrill slaves—and worse yet, his cubicle was just a few yards away from the open-door office of his tight-ass thirty-year-old boss, who would have loved nothing more than to make an example of David in the first week to scare the hell out of the other firsties. No, David was better off risking suspicion by sneaking off to the library every few hours on some bullshit "research" excuse than getting himself fired by making these calls from his cubicle.

He leaned back in his chair, twirling the phone in front of him. The library office was small and stark—just a wooden desk, a few bookshelves, a pair of IBM workstations, and the phone. Still, David would have died for an office like this, somewhere he could just go and think, away from the constant noise of the banking floors. The other first-years were okay guys, he guessed; a few of them he knew from HBS, and the rest were pretty much carbon copies from Wharton, Stanford, MIT—wherever they were churning out kids like him, poor saps who'd entered business school at exactly the wrong moment in history. David often wondered where he'd have ended up if those fuckers hadn't chosen to crash those planes right at the start of his final year at HBS. Certainly he wouldn't have been at Merrill making seventy-five thousand per annum the hard way.

Pushing papers and making cold calls would have been heaven compared to what his job had actually turned out to be. By the end of the first day, he had been shifted from investment analysis to private banking. When he'd first heard the words, he'd thought maybe he was getting a break. Maybe he'd be meeting with celebrities and professional athletes and rich CEOs, discussing their investments. But he'd been dead wrong. His boss had him visiting old-age homes, sitting down with ninety-year-olds talking about retirement funds. He was spending his evenings reading up on IRAs and estate planning, and his days trucking across town to places he could only describe as death's waiting rooms. It was quite literally the worst job he could have imagined.

The only bright light in his professional life was that robin's-egg-blue card taped to the underside of his cubicle. Every morning at 6:00 A.M., a full hour before the other first-years arrived, he took the card out, stared at the name and number, and hurried to the library to make that first phone call. And every morning it had gone the same way. *Mr. Giovanni's in meetings all day today, he won't be able to fit you in. Mr. Giovanni's on his way to Chicago for a lunch. He won't be back in the city until tomorrow. Mr. Giovanni is playing racquetball this afternoon. He won't be getting any messages from some punk-ass kid he met at some dinner, a kid he's probably already forgotten about. . . .*

David closed his eyes, put the phone back in its cradle, and lowered his head to the desk. The wood felt cold against his cheek, and he could hear the quiet whir of the IBMs through the bones in his skull. He was at a loss for what to try next. More flowers? Maybe some jewelry? Fuck, he'd already won Harriet over. She'd probably go on a date with him by now if he were single—and maybe a decade or two older. How was he going to get past her to that bastard in the big office—

A high-pitched ring reverberated through the desk and nearly made David cough up that morning's coffee. He lurched back, almost overturning his chair in the process. Then he stared at the phone. In seven days, the hunk of plastic had never rung. David hadn't even realized that the thing could take incoming calls. For a moment, he wondered if he should answer it. He looked back over his shoulder, at the closed door. He hadn't seen anyone else in the library as he'd made his way to the office. He shrugged and reached for the receiver.

"David? Did I find you?"

David felt his eyes roll back in his head. *Just what he needed.*

"Mom, how the hell did you get this number?"

"A nice young man forwarded me over here when I called the number you gave me last week. Do you have two offices? That's great, honey, you're a real Manhattan big-shot now, two offices in one building—"

"I don't have two offices. This is the library. And I probably shouldn't be talking to you here."

David felt like putting his head through the desk. He was pretty sure his mother had been forwarded to the library phone by his boss, as nobody else would have been rude enough to answer his phone. That meant his boss was probably hovering around his cubicle, wondering where he was. *Great.* One week into his first real job, and his mother was already getting him into trouble.

He couldn't blame her, of course, because he knew her well enough not to be surprised by the call. She had always been a "hands-on" kind of mom. Especially since his father's accident, the family had been incredibly close-knit. David's going off to England for the two-year program at Oxford had nearly sent his mother to the hospital with fainting spells. As far as he knew, his mother had never been on an airplane, had never left New York State. It wouldn't have been a stretch to say she lived through her only son, and it had taken all of David's resources not to grow into one of *those* types of "only sons." Although sometimes Serena would argue that even his most herculean efforts hadn't been enough.

"Well, I just wanted to check in and see how the job is going. And make sure you're bringing Serena to dinner this Sunday night. You know it's a very special day for your father."

David felt his lips tugging down at the corners; he really didn't want to think about his father's special day at the moment, because it was still hard for him to accept what had happened and how it had changed things at home. One year of high-intensity therapy finished was no small feat, and his father deserved to celebrate—but David wanted his mind clear to deal with his current dilemma.

"I know, Mom. We'll be there."

Before his mom could respond, a loud beep signaled that there was a second call on the line. David raised his eyebrows, wondering how the hell he could get two calls in one day on a phone that had never rung before. Then he realized it was probably his boss. Maybe he was about to get fired. Well, considering that he was supposed to visit two old-age homes later that afternoon, he wasn't sure that would be such a bad thing. Then again, seventy-five thousand dollars was seventy-five thousand dollars. And even with his scholarship from the Italians, he had loans to pay back.

"I gotta go, Mom," he said quickly, clicking over to the other call before she could say anything else. "Hello? Just finishing up here, I know I've been away from my desk a while and I'm really sorry—"

"David?" a woman's voice interrupted, and David suddenly realized it was Harriet, Giovanni's assistant. "You still there? I tried your office number and some unpleasant young man sent me over here."

David could picture the smoke coming out of his boss's ears—two calls forwarded over to David in a matter of minutes. He probably thought David was running some sort of phone sex line out of the library. But David didn't care about his boss at the moment, because if Harriet was calling him back it had to be good news.

"I'm here. Did I get through?"

"Morton's, in two hours. The table is under his name. Don't be late." With that, she hung up.

David slapped the phone down, blood rushing to his ears. Then he looked at his watch. He'd have to cut out of work an hour early. Shit, he'd definitely get in trouble, maybe even fired. But Anthony Giovanni had invited him to dinner.

Or had he? David couldn't be sure that Harriet hadn't simply snuck him onto the reservation. Dinner at Morton's certainly wasn't the sort of meeting David had expected when Giovanni had told him to try to get on his schedule.

Well, it didn't really matter, because David wasn't going to miss that appointment. Not even an army of Merrill Lynch middle managers armed with rapidly expiring retirement accounts could have kept him away.

Chapter 5

Geography aside, it was hard to tell where Wall Street ended and Morton's began. The minute David stepped through the door of the hallowed steak house cum financial hangout on Forty-fifth and Fifth, he was accosted by a cacophony of sounds and scents that reminded him of the social outings he'd endured back at HBS. The air was so thick with clouds of cigar smoke that David would have needed a gas mask to make out the old-world Chicago decor, and the overwhelming mixed scent of whiskey, bankers, and roasting dry-aged meat was so intense that he wasn't sure whether he wanted to salivate or vomit—maybe a little of both.

The place was crowded, even though it was barely 6:00 P.M., and it took David nearly five minutes to get the attention of the overdressed, overweight host with the restaurant's coveted seating chart. Of course, the rotund man didn't need to consult the chart to direct David toward Giovanni's table; though there were four corners to the rectangular steak house, there was only one "corner table."

David did his best to compose himself as he made his way through the crowded restaurant, navigating carefully between the tables that seemed dangerously close together, especially considering that most of the waitstaff were obese and most of the clientele were already three whiskeys deep. David hoped he wasn't sweating too much beneath his herring-gray Brooks Brothers suit. He was pretty sure he had escaped Merrill without his boss noticing his early departure, but the five-block record-breaking journey to the restaurant was a blur of near-death experiences involving taxicabs, pretzel vendors, and tourists. At least now the tourists had something to tell their friends back home about—the crazy fucking kid in a banker's monkey-suit sprinting through red lights while a guy in a vendor's apron screamed after him, tossing pretzels at the back of his head.

Somehow he'd made it, with a few minutes to spare. Following the directions the maître d' had given him, David spotted his quarry, mentally taking in the corner table with quick flicks of his eyes. Anthony Giovanni was seated at the center, his hair and suit immaculate, a glass of scotch at his lips and a cigar in his outstretched right hand. To Giovanni's left was a man David vaguely recognized from the financial newspapers: Jim Lowell, a preppy, midforties banker and near-billionaire who was currently trying to buy the New York Knicks. To Lowell's left was another almost familiar face: Doug Masters, the head of a consulting behemoth that had rejected David's résumé—thank God, as David had no interest in the world of consulting—a few months before he'd landed the Merrill job.

On Giovanni's other side was a man David didn't recognize: dark hair, dark eyes, wide shoulders, young—maybe late thirties, definitely under forty—and handsome in a Baldwinesque sort of way. Not exactly Alec, but somewhere on the way to Billy. The unknown man spotted David first, nudging Giovanni in a manner that immediately told David the two were colleagues, if not equals.

"There he is," Giovanni said, waving his cigar and kicking out the empty chair closest to David. "Right on time and not a hair out of place. Gentlemen, meet my assistant's newest crush, David Russo."

David tried not to blush as he shook hands all around, then lowered himself into the free seat, directly across from Giovanni.

"I'm not kidding," Giovanni continued, grinning. "Harriet's got your fucking picture taped to the wall above her desk. Chocolate and flowers? I like a kid who gets creative, but now your girlfriend's got a real fight on her hands."

David laughed as a waiter placed a glass of scotch in front of him, then passed out poster-sized menus. After the waiter had explained the specials, Giovanni waved him away, then finally introduced the man to his left.

"Nick Reston, youngest president in the history of the Merc Exchange. He's my right-hand man, and I'd have resigned as chairman long ago if I didn't have Nick around to keep the fucking traders out of my hair. Now that that's out of the way, no more business until after we eat. You boys need to realize that to gavones like me and David, eating is religion. You don't sully religion with business."

The next hour went by like a blur as David did his best to keep up with the conversation while wolfing down a piece of steak big enough to hang from a meat hook. True to his word, Giovanni kept the dialogue away from business—which was a good thing considering that David was so far below these men in terms of pecking order, he should have been wearing an apron and telling them about the dessert specials. During the meal, David spent much of the time taking mental notes about Giovanni and the others—especially Reston. He still didn't really know what the Mercantile Exchange was all about, nor did he have any idea what Giovanni and Reston did as chairman and president. But he could tell, even from the nonbusiness conversation, that Reston was sharp, polished, probably a genius. He had a bit of a Texas accent and a little bit of cowboy toughness in his speech patterns, but even so, David could see that the man was as smart as anyone he had gone to school with. From snippets of conversation, he found out a bit about the man's history. Ten years ago, in his midtwenties, Reston had been some sort of rock-star trader for an oil company in Houston when he'd been invited by an associate he'd met at a conference to work at the Merc. He'd taken the opportunity, even though it had meant a huge pay cut and a major change in lifestyle. He'd quickly risen in prominence, making a small fortune on the trading floor—and catching Giovanni's eye. Giovanni, who'd first made his fortune in real estate and then doubled it on the trading floor, had already grown to prominence as a key member of the board that ran the Merc. Recognizing Reston's abilities, the older man had yanked him under his wing. Together, they had built a power base among the board, and when Giovanni had been elected chairman, it hadn't taken long for him to get Reston the president's seat, despite the Texan's age.

Reston seemed like a straight shooter, brilliant but also hard as nails. David noticed that Reston was somewhat ignoring him during the meal, not openly—nothing rude—but he never seemed to address David directly. It kind of reminded David of the kids at Oxford who wanted nothing to do with the little shit from Brooklyn, so they just pretended he wasn't there. David couldn't help wondering if Reston was going to be a problem.

After the meal was finally cleared away, the billionaire and the consultant demigod excused themselves, and David found himself left alone at the table with Giovanni and Reston. Giovanni quickly ordered another round of scotch; it would be David's fourth—difficult, but hopefully not disastrous. He'd learned to drink at Oxford, of course, but he'd lost some of his skills over the past two years.

When the drinks arrived, Reston surprised David by suddenly turning to face him head on, his own drink raised.

"So, kid," he said, which seemed kind of funny considering he didn't look that much older than David, "what do you know about the Merc Exchange? The NYMEX?"

David touched his scotch to Reston's, then took a long sip. He could feel Giovanni watching, amused.

Maybe it was the booze, or maybe it was the massive hunk of meat in his stomach, but David decided it was time to stop being intimidated by these guys just because they were richer, more powerful, smarter—well, goddamn *intimidating*.

"Not a damn thing," he answered.

Reston laughed.

"Good fucking answer. Well, it's not rocket science. An exchange is like a soccer field. It's where the game takes place. We're the officials who make sure that the game is played fairly, that everyone follows the rules. The NYMEX started as a potato exchange. That's right, people came to us to trade potato contracts. Then orange juice and sugar."

"And now?" David asked.

"Energy," Reston said, slamming his emptied glass of scotch onto the table in front of him. "Ener-fucking-gy."

"Nick," Giovanni chided, "you always gotta complicate things. Oil, David. We trade oil on the NYMEX. Oil is energy, yeah, but it's more than that. Oil is money. Oil is power. Oil is everything. That's why we're the most important institution in the city—fuck it, in the world."

David leaned back in his chair, watching the two of them as they played off each other.

"Nine-eleven," Reston said, waving a hand above his head as if conjuring it all with one gesture. "You know what one of the first businesses in New York City that reopened after the disaster was? The NYMEX. Not the banks, not the supermarkets, not the schools. The Merc. Because oil is the lifeblood of this country. Our economy runs on it. Hell, oil is the new currency."

"And you guys trade oil," David said, but Giovanni shook his head.

"No, we run the exchange. The traders trade. Both Nick and I used to be traders. I spent twenty-five years on the floor. Nick put in ten. The traders technically own the NYMEX. But we run it."

David nodded. He had a vague notion about the trading world—Merrill Lynch had traders too, guys in suits and suspenders who spent their days on the chaotic New York Stock Exchange, shouting out the orders that were sent down to them via phone and computer from the big boys in the corner offices. Even though he'd been to business school, David knew very little about their work—really just what he'd seen in movies and on TV. But Giovanni and Reston were talking about traders who traded oil, which he guessed was a very different game. Even the word itself, *oil*, invoked emotion, considering how much it was talked about in the news and on the streets.

"So the traders control the price of oil," David started, putting it all together.

"No," Reston corrected. "Like on any exchange, supply and demand control the price of oil. The traders try to predict that price, try to react to that price, and try like hell to get rich from that price."

"Look," Giovanni suddenly interrupted, "don't worry about that right now. Worry about it on Monday, because starting Monday, you work for me."

David stared at him. Giovanni finished his scotch, stood up, and walked away from the table, heading right for the restaurant's front door. David watched in shock, realizing that Giovanni wasn't coming back. Just like that—*starting Monday, you work for me*—no title, no salary, just the statement hanging in the air.

Reston grinned at him.

"You don't get it, do you? He wants you to be one of 'Giovanni's Kids.' Make some fucking phone calls, ask around. This is what he does. He finds young guys like you, senses energy in them. He trains you on the Merc and eventually puts you in charge of one of his companies. It's a golden fucking ticket. But you only have twenty-four hours to decide."

Reston reached into his pocket and pulled out a wad of hundred-dollar bills. He rose from his seat, throwing the bills onto the table to cover the check.

"Usually I grow to hate the kids Giovanni throws at me. Little Ivy League brats who end up being way more work than they're worth. A huge fucking waste of my time. The Merc isn't something you learn about in some classroom. It's a battlefield. So don't take this on lightly. Russo, you know what the difference is between oil and potatoes?"

He leaned close, grinning like a Cheshire cat.

"Nobody fights wars over potatoes."

SIX HOURS LATER, David sat on the floor of his apartment, his cordless phone resting precipitously on his lap. The lights were off, the small, spartanly furnished living room bathed in the pseudo-darkness of Midtown at 2:00 A.M. He could hear Serena's quiet breathing from the bedroom; she had fallen asleep sometime after midnight, after listening to him agonize about the decision for nearly three straight hours. He knew he had a whole day to decide—but he also knew that he wouldn't get a second of sleep until he made the call, one way or the other.

He took a deep breath and dialed Giovanni's office number. Straight to voice mail, Harriet's matronly voice echoing in his ear:

"Leave a message for Mr. Giovanni after the tone."

David ran a hand through his hair, the decision made.

"Mr. Giovanni, I'm quitting my job at Merrill tomorrow. I'll be there Monday morning."

He could barely fucking believe it.

He was now, officially, one of Giovanni's Kids.

Chapter 6

Monday morning, 8:59 A.M.

At first, silence.

A moment frozen in time, like a reflection caught on a pane of glass. Air choked with electric tension, every atomic particle seemingly on the verge of sudden and catastrophic motion. A massive hall with impossibly high ceilings, a warren of low computer tables and cubicled workstations spiraling out from a half-dozen circular pits. And the pits themselves, a few feet descended into the floor of the hall, crowded with men in strange bright jackets—blazers in patterns ranging from dark solids and pastels to intricate stripes and even plaids, some approximating a Jackson Pollock of swirls and even spots, all the colors of the rainbow. A rainbow frozen and hushed like the air around, pregnant with anticipation, exhilaration—and maybe even a little fear.

Then—chaos.

It began with a bell. Piercing, metallic, a sound that cut through the tense air and instantly shattered the metaphorical glass. Suddenly, the room exploded. The men in the Jackson Pollock jackets were shouting and physically shoving each other, jockeying for position. Hands were up in the air, fists clenching tiny slips of paper, hoarse voices shouting to be heard over the scuff of shoes, the whir of computers, and the metallic echo of the bell. The fists swung back and forth, the voices cried out, and the tiny slips of paper rained down toward the floor like confetti. Above it all, lights flashed and numbers splayed out across a magnificent, luminescent digital board that hung, precariously, from the ceiling.

"Welcome to the asylum," Reston whispered in David's ear as they stood at the edge of the biggest of the pits, watching the chaos. David jumped back just in time to keep from getting clocked by a wildly gesturing trader in a barber-pole jacket. Reston grinned at him. *The asylum.* David thought it was a pretty good description of the place. Barely a blip on the radar of the outside world, this frantic trading floor known as the NYMEX was like nothing he had ever seen before. It had taken him twenty minutes slogging up and down the windswept streets of Lower Manhattan to find the place. Finally a cop standing in front of a barricade that had probably been up since 9/11 pointed the way. Lodged in one of the most secure buildings on earth—protected by dozens of armed guards, multiple X-ray scanners, a veritable pincushion of security cameras—and located at the very southernmost tip of Manhattan—as far south as David could go without tasting the Hudson—it was really like something out of a Hollywood movie. Reston had met him by the scanners in the lobby, then led him straight to the trading floor.

"May as well start at the heart," he'd said simply, "then work our way up to the brain and the soul."

The heart of the Merc seemed like a cardiac arrest waiting to happen. The traders in their brightly colored jackets were shouting so loud that their voices blended into one ear-shattering roar. The slips of paper that represented the only real record of their trades were already ankle-deep across the floor, and it was only a few minutes into the trading day.

"Christ," David said. "How does this possibly work?"

"Biggest casino in the world. These meatheads are trading billions of dollars a day. It looks like pure chaos, but it's coordinated."

As Reston was talking, one of the meatier of the bunch turned to face them from the pit. A kid really, probably not even David's age, in a red-and-orange-striped jacket.

"Hey, Nicky," he shouted, his voice raspy and used. "I see you brought your girlfriend to work with you."

"That's right, Vitzi," Reston responded. "This pretty thing is David Russo. Giovanni's newest pain in my ass. This one's a Harvard boy."

David groaned inwardly. He knew, instinctively, how that was going to go over. Looking around the room at the traders, he felt like he'd suddenly raced backward in time to his childhood split between Staten Island and Brooklyn, to the family reunions and grade-school playgrounds and neighborhood streets. Giovanni and Reston hadn't been kidding about the makeup of the trading floor. Their ages seemed to range from early twenties to late forties—even a few fifties and sixties in the mix—and it was almost entirely male. Tough guys, from the looks of them, despite their Day-Glo-colored clothes.

Two more of the traders turned around to look at David, both young men in their twenties like Vitzi, both obviously Italian and more than a little rough around the edges. One was burly, with a protruding paunch and wild brown hair. The other was thin and lanky, with at least two days' beard growth on his jaw.

"Just what we need. Another rocket scientist. How long did the last one make it? A week?"

"I think his mommy came to rescue him by day three," Vitzi joked back.

David felt like he was about to get eaten alive. He wanted to respond, nip this shit right from the start—maybe even swing at one of them just to set things right—but he kept his mouth shut. He didn't want to get fired five minutes into his first day. Especially considering the bridge at Merrill was still burning, and, as far as he could tell, the financial job market hadn't gotten any better over the weekend.

Reston responded before he had a chance. "I'm guessing this one is gone by tomorrow, but I'm hoping he makes it a bit longer. Nothing worse for me than having to deal with you boneheads face-to-face."

With that, he led David off the trading floor, straight to a bank of elevators. Once they were secure in the ascending steel box, Reston turned to look at him.

"Those guys are right, you know. You can take your Harvard degree and shove it up your ass."

David felt his cheeks turning red. *This was going great so far.*

"This place bleeds Brooklyn," Reston continued as the digital numbers on the elevator readout blinked upward. "This place sweats Queens. This isn't the New York Stock Exchange. You can't just get a fancy degree and apply for a job at the Merc. This place is an apprenticeship system, like a fraternity, with secret handshakes and hazing rituals. Those guys are going to call you my girlfriend until you prove to them that you're not."

David wanted to melt into the elevator wall. When he'd met Reston at Morton's, he'd sensed some animosity, but he'd assumed that it was something he'd be able to work through. He wasn't so sure anymore.

"That meathead Vitzi," Reston continued, "is one of the hottest kids on the floor right now. And he came from fucking nowhere. He'd tell you himself—if he wasn't doing this, he'd be selling shoes. Grew up on the street in Bensonhurst, stealing car radios and knocking over ATM machines. Somehow stayed out of jail long enough to worm his way into a clerk job here—maybe a cousin or an uncle brought him in. Got paid ten thousand a year to be someone's bitch—the shittiest fucking job in the world. But he was smart, sharp as a fucking tack. Now he's playing in the game—and if all goes well, he'll make fucking millions."

David blinked, taking it all in as best he could.

"I get it. They're going to haze the hell out of me until I prove myself. You went through this in the beginning too?"

Reston laughed. "Hey, don't lump me in with you, Harvard. I'm an Irish kid from Plano, Texas. I nearly flunked out of high school and got into college because I'm good at throwing a baseball. After college, I found out I was good at something else—trading. When I got the offer from the Merc, I'd never been out of Texas—but I hopped on a plane the next day."

David tried to imagine getting on that plane, heading off toward the unknown; it wasn't that hard for him, considering that he'd done the same thing when he'd gone to England, crossing an ocean for the first time.

"I met my wife on the flight to my first interview," Reston said. "I became a trader and a New Yorker all in one week. I got my ass handed to me so many times by this place and this city, fuck, you have no idea."

"But you hung in there," David said. He wasn't just kissing ass, he was truly a bit unnerved by the chaos of the trading floor, and especially the character of the traders he'd seen. He hadn't expected Ivy Leaguers, but he hadn't expected a high school locker room either.

"They have a saying here: from garbagemen to millionaires. Guys like me and Giovanni and Vitzi come to this place with nothing, scratching and clawing our way through the front door. And if we're smart, if we're lucky, if we've got the balls—we get rich beyond our wildest dreams."

David didn't know if it was hyperbole or bravado, but if Giovanni was any indication, there had to be some truth to the saying. David had to admit that he liked the sound of it: garbagemen to millionaires.

"Well, it won't be the first place I've ever been where my education was a negative. That trading floor looked like my family reunion."

Maybe he'd have to revert to the person his parents had spent a hundred grand to get rid of—but David wasn't going to give up as easily as the last Giovanni Kid.

"Well, don't throw away your gray matter just yet, boyo, because your office isn't in the heart of the Merc."

The elevator came to a stop, and Reston pointed to the digital readout.

"Fifteenth floor. This is where you work. The brain."

Chapter 7

The first thing David noticed as he stepped out onto the fifteenth floor was that it was quiet. Wonderfully, soothingly quiet—such a stark contrast from the trading pits downstairs that it was hard to believe both were encased in the same fortresslike building. The second thing he noticed was that straight ahead, at the end of a long, carpeted hallway banked on either side by low cubicles, hung a picture of himself. Eye level, maybe a little crooked, directly above a glass desk behind which sat the woman he'd been picturing for an entire week. He hadn't been that far off considering that he'd been working only from her voice. She was matronly but pretty, more curves than edges, with overflowing, reddish-brown hair barely controlled by what seemed to be a mix of hair spray, barrettes, and prayer. Though she was wearing a gray suit that looked expensive, her thick makeup and blood-red lipstick and nails told David that she had probably grown up on the same streets as his cousins—well, maybe not Brooklyn, but probably New Jersey. And if she was anything like David's cousins, although she seemed sweet as sugar, she'd probably have no problem clawing your eyeballs out if you looked at her the wrong way. At the moment, she was all smiles, already up and out of her chair by the time David and Reston had made it half-way down the long carpeted hall.

"Glad to see you survived the trading floor with all four limbs still attached," she said by way of a greeting. Instead of a hand-shake, she offered David a manila envelope. "Here's your employment package. Nothing too confusing in there, I promise, just a W-2 and a welcome letter. We like to keep things simple up here."

Reston patted David on the back. "Harriet will take care of you. She's like our den mother—none of us would have survived without her. After you get settled—ten minutes should cover it—meet me back at the elevator, and we'll continue the tour."

Reston headed toward a row of doors beyond the cubicles.

"Those are the board members' offices," Harriet explained as she came around her desk, straightening her suit with quick sweeps of her long, brightly painted nails. "Mr. Reston's office is next to Mr. Giovanni's—who, by the way, won't be in today, as he's flying back from London this evening. But he'll be there at the board meeting tomorrow, so make sure you aren't late. Your first board meeting is an important event, and you'll want to make a good impression."

She spoke much faster in person, the words running together in some places, and David noticed for the first time that she did indeed have a hint of a Jersey accent, something that hadn't come across over the phone. He let her lead him to one of the cubi-cles—directly outside of the two doors that she'd indicated led to Reston's and Giovanni's offices.

"This is your desk for now. You'll be spending most of your time in Mr. Reston's and Mr. Giovanni's offices, or running up and down to the trading floor."

David took in the cubicle: desk, chair, IBM workstation, and a steel telescoping lamp. He could have been right back at Mer-rill—except the other cubicles surrounding his seemed to be va-cant, no signs of life clearly visible, no pictures tacked to walls or sad little plants trapped in equally sad little pots.

"Where is everybody else?" David asked.

"There is no everybody else," Harriet answered, turning back toward her desk. "The other board members' assistants have cubicles on the fourteenth floor. The traders live in caves and eat their assistants during the cold winter months. The fifteenth floor is just for board members. And me."

She smiled back at him, chasing an errant, oversprayed lock out of her eyes.

"And now you."

David blushed. She saw the color in his cheeks and laughed.

"You're cuter in person, David, but don't get the wrong idea. I didn't put your picture up above my desk—Mr. Giovanni did. The old man has an odd sense of humor sometimes. Though I really did like the flowers and chocolates."

When she was gone from view, David lowered himself into his chair, testing the springs, getting the feel of yet another cubicle. They never taught you about cubicles in business school. Maybe that was because, until a year ago, business school grads didn't have to deal with cubicles.

David put the manila envelope on the center of his desk and went to work on the metal clasp. The W-2 came out first, followed by a letter from the Merc, welcoming him and laying out his payment package. He took a deep breath as he searched for the numbers—then exhaled as they hit him like a club to his gut.

Fifty-eight thousand dollars, plus benefits. Nearly a third less than what he was making at Merrill Lynch. He knew that money wasn't everything—but hell, with his school loans and his apartment and his girlfriend, it was going to be a tough year.

Sometimes you gotta move lateral before you move forward, he sighed to himself, repeating one of his dad's mantras. The thought brought him back to the night before—to the party celebrating his dad's completed year of therapy. It had been quite a Russo affair: aunts, uncles, cousins, food flying everywhere, little kids running around with snot running down their faces, David's mother making everyone toast again and again—hell, the whole group would have been thrown out of the restaurant in the heart of Little Italy if it hadn't been owned by a distant cousin. David smiled inwardly as he remembered how elegant Serena had looked in the midst of all that Russo chaos, sitting right next to his dad the whole time, matching every toast glass to glass. And David's dad had truly looked so good, it was hard to believe that a year ago he was in that hospital, the panic attacks that had resulted from the accident so fierce that his heart had literally seized in his chest—David shook the thought away. Lateral motion— that's exactly what his dad had called the monstrous thing that had ended his career at the accounting firm, because, well, it had ended the accounting firm as well. And he truly was moving forward again, putting himself back together emotionally, rebuilding his career at a new company that was kindly letting him work at home until his rehabilitation was over.

So what the hell did David have to complain about? Fifty-eight thousand dollars was a hell of a lot better than not being able to do the simplest things in life, like get into a compact car or walk down a set of stairs—

"Is it that ugly?" a voice interrupted David's thoughts—a damn good thing, considering where those thoughts might have taken him—and David turned to see a smiling face peering over the edge of his cubicle. Midfifties, ethnically Jewish, with a receding hairline graying at the edges and ears that stuck out a little too far.

"Alex Mendelson," the man said, extending a hand, which David shook. "Board member. Crude oil was my game until I hung up my trading jacket and took a seat with the brain trust up here. You must be Giovanni's Harvard boy."

David instinctively rolled his eyes. Had Reston made an announcement over the PA or was he using a fucking bullhorn? David may as well have worn his Harvard tie.

Mendelson laughed. "It's okay, I'm class of '69 myself. Yeah, that's right—Summer of Love and somehow I ended up in banking. Thank God I discovered this place before I was too old to throw a good punch."

David slid his employment package back into the manila envelope and rose from his chair.

"You need to know how to punch to get by here?"

"Hell, yeah. You'll learn soon enough. This place is a cockfight. Sometimes literally. There are fistfights on the trading floor every now and then. But you look like you can handle yourself."

Mendelson started toward the elevators, and David followed.

"What about up here? Do you have to fistfight to get by up here too?"

Mendelson grinned at him. "No, up here it's full-fledged warfare. Armored tanks and AK-47s. You'll see soon enough. Your first board meeting is tomorrow, right? Well, don't worry, Harvard, I've got your back."

He made a pistol with his hand, fired off two faux shots at David's face, then cut left toward an office on the other side of the room. David watched him go—and realized, for the first time, that Mendelson wasn't wearing any shoes. His suit was tailored and obviously expensive, he had on a Rolex watch and a tie that could have been Prada or Gucci, but his feet were bare and he was padding along the carpet like a kid on Christmas morning.

David was still staring after him as he reached the elevators. Reston was already there, a grin on his face.

"Yeah, Mendelson's a character," he said, holding the elevator door open for David. "He made a fortune trading crude. He was so good that some of the other traders got together, made a million-dollar bet with him that he couldn't make three times that in a single afternoon. Mendelson was so sure he'd win that he even raised the bet by throwing in a pair of his favorite shoes."

David raised his eyebrows as he stepped into the elevator, Reston right behind him.

"Mendelson lost?"

"By one hundred thousand. He made 2.9 million, had to pay a million of it to the other traders—and he never wore shoes to work again. Still, he came out with 1.9 million for himself, so don't feel too bad for the guy."

The elevator doors slid shut. Again, the digital readout blinked upward. Before David could ask any questions about Mendelson or the traders or his measly employment package or tomorrow morning's board meeting—which obviously was a big deal—the elevator was already slowing down. He glanced at the readout and saw that they had come to a stop on the eighteenth floor.

"You've seen the heart and brain of the Merc," Reston said as the doors slid open. "That only leaves the soul."

Chapter 8

David stepped out into what looked to be a lounge, with a restaurant off to his left and an outdoor patio located through a pair of glass doors straight ahead. There was a long wooden bar off to the right, complete with bar stools and a great pyramid of liquor bottles inside a huge glass cabinet. The lounge, restaurant, and bar area were all decorated in muted colors, with leather-lined chairs and sofas, elegant carpeting, and oil paintings on the walls. The decor was in stark contrast to the garrulous traders who crowded together in cliquish groups, different-colored jackets congregating in different corners of the L-shaped floor. Even though trading was in full swing downstairs on the trading floor, there were obviously enough traders taking breaks to give the upstairs lounge the feel of a rowdy downtown bar.

As Reston led David through the throngs, he got a few sideways glances, but mostly the traders continued with their conversations. David caught snippets of their dialogue; he wasn't trying to eavesdrop—it was just that the traders talked so damn loud, probably a consequence of days spent screaming at each other down on the trading floor. He passed one group talking about a weekly poker game with stakes so high David could hardly believe it was real. Another group was talking about where they were going to go when the trading day ended; David caught something about some sort of club that employed women who danced in cages.

Reston took a seat at a small table by the windows, with a pretty good view of the river and New Jersey beyond. David sat across from him, trying to look comfortable as he sank into the leather chair. David could see tugboats churning through the gray waters eighteen floors below. He wondered how many kids in Harvard ties bobbed up and down in their wakes.

"So how basic do we have to get?" Reston asked as a waitress brought them each a beer in a tall, frosted glass. "I know this is your first day, but where do we need to start? You know what an exchange is?"

David wondered if it was a trick question. He thought back to the analogy Reston and Giovanni had given him at Morton's— that an exchange was like a soccer stadium. To be honest, he wasn't entirely sure what that meant. If this had been a class back at Harvard, he would have tried to bullshit his way through. Instead, he decided to table his ego for the moment and let Reston lead him wherever the Texan wanted him to go.

"A place where traders come to trade," he responded, as simply as possible. "Here they trade oil."

"Wonderful." Reston sighed, taking a long swig from his beer. "So that's what two years of business school comes down to."

David felt a bit of heat rising into his cheeks, but quickly pushed his emotions away. For the moment, he was here to learn; he'd have a chance to prove himself as time progressed. Still, a little attitude never hurt anyone.

"Pretty much. I also know that oil is what makes cars go fast, but I figured I'd save that for my second day."

Reston looked at him, then grinned.

"Okay, the basics it is. Yes, you're right, exchanges are, as the name suggests, meeting places for people to trade goods for other goods. Historically, exchanges sprang up near ports, where people naturally gathered together with whatever wares they had to hock. The gathering together was important, because being face to face restricted the ability to get screwed; when you could see the transactions going on all around you, you had a sense for what the market rate was, and therefore it was less likely you'd get taken for a ride."

David nodded; it was all pretty seventh-grade textbook, but he didn't want to rush Reston. The chaotic scene he'd witnessed downstairs on the trading floor seemed terrifyingly complex, and he didn't want to skip any steps that would help him make better sense of how the Merc operated.

"For a long time," Reston continued, "exchanges traded in the physical—'spot'—market. That means, in the immediate transfer of goods for goods. I give you a sack of potatoes, and in return you give me money. Now, that worked fine for commodities with short shelf lives, but as you moved into things that you can store—such as, well, oil—you wanted longer-dated purchase agreements. That's where futures come in."

Of course, David had learned about futures in business school. They were pretty self-explanatory: you contracted to buy or sell items in the future at a price determined now.

"Sure," David said. "I agree to sell you one gallon of crude oil in one month for fifty bucks. The current price is forty nine. You believe the price is going higher, so you agree to the deal. I think the price is going down, so I also agree. If, in one month, the price is below fifty bucks, you lose and I win. If it's above, you win and I look for another job."

Reston leaned forward over his beer. "And what if that month goes by, the price of oil tanks to forty bucks, but I say, fuck you, and refuse to pay you the difference? Well, that's where the exchange comes in. The exchange acts as insurance to make sure the deals go through smoothly. For that service, the exchange takes a clearing fee and a trading fee. The more oil that gets traded, the more money the exchange makes. But the brilliance of the whole

thing is that the exchange doesn't take any of the risk—the risk
is all on the traders. They're the ones speculating on the price,
deciding whether to bet that whatever they're trading is going up
or down."

"So the exchange is like the house, the casino," David said,
parroting back what he'd heard Reston say earlier. "The traders
are the gamblers."

Reston nodded. "Though it's a little more complex than that.
As the markets developed, got bigger, faster, and more complicated, brokers stepped in—guys who made it their business to
control the transactions for a commission. The brokers represent
the people selling the oil as well as the people buying it. The
brokers interact with the traders, who are essentially speculators
who squat in between the buyers and sellers. A barrel of oil being
pulled from the coast of Louisiana—destined for your car's gas
tank—can change hands dozens of times along the way as various people take different views of the short-term price direction.
That one barrel of oil, which we've bought and sold for fifty
bucks, can actually generate thousands of dollars of profit and
loss for people in the middle before it gets turned into exhaust."

Somehow the basics had gone from seventh-grade textbook
to somewhere in the stratosphere, but David was sure he'd get
the knack of it all before long. At least, he hoped so; he doubted
Reston was the kind of guy who liked explaining things more
than once.

"And that's what you saw going on down there in the pit.
All that yelling is actually coordinated communication. Signals
being passed between traders that communicate the prices and
sizes of crude oil contracts—buys and sells—based on whatever
speculative magic each individual trader brings with him to the
floor. Been going on like that since 1983, when crude took over
as the main commodity of the Merc. Before that, it was potatoes.
Before that, butter and cheese. That's right, the Merc opened in
1872 as the Butter and Cheese Exchange of New York. After
World War II, potatoes overtook dairy—and in '83, oil trumped

potatoes. But even though the commodity that's being traded has gone from butter to oil, the traders and exchange haven't changed much in a hundred and thirty years."

David leaned back in his chair. The madness he'd witnessed downstairs had been going on for more than a century. And now he was going to be a part of it all.

"If you haven't quite figured it out yet," Reston continued, nursing his beer, "there's a real divide between the board and the traders. It really boils down to the age-old antagonism between workers and management—between the guys who feel they make the cars, and the guys who wear suits and take credit for making the cars. The traders trade, and we make money off of them— and they hate us for it, even though most of us were once floor monkeys just like them. Part of your job is going to be bridging that gap—so you'll be spending plenty of time up here. This is where the upstairs guys and the downstairs guys come to relax. If you can call it that."

David finally turned away from Reston and watched two young traders—maybe late twenties, maybe even younger—shoving at each other back near the bar. A third trader intervened just before punches started to fly. David pictured the trading floor downstairs, how all the guys were jammed together, screaming and yelling—Christ, it really did seem insane that an exchange could work this way. David really felt like he had been plunked down in some bizarre nightmare from his youth, surrounded by the tough kids he had grown up with—who had simply traded in their jeans and leather coats for colored trading jackets.

"You guys weren't kidding about the ethnic connection here," David said, thinking back to the night at Morton's.

"It's the culture of apprenticeship," Reston replied, taking a deep swig from his beer. Even though it was barely ten in the morning, David followed suit. He didn't think he'd be getting much work done on his first day, considering that Giovanni wasn't even in the office. Not that he had any real idea what he'd be doing day to day anyway.

"Like I said," Reston continued, "it's been going on for more than a hundred and thirty years. Traded down from father to son, almost forever. A real family business. Like we told you, you can't just walk into the Merc and try to get a job. And even if you did, you wouldn't survive without a mentor. It isn't something you can learn at Harvard Business School. We've all seen it before, the Ivy League kids who hit the trading floor and fall completely apart. You have to have the heart to do this, as well as the mind."

David nodded. Reston really seemed to have a stick up his ass about David's degree. Maybe Reston was letting him know that he wasn't going to get any special treatment—that just because he was Giovanni's newest kid, that didn't make him a de facto star. Or maybe Reston simply didn't like him. Either way, David knew he was going to have to work to earn Reston's respect.

Their conversation was interrupted, briefly, as the two traders who had shoved each other a few minutes ago went at it again. This time one of them had to be pulled away by two others in similar bright blue jackets. David heard at least one ethnic slur in the shouting that followed—but it was one Italian talking to another, as far as he could tell, so it didn't go any further than that.

"Christ," David said, only half-joking, "I might need to bring my boxing gloves if I'm going to be spending a lot of time with the traders."

Reston shrugged. "The Merc is a real physical exchange, a street fight. Trading on the Merc truly does involve physical confrontation. There are real bodily limitations to the floor. Where you stand—being closer to certain traders looking for certain positions—can mean the difference between millions of dollars. Fistfights are not uncommon, downstairs or up here. Certainly, pushing and shoving is a daily thing. There's one trader, Bobby Maroni, a little guy, maybe sixty years old and shrinking every week, who has two clerks paid to actually stand behind him, holding him in the pit so he doesn't get tossed out when things get frantic."

David laughed, then realized Reston was serious. It was

amazing to think that a modern exchange worked this way—men physically fighting for space as they traded millions of dollars worth of energy futures. And further, that this seemingly archaic battle had far-reaching implications, because at its heart was the price of the ultimate commodity.

"See, but it makes sense," Reston continued, as if reading David's thoughts. "Oil is volatile. To trade oil, sometimes you have to be equally volatile. The traders on the floor are working with millions of dollars per day. And sometimes they don't hold their positions very long at all—some hold for only a few seconds, others a few minutes, while some hang on overnight. And the price is always changing. And not just little changes like with the stock market—huge swings that seem to come out of nowhere. So these guys, they're really gamblers at heart. The biggest gamblers in the world, playing in the biggest casino you can find."

"Why does the price of oil change so much?" David asked, hoping it wasn't too stupid a question. Reston seemed happy to answer—maybe happy that the Harvard brat had realized he had to ask questions, because this was as foreign to him as Harvard was to most of these guys from Brooklyn.

"Most of our oil comes from certain specific regions of the world, while the demand is ubiquitous. A variety of triggers can vastly affect the price. Hell, you know what one of the most influential triggers is to the price of oil?"

David's first thoughts were war, maybe unrest in the Middle East. But then it dawned on him—something much more commonplace probably had a much bigger effect.

"The weather?"

"You win another beer, whiz kid. Yeah, the weather is enormous here. In the traders' offices, they've got it on their TV screens all the time. They even have a meteorologist on staff."

Intuitively, David realized, it was easy to understand: A cold front hits Manhattan, and suddenly the demand for oil skyrockets. The trading floor becomes a churning mob scene as the traders take advantage of the price movement, and the volatility increases, building on itself. Millions of dollars are made in minutes, sometimes seconds.

"So when the weather goes crazy—"

"This place turns upside down. Funny story. About four years ago, when I was still trading full-time, I was at a rehearsal dinner for my niece's wedding. Cute girl, Fiona, my older brother's kid. Anyway, I was about to make a toast when I caught sight of a TV in the background. A hurricane had just earned its name, and the weatherman was predicting that eventually it was going to hit the Gulf. Everyone else at the wedding was laughing and smiling, but I was fighting back tears. I was in a deep position on crude, and I was going to lose millions."

David shook his head, laughing. He tried to picture Reston as a trader. The Texan, as tough as he was, seemed so much more refined than the guys in the jackets who surrounded them. David's eyes searched through the crowd, trying to see if there was anyone Reston might have fit in with—and noticed a table about twenty yards to their right, close to the glass doors that led out to the patio. The table was surrounded by a half-dozen young men in jackets with what looked to be zebra stripes, all standing while they drank from frosted mugs. Only one trader was seated, his feet up on the table as he leaned back, arms clasped behind his head. He was older than the rest—in fact, maybe even as old as Mendelson and Giovanni, certainly late fifties, maybe closing in on sixty. His hairline was receding, a ring of wispy, silver-gray locks sticking up behind his ears like some sort of demented halo. He had dark rings around his eyes and thick, chalky lips, clamped down around a cigar. Nobody else seemed to be smoking indoors, though the outer patio was obviously smoke-friendly. But this guy seemed somehow above the rules. And it wasn't just the cigar that gave David that feeling—it was the way the younger traders milled about him, not just the guys in the zebra jackets that matched the old man's but the other traders as well. As an Italian, David had been trained to recognize the signs of that sort of respect from a very young age.

Reston noticed where David was looking and leaned forward over the table between them.

"You've got a good eye, kid. His name is Dominick Gallo. He's the biggest trader on the floor—hell, maybe the biggest in the history of the Merc. He's been here even longer than Giovanni—fuck, he was born on that trading floor. Worth about three hundred million, maybe even more. We call him 'the Don.'"

David raised his eyebrows. That was just too much.

"You're kidding, right?"

"Not to his face. But, yeah, among the board. I told you, this place is a family business, and Gallo's family has been in this since the beginning. He's got immense power over the traders, especially the older guys, the ones who came up with him. He's like a god on the trading floor. And he's a real mean bastard. He comes to all the board meetings, just because he can. And that often turns the board meetings into pitched battles, sometimes all-out wars. See, technically, the traders own the Merc, even though we on the board run it. So if the Don doesn't agree with something, we often have to cater to him."

David realized with a start that Gallo was now looking right at him and Reston. The cigar jerked up and down in the man's chalky lips as those eyes gave David the once-over.

"His power base extends way beyond this place," Reston said, waving past David at the older trader. "He's used his money to buy up journalists, politicians—whoever he needs. And the amount of money he moves through this exchange puts the banks and even Big Oil under his skirt. So we don't fuck with him, and he doesn't fuck with us. Usually."

David watched as Gallo took the cigar out of his mouth and suddenly pointed it right at him.

Reston kicked him under the table.

"I think the Don wants you to come over and kiss his hand."

David looked at Reston, who shrugged. David wondered once again what the hell kind of world he had gotten himself into. A place like Merrill Lynch had been easy to figure out:

there were bosses, and bosses' bosses—a clear hierarchy. Here it seemed more like warlords and barbarians, all crashing into one another. Still, it was exciting to think about how much money was being made downstairs and what was at the core of all this insanity—oil.

"I'm kidding about the hand," Reston said as David rose from the table. "Just go over and introduce yourself. And try not to say anything that pisses him off."

David nodded, though he knew that sometimes he had a knack for that sort of thing. He pushed his way through the crowded lounge, heading straight for the zebra jackets.

The young men parted as he arrived, making room for him across the table from Gallo. There wasn't a chair, so David stood, assuming that was the protocol. Gallo never changed position, his feet still up on the table, the cigar back in his mouth, his hands clasped behind his head.

"So you're Giovanni's new kid," he grunted, more a mumble than anything else.

David held out his hand.

"David Russo. It's an honor to meet you. I'm just learning the ropes around here, but any advice you have for me would be greatly appreciated."

Gallo looked at David's outstretched hand like it was a hunk of rotten fish, making no move to reciprocate. David heard snickers behind him from the younger traders watching like a gang of fucking hyenas.

"Every year Giovanni brings in an Ivy League piece of shit kid like you," Gallo said, never removing the cigar from the corner of his mouth. "Coming up with all sorts of Ivy League ideas about how we could make the place more—what's that faggy word you HBS guys are so fond of? Oh yeah, *efficient*."

There was real laughter now coming from the traders, and Gallo seemed to be enjoying the moment. He rolled his eyes, black marbles spinning in the center of those ominous, dark circles.

"Well, let me save you the trouble, kid. I've been trading here

since it was potatoes and Reston over there was a gleam in some
bull-riding, whiskey-drinking Mick's eyes."

David had already figured out that there was a divide between
the heart and the brain of this place—but was shocked at the
outright hostility coming from the man Reston had called the
Don. David had barely said a word, and already this guy seemed
to hate his guts.

"You want advice?" Gallo continued, finally taking the cigar
out of his mouth to jab it like a knife in David's direction. "Keep
your ass up on the fifteenth floor, and your head in Giovanni's
lap. That's the best way for you to stay out of trouble."

With that, he waved David away. David stood there for a brief
second, stunned. Then the raucous laughter from the traders
broke his trance, and he quickly made his way back to Reston's
table. Reston was grinning as David shakily lowered himself back
into the seat.

"Don't worry," Reston joked, obviously getting the gist of
what had gone down from the look on David's face. "His bite is
way worse than his bark."

"I don't think he likes me very much," David managed.

"Hah. That old fuck doesn't like any of us, but me and
Giovanni—and by extension, you—have a special place in his
heart. See, we're not just suits fighting a turf war with the traders; we represent something even worse—change. Gallo has built
up his fiefdom for fifty years, he's made a fortune, and his family
has had this place all to themselves for three generations. Now he
thinks we're threatening all that. Modernizing the exchange, going international, automating trading—hell, one day, if we have
our way, there won't even be a trading floor, and guys like Gallo
will have a hell of a time adapting. You think the Don knows
how to work a fucking Mac? This is his home, he understands
it—and he thinks we've come here to take his home away. And
you know what? Maybe he's right. But that old fucker won't be
around forever."

Just long enough to make my life miserable, David thought to himself. His hands were trembling under the table. He'd never been overly intimidated by assholes before, no matter how powerful they were. But something about Gallo scared the shit out of him.

"Maybe you can think of a comeback by the board meeting tomorrow morning," Reston suggested. "Gallo will be there, you can bet on that. And from the looks of things, he's gunning for you right from the start. Usually he gives Giovanni's kids a week or two to get acclimated before he knocks 'em down a peg. So consider yourself special."

Reston seemed more than a little pleased, and David questioned for the first time if he'd acted a bit impetuously, shifting jobs without doing a little more research. He reminded himself that Giovanni was in charge here, not Reston or Gallo. And he was here to work for Giovanni—his idol, the man he one day wanted to be.

Still, looking over at Gallo and the laughing, zebra-jacketed hyenas, David wondered what it really took to thrive in an environment like this. With his first board meeting less than twenty-four hours away, David had a sinking suspicion he'd find out soon enough.

Chapter 9

The view was like something out of a science fiction movie. A veritable forest of massive cranes, spanning as far as the eye could see, each one attending to futuristic monsters of concrete and steel, rising up toward the heavens like fingers reaching for God. Lush greenery interspersed with sweeping glades of sand, man-made fountains and waterfalls and beaches mingling with twenty-first-century roads, bridges, and tunnels. Camels on dirt paths just twenty yards from Ferraris on superhighways, Arabic men and women in traditional robes and burkas strolling past Europeans in Armani suits and the latest fashions of the Parisian runways. London was cosmopolitan; this was simply another planet altogether.

"Like a dream," Khaled said as he touched the floor-to-ceiling windowpane with his outstretched fingers. Directly ahead, in the distance, he could see the great Burj Al Arab Hotel rising up above the coastline, its beautiful billowing sail soaring a thousand feet into the air. Khaled had checked into the world's only seven-star hotel the night before—and the miraculous construct had been even more mind-blowing at night, surrounded by dancing sculptures of water and fire. Beyond the Al Arab, he could just make out the palm tree–shaped man-made island, Palm Islands—still under construction, but already one of the great wonders of the modern world. And closer, nearly straight down from where he was standing, he could see the great arched, three-hundred-foot-high, glazed-granite building that acted as the entrance to the city's work-in-progress financial center, the Gate.

Khaled shook his head, stepping back from the window. The scale of it all was almost dizzying. Especially from twenty stories up in one of the most modern office buildings in the world.

"Indeed, it is a dream. Though at times, you'll see, even the most wonderful dreams have a way of keeping you awake at night. The work here never ends."

Khaled smiled as he turned to face the portly deputy finance minister. Minister Hakim Al Wazali was a good head shorter than Khaled, with a round, amiable face, puffy cheeks, and thick, sausagelike lips. His white ceremonial robes did not help his appearance, making him seem more marshmallow than man—but Khaled knew that this marshmallow was actually one of the more powerful people in the region, and truly deserving of his post at the forefront of one of the greatest financial miracles in Middle Eastern history.

"It is an absolute honor to be here. I thank you for the opportunity from the bottom of my heart," Khaled responded, and he truly meant what he said. Looking around the glass-walled office, at the sophisticated decor that included a glass desk with inboard computer, multiple flat-screen TVs, bookshelves filled with finance texts resting side by side with religious literature and political tomes—it was a dream come true.

He could hardly believe that this office was now his own.

"No need to thank me," Hakim said, waving a thick hand in the air. "Your résumé is nothing short of spectacular. Top grades at Cambridge and the University of Geneva Business School. Five languages, proficiency in computers, mathematics, and religious law—we were lucky to find you."

Khaled nodded, accepting the compliment, though inside he felt a slight tinge of guilt. He knew his résumé was only part of the reason he had been offered the position, working directly beneath the finance minister in this office in the staggeringly modern Emirates Tower, just two floors below the minister's own. The truth was, his uncle was a great friend to the nation as a whole, and a personal friend of Sheik Maktoum bin Rashid Al Maktoum, the all-powerful emir of the magical city-state. Sheik Maktoum and his brother, Sheik Muhammed, had created this futuristic oasis by sheer force of will; Khaled's uncle had sent Khaled to work for them because, in his mind, there was no greater place for a young man to grow into a true leader.

"Anyway," Hakim said, pulling his robes around him as he headed for the office's smoked-glass door, "I'll give you a chance to settle in before afternoon prayer. After prayer, I'll take you to meet the rest of the staff. You'll see that we have a top-notch operation—you'll fit right in, I'm sure."

Khaled thanked the man again and watched as he waddled away in a swirl of white robes and jiggling limbs. Then Khaled turned back to the magical skyline.

He only hoped he could live up to his résumé and his uncle's connections. He was determined to repay his debt tenfold.

Watching the endless traffic of people, cars, and commerce in the magnificent city down below, he felt a burst of adrenaline. He was staring at what could only be described as the future—not just of the region, but perhaps of mankind as a whole.

Khaled prayed to Allah that somehow he would be an important part of that future. That somehow he would find a way to make a real difference—for the sheik, for his father, and for himself.

Chapter 10

Are you sure about this?"

David closed his eyes as he pressed his face against the cool glass of the VW Bug's side window. He could feel the sweat pooling beneath the stiff collar of his Oxford shirt. He placed a hand against his stomach, right where the shooting pains seemed to be coming from—then grimaced as the pain seemed to get worse at his touch. He angrily pulled his hand away, gave Serena a quick peck on her worried cheek, then reached for the door handle.

"I'm not missing my first board meeting because of a stomachache," he said as he pushed the door open. An icy breeze swept into the car from the direction of the river, sending a shiver down his spine. "I'll be fine."

"Maybe you're just nervous," Serena responded, her hands still on the steering wheel, but he could tell from the way she said it that she didn't believe it herself. She knew him better than that. Sure, he got nervous, but he was also the most driven guy either of them knew. Nerves had never brought him down before. And nerves couldn't possibly explain the waves of nausea that were moving up his body.

Of all the days to get food poisoning, this had to be the worst. It was like some supernatural sick joke. At least Serena had been able to borrow her sister's car to drive him down to the Merc—or at least as close as they could get to the bright blue police barriers that kept traffic away from the fortified building—so that he didn't have to take the subway, which would have been a real adventure, considering how rotten he felt. Anyway, there was no way he was going to miss his second day of work. Especially since Giovanni would be there.

"I'll survive," David said, managing a forced smile. He shut the car door and hurried past the police barricades. More pain shot through his stomach as he half-jogged the two blocks to the front entrance of the Merc, but he refused to acknowledge it, refused to let it slow him down. At the very least, he was determined to make it through the morning. He'd reassess the situation after lunch.

After getting buzzed through the glass revolving doors, David made short work of the security procedures, passing through the twin metal detectors and showing his brand-new work ID to the armed guards stationed outside the lobby elevators. David also had a trading-floor ID pinned to the lapel of his understated, off-the-rack, gray-blue suit jacket, but he hoped he wouldn't be seeing the trading floor anytime soon. He doubted his upset stomach would be able to handle the chaos at the moment. It was going to be hard enough coming face to face with Gallo again after the episode of the night before.

Leaning against a corner of the elevator as it rose upward through the building, David went over the scene again in his head. He'd relayed the entire episode to both Serena and his mother after he'd gotten home from work, and neither of them could believe how over the top the guy had been, or how Reston had simply laughed it off—as if that sort of animosity was expected and even condoned. David was glad his father hadn't been on the phone as well—knowing him, David figured his advice would have involved a baseball bat and an inevitable assault charge.

David knew he got most of his hotheadedness from his father; the women in his life were his counterbalance—or at least as much counterbalance as a fifty-year-old Sicilian fireball and a twenty-five-year-old Latina bombshell could be.

Both had eventually suggested to David that Gallo's posturing was just that—a bit of dramatics to impress the traders who worked for him. David had an instinctive feeling that it was more than that—and that the turf war between Giovanni and the board and Gallo and the other traders was real and problematic—but he assumed he would learn how to stay out of the line of fire. Until then, he'd have to keep his eye on Gallo, at least until the guy accepted him, and do his best to prove himself upstairs and downstairs. Despite what Reston and Gallo might think, he wasn't just another Harvard boy slumming under Giovanni's wing; he came from the same place as Gallo and the traders, so he was in a unique situation of having a foot in both worlds. If he could figure out how to use his background and his skills, he was certain he could thrive.

But first, he had to survive his second day at work. The minute he stepped out onto the fifteenth floor, he saw that things were different in the brain on the morning of a board meeting. The place was full of people—mostly men in their forties and fifties, well dressed in suits and ties, all heading toward one of the doors at the end of the long hall lined with cubicles. Harriet was standing in front of her desk, handing each of the men a thick envelope as they passed by. When she saw David coming toward her, she rolled her eyes and waved one of the envelopes in his direction.

"Notes from last week, new business, holiday pledge drive, etcetera," she said. He noticed she was chewing gum, and despite the pain that was still rising up from his stomach, he had to smile. He liked her more and more.

He took the envelope from her and glanced at the steady stream of men in suits.

"So this is the board?"

"Everybody's here. There are thirty of them altogether. And

the Don, of course, who always makes an appearance. He's inside already. Mr. Giovanni too. You probably should have gotten here a little earlier today, but you'll know better next time."

David nodded. He would have gotten there earlier if he hadn't been busy throwing up in a corner of the parking garage where Serena's sister stored the VW. He glanced past Harriet at a blank spot on the wall above her desk.

"What happened to my picture, Harriet? Are you moving on to someone else already? I thought I'd last in your heart at least a week."

Harriet smiled, then shrugged. "Actually, it was gone when I got to work. I guess Mr. Giovanni wanted to make room for another kid, just in case you don't work out."

David was pretty sure she was joking.

"I'll bring you a new one if I last the month," he said, and he moved past her with a wink.

The fifteenth floor's main board room was pretty much what David had expected, having spent a fair amount of time in similar rooms at various investment banks and consulting companies during the hellish job interview process before business school graduation. Rectangular, antiseptic, with high ceilings and stark white walls, except for one side that was nearly all tinted glass, overlooking the river down below. A huge oak table, surrounded by high-backed matching wooden chairs, took up most of the room. Most of the seats were already occupied; a good dozen more men had also congregated at the back of the room, where a table of bagels, doughnuts, and trays loaded with Styrofoam cups of coffee had been set up.

David quickly located Giovanni at the head of the table, deep in conference with Reston, who was leaning over his right shoulder. Mendelson was a few seats down from Reston; David would have had to go under the table to see if Mendelson was still barefoot, but he had no reason to believe otherwise. Mendelson saw him, smiled, then pointed to a chair that was placed a few feet behind Giovanni's commanding position, right beneath a huge, blank blackboard. David silently thanked the older trader and quickly made his way toward the chair.

Giovanni saw him as he passed by and gave him a quick wink and a thumbs-up. David smiled back, relieved that the daggers in his stomach had momentarily subsided. Maybe whatever he had eaten had finally surrendered, and anatomical peace had been restored.

As David lowered himself into his seat beneath the blackboard, his eyes wandered to the far end of the long wooden table, directly across from Giovanni's roost. It didn't take him long to spot Gallo: the dilapidated crown of steel-gray hair, the deep-set dark eyes, and, of course, the cigar clamped between his teeth. Gallo was also the only man in the room not wearing a suit; he had traded his zebra-striped jacket for what looked to be a velour zippered pullover. David could only guess that the man was wearing matching sweatpants. Christ, what his father would have said at the sight of the old-school multimillionaire powerbroker. Gallo really was something right out of the goddamn *Sopranos*.

Giovanni cleared his throat, and the board members milling around the breakfast table quickly took their seats. Reston started the meeting off by reading from a prepared list of items, most of which David did not understand because they had to do with regulatory policies and day-to-day exchange business. It wasn't until Reston got into the more esoteric subject of where the exchange was heading that David really perked up and listened. A difficult task, considering that his stomach had started bubbling again, and there was now a strange rushing sound deep in his ears.

"As you all know," Reston was saying, "the future is coming at us pretty fast. Trading software is getting more sophisticated by the day, and it won't be long until a fully automated energy exchange is possible—"

"Over my dead body."

Even through the rushing in his ears, David recognized the voice immediately. It had been seared into his skull the night before. Gallo had both hands splayed out on the wooden table in front of him and was giving Reston and Giovanni a look of pure hatred.

"I said 'possible,'" Reston repeated. "Whether we want to go in that direction or not is something to study and discuss—"

"Study and discuss all you want," Gallo interrupted again. "Meanwhile, we traders will continue to trade, making millions for ourselves and for you fat cats up here."

There were whispers moving around the room as other board members glanced at Gallo angrily but didn't dare to speak up. Giovanni put a hand on Reston's shoulder, then smiled across the table at Gallo.

"We're not here to argue about the future, just to take a look at where it's heading. We might just already have the most efficient way the world knows to price oil—for all the chaos, I know as well as you that the system works. A perfect market, in a way, with purposefully imperfect parts. But that doesn't mean we stick our heads in the sand. We keep our eyes open, we study the changes that are happening around us, and we react if we have to."

Gallo rolled his eyes, then tapped cigar ash toward the carpet.

"Whatever floats your boat. Have your new Harvard kid write up a few hundred pages for all of us to look at. I'm still using the papers your last kid drew up to insulate my beach house."

There was laughter all around. David would have blushed at yet another mention of his degree had not the rush in his ears suddenly become a dull roar. It was so bad that when he felt a buzz in his pants pocket he thought maybe it was something else internal erupting—then realized it was actually his BlackBerry going off. He thought about ignoring it, but then decided that the tension was so obvious between Giovanni and Gallo, nobody in the room would be looking at him.

He slid the BlackBerry out of his pocket and glanced at the screen. To his surprise, the text was from Reston:

You look like shit.

David looked up, but Reston was facing the other direction. David reached a hand to his forehead—and felt a sheen of sweat so thick it drenched his sleeve. The roar in his ears was so loud now that he could barely hear Giovanni responding to Gallo— something about the exchange needing to get out of the dark ages—and then he couldn't hear anything at all because the daggers of pain in his stomach suddenly exploded in full force. He felt like he was being torn in half. He screamed, then saw the floor rising up at him. The next thing he knew he was lying on his back on the carpet, surrounded by board members. He struggled to focus and found himself staring right at a pair of bare feet.

Then Reston had one of his arms and Mendelson the other, and they quickly half-dragged, half-led him out of the board-room. Giovanni was a few feet behind, shouting into his cell phone, something about having the car ready to take David straight to the hospital. David tried to say something, but Harriet put a damp washcloth over his face and took over for Reston and Mendelson. She was obviously much stronger than she looked, as she had no problem guiding him into the elevator. David's last view of the fifteenth floor was from behind the washcloth: the board members peering out through the open boardroom door, while Reston, Mendelson, and Giovanni returned to the meeting, Giovanni shouting at the gawkers that everything was under con-trol. Then the elevator doors slid shut, and David was alone with his pain, mortification, and Harriet.

"Don't worry, Mr. Giovanni's limo is waiting by the lobby doors. The driver will take you right to the hospital. I got your mother's number from your employment forms, and she already called your girlfriend. I'm sure you're going to be okay."

David tried to thank her, but the pain was so intense that it took all of his strength not to curl up on the floor. After an eter-nity in the elevator, they finally reached the lobby. As Harriet handed him off to a pair of security guards to take him to the limo, she whispered in his ear:

"Now that's what I call making a first impression. First time I've seen the Don drop his cigar in fifteen years."

David didn't have time to enjoy her sense of humor, as suddenly his knees buckled and his world went pitch-black.

Chapter 11

David came awake to the sound of classical music.

He was lying flat on his back with a piano on his chest and thick white tape over his eyes. Someone was repeatedly kicking him in the stomach, and he was pretty sure at least two other people were busily drilling holes in his skull.

Or at least that's what it felt like. In actuality, when he finally managed to force open his stuck-together eyelids, he saw that he was lying in a hospital bed with an IV line in each arm and bandages covering most of his bare stomach. Bright fluorescent ceiling lights brought tears to his dry eyes, and he had to blink a few thousand times before he could barely make out the rest of the small private hospital room through the haze of his anesthesia hangover; the stark white walls with poorly placed artwork, the shelves that seemed to be lined with medical equipment, the TV hanging from a telescoping arm attached to the ceiling, the small, shuttered window with bars on the outside. He wasn't sure what the bars were for, but the way his stomach felt, he was kind of glad jumping to his death wasn't really a viable option. Of course, even without the bars, he would have had to make it past Serena, who was standing at the edge of his bed, a concerned look on her face. She had something in her hands, a strange, tubelike device with a bag on one end made out of bright red plastic. David blinked again, wondering if his vision was still fucked up from the anesthesia, but he couldn't quite make out what the object was.

"You've got some interesting work friends, David. They could have just sent flowers."

Then David realized with a start that the thing Serena was holding was an enema. He looked past her, again taking in the small hospital room, and realized that his eyes had played tricks on him—that wasn't art on the walls or medical devices on the shelves. Enemas, literally hundreds of them, were piled up in every corner of the small hospital room, covering the windowsill and the shelves, hanging from the walls like makeshift modern art.

David let his head fall back on the pillow. He almost had to laugh, even though it hurt to even think about laughing. His appendix bursts, he nearly dies on the way to the hospital—and some sick fuck fills his room with enemas? Scratch that, it had to have taken half a dozen people to outfit his room like this—and to do it all while he was in surgery, getting his abdomen suctioned out—Christ, whoever was behind this was really twisted.

"How do you know it was someone from work?" David finally managed, coughing out the words.

Serena walked around the side of the bed and held something over his head, so that he could see without moving from the pillow.

It was the black-and-white picture from above Harriet's desk. David's face had been disfigured by a note written across his forehead in bright red indelible ink: WELCOME TO THE MERC.

Beneath the scrawl was a signature. It took David a few seconds to make a name out of the dramatic, swirling letters: DOMINICK "THE DON" GALLO.

David tried to raise a hand to take the picture from her, but the IV line held him back. He was too weak to crumple the thing into a ball anyway. He could hardly believe Gallo had done something so juvenile—but then, that seemed to be the culture of the traders. Giovanni had put the picture up on Harriet's wall in the first place, after all. David decided he'd just have to write the enemas off as a form of hazing. Still, he was pretty sure it was going to be a story he'd have to live down for the rest of his time at the Merc. Keeling over in the middle of his first board meeting, then having his hospital room filled with enemas. He was only glad that his mother wasn't there to see the practical joke. Though she and his father would certainly be there within the hour—Serena was going to have a hell of a job getting rid of the evidence before they arrived.

"I know," Serena said, as if reading his mind. "I'll get some orderlies to help me clear it out. David, are you sure that this job is really for you?"

David gritted his teeth. He was guessing that both his father and mother would be asking the same question when they arrived. Not only was the Merc obviously full of maniacs, but David was taking a pay cut to be there. And Giovanni, his hero—well, the man had gotten David to the hospital and had obviously called ahead, because one of the top surgeons in New York had been waiting when David arrived. The doctor had explained what was going on even as the anesthesiologist was putting him under—that he was about to have an emergency appendectomy, that they were lucky to have gotten to him in time. But it wasn't Giovanni waiting in the hospital room for him when he woke up—it was Serena and Gallo's enemas.

Mindful of the IV tubes, David reached for Serena's hand. Her skin felt warm, and he could see the concern in the corners of her dark eyes.

"This could have happened anywhere. It was just bad luck—"

"I'm not talking about your appendix," she said, shaking her dark curls. "David, this Gallo, and the traders, and even Giovanni. When you told me about them, I thought you were exaggerating. Now I see that you weren't. If you had gotten sick at

Merrill, you think this would be the response? I feel like you're taking a long step back."

David gave her hand a little tug. She leaned forward so that he could touch her lips with his.

"I've got to at least give it a little more time," he said.

The truth was, there was no way he was going to quit after two days. Because that's exactly what Gallo and the other traders probably expected him to do. Even Reston, he guessed, wouldn't have been that unhappy to see him go. To them, he was just Giovanni's new kid. A pawn in the strange political battle between the board and the trading floor. A Harvard geek who'd taken a wrong turn somewhere and somehow ended up in the middle of a street fight.

Well, if that's what they thought, they'd seriously underestimated him. They didn't know anything about him, about how hard he'd worked to get there, about what his father had gone through—they didn't know who David Russo really was, deep inside.

Through the pain, David grinned up at Serena, and she sighed, because she knew that look in his eyes. They didn't know who David Russo was—but they were about to find out.

Chapter 12

Monday morning, 9:10 A.M., the New York Mercantile Exchange.

The trading floor was in full swing.

Bodies crashed into bodies as the Technicolored jackets jockeyed furiously for position. Outstretched hands grasped after the hailstorm of trading tickets, screaming voices erupting from painfully hoarse throats as the numbers on the great board above flashed upward, downward, side to side. *Crude oil, gasoline, heating oil, natural gas*—the four biggest energy commodities, rising and falling with the fate of the nations that produced and depended on them, while a thousand fanatical men in brightly colored jackets fought a veritable gang war in their wake. *Crude oil, gasoline, heating oil, natural gas*—the four commodities that propped up the modern world, deconstructed into bright red digital numbers to be digested and reacted to: buy, sell, buy, sell. Fortunes made and lost in the blink of an eye, the flutter of a little white piece of paper, the collision of one shoulder with another. The chaos of a real, true, physical market in the form of a pitched battle between real, true, physical market forces.

Gladiators at dawn, David whispered to himself as he strolled through the back doors of the vast, football field–sized room and headed directly toward the trading pits. Deep down, he was terrified, but his eyes remained straight ahead, his face completely calm. He could still feel the stitches pulling at the skin of his abdomen, but the pain was gone, and with it any qualms he had entertained during his brief four-day recovery at home, swathed in the nearly suffocating realm of his overprotective mother and equally zealous girlfriend. This energy, this electricity in the air— it simply didn't exist in any other business. This was where David belonged.

As he reached the edge of the trading pits, he saw the heads begin to turn. At first, the attention was fairly innocuous, curious eyes watching him as he strolled behind the traders. But then the attention became more focused, the eyes more narrowed. Traders grabbing one another and pointing, more heads turning, faces showing mixtures of emotions: confusion, surprise, and, of course, pure anger.

David braced himself as one of the traders suddenly separated himself from the throng and started toward him. David recognized the kid from his first day at the Merc—Michael Vitzioli, the oversized thug in the red-and-orange-striped jacket. He had a cherubic face and a childlike shock of dark brown hair, but fists the size of lamb shanks. At the moment they were cocked and rising, and David knew he had only minutes to defuse the situation. Except, David wasn't there to defuse anything. He was there to make a statement.

"What the fuck do you think you're doing?" Vitzi snarled as he kept coming forward. At least fifteen other traders were gathered close enough to hear. Most had momentarily forgotten about the great board up above and the never-ending rain of trading tickets.

David let Vitzi get to within a few feet before he responded.

"I'm learning about the oil business."

Vitzi's face reddened. He jabbed at David with a thick finger.

"No, I mean the badge. You think that's funny?"

David glanced down at his own lapel. He had affixed the trading badge right in the center, where he'd seen the traders wearing theirs. He then looked over at Vitzi's badge, which had the kid's nickname in big block letters: VITZI.

He shrugged. "Mr. Giovanni told me to choose a nickname, because that's what you meatheads do down here. So I chose myself a nickname."

Vitzi sputtered, trying to find words. David glanced down at his own trading badge again. The single word stared up at him: DAGO.

"You know what that fucking means?" Vitzi half-shouted.

David knew exactly what it meant. In fact, David had debated with himself for a full hour whether he should go with "Dago" or the equally derogatory "Guinea." He had settled on Dago because it just felt better rolling off the tongue.

"Look, man, of course I know what it means. This is a badge of honor to me. I'm a poor kid from Brooklyn with a dago mom and a dago dad, and I'm a proud goddamn dago too. So you can take it or leave it, I really don't give a fuck."

David could feel the tension rise around him as his little section of the trading floor suddenly went dead silent. He wondered if he had gone too far. *Well, fuck it,* he thought to himself. They weren't going to remember him as the guy whose hospital room was filled with enemas after his appendix burst during a board meeting. They were going to remember him as the guy who demanded respect right from the beginning. Either that, or the guy who got his ass kicked all over the trading floor by a Neanderthal in a red-and-orange-striped jacket.

Vitzi glared at him for a good five seconds. Then, finally, something crazy happened. He grinned and reached forward with one of those lamb shanks and gave David a big paisan handshake.

"You're all right, buddy. I nearly knocked your fuckin' head off, but you're all right."

David's heart was pounding as he accepted the handshake,

then separated himself from the thuggish trader. He shook a couple more hands, then quickly headed off the trading floor. As he reached the elevator that led up the spine of the building to the higher, more civilized floors, he detached the offending badge and shoved it deep into his back pocket. He doubted he'd ever have to wear it to work again.

TEN MINUTES LATER, he was still breathing hard as he took a seat on the massive antique leather couch that took up most of the back wall of Giovanni's corner office. There was a cup of coffee on the glass table by his knees, next to a plate of pastries that seemed vaguely familiar, pricking at memories from his childhood excursions to the old-world Italian markets where his mother had done most of her shopping.

Giovanni pointed at the plate from behind his huge wooden desk on the other side of the long rectangular room, but David shook his head. Giovanni shrugged, going back to his phone call. He had been on the line when Harriet first ushered David into his office and hadn't come up for air since. David was glad to have the free time to admire Giovanni's office, which was decorated nearly floor to ceiling with one of the best collections of New York sports memorabilia David had ever seen outside of a museum.

The largest portion of the collection was housed in a glass shelving unit that spanned the length of the office's enormous picture windows. David counted at least a dozen baseballs signed by various Yankee rosters, most notably one signed by the entire 1958 World Series team and another signed by the 1996 winning team. There were two Darryl Strawberry jerseys and three mitts signed by Joltin' Joe DiMaggio himself. There were also basketballs signed by various incarnations of the Knicks, hockey sticks and pucks from a Rangers fan's wet dream, and photos galore of Giovanni with various stars from at least three different generations, perhaps more. It was really an impressive gathering of material, and David could only imagine how much it was worth. Not that Giovanni would be selling it anytime soon; it was the kind of collection that a die-hard New Yorker took with him to the grave.

The more David learned about Giovanni, the more he was in awe of the man and what he'd accomplished. During his recovery from his appendix bomb, David had had a chance to refresh his knowledge of the man he'd come to work for—a sort of "eye on the prize" exercise he'd put himself through to erase the bad taste of Gallo's prank with the enemas. Seeing this incredible sports collection—and knowing that, as a kid, Giovanni would sneak into Brooklyn Dodgers games because his parents, immigrants from the old country, couldn't afford to buy him tickets to see his beloved team play—was inspiring. David knew that Giovanni had switched his allegiance to the Yankees around the same time he'd dropped out of high school to start a landscaping company with two cousins who'd been Yankee fans from the start. After he'd rolled his landscaping profits into his first real estate success—a run-down tenement building in Borough Park he revamped and sold back to the city for twice what he'd paid for it—he'd bought season tickets, and his true love affair with the championship team had begun. Now that his family—three sons, two daughters, and six grandchildren between them—had inherited his passion for the team, he'd exchanged the season tickets for a box, which alone was no doubt more expensive than the first home he'd shared with his wife of thirty-one years. Giovanni was a true American success story, and his chairmanship of the Merc was just one more exclamation point on a résumé that spanned half a century.

Another few minutes went by as David alternately eyed the sports paraphernalia and the Italian pastries; both seemed equally off-limits, the trappings of a world he hadn't yet earned his way into. He contented himself with watching the seagulls dart and spin by the picture windows, flashes of glorious life in an otherwise characteristically gray sky.

Finally, Giovanni finished with his call and came around the side of his desk. Instead of sitting across from David, he put a hip against the windowsill, palming the hilt of a Louisville Slugger miniature baseball bat that even from a distance David could see had been signed by none other than Mickey Mantle.

"Everyone's talking about your exchange a few minutes ago on the trading floor."

David raised his eyebrows. That was fast. Giovanni grinned.

"This place lives on stories, rumors, and innuendo. Interesting tactic, kid. *Dago*. Personally, I probably would have decked you. But it was smart thinking. That trading floor is a schoolyard, and you gotta play by schoolyard rules."

David blushed, embarrassed that Giovanni knew about his trading badge, but thrilled that the man had complimented the thought behind it. And if Giovanni had heard the story, by now everyone in the building probably had too.

"Don't worry about Gallo," Giovanni continued, reading his mind. "He's a pathetic dinosaur. It might surprise you to know that we're about the same age. I know he seems three decades older—because while I've been swimming forward for the past fifty years, he's been treading water in this lucrative swamp of his. He's made a fortune in this place—and he doesn't see any reason to let anything change. From dairy to potatoes to heating oil to crude, these guys were tucked away in their insulated little corner of Manhattan, and nobody was watching—they had it all to themselves. Getting to work at nine-thirty and leaving at two. If they didn't have the NYMEX, they would be shining shoes. Gallo's got to understand—things *are* changing, David. Fast. Which is why I hired you in the first place."

David watched as Giovanni lifted the little baseball bat and twirled it in his hands.

"Anything I can do to help," David said, though it had sounded much less lame when it was just a thought in his head. "I've been reading up on oil and the exchange nonstop since my appendix exploded—but I think it's still going to take some time before I'm up to speed."

Giovanni laughed. "It took me ten years to get up to speed. But it's a different world now. And that's my point—it's the whole fucking world, not a little trading floor in a forgotten corner of New York. Oil is the biggest thing going, and it's only getting bigger. The whole world is watching—and guys like Gallo are going to have to learn to adapt."

Giovanni swung the bat in a low arc, nearly knocking a picture of George Steinbrenner off the glass shelves.

"Adapt to what?" David asked.

Giovanni winked at him. "That's what you're here to help figure out. How does this exchange fit into what's going on in the rest of the world? What's next? Automation? Expansion? Exchanges are springing up all over the place. Business is spreading. London, already big and growing every day. What's next? Hong Kong? Tokyo? I don't have a fucking clue. I'm an old guy in an old suit taking care of the other old guys in their old suits. But you and Reston, you're the future, and you're going to be my eyes and ears. Here at the Merc, and around the world."

David's heart was pounding again. A week ago he was looking forward to visiting old-age homes and calculating estate taxes; now Giovanni was talking about big issues, worldwide possibilities. He wasn't sure, specifically, what his role was going to be, but he liked the sound of it so far. Sadly, more edification was going to have to wait, as Giovanni was suddenly pointing the baseball bat toward the door.

"Now get your dago ass out of here, so I can get some work done. Harriet has some crap for you to go over for a meeting with some Washington politicos I'm taking tomorrow morning, so don't waste any more of your time getting into fights with the animals downstairs."

David hurried toward the door. As he passed through, Giovanni shouted after him:

"And, kid, I'm glad you didn't die at the board meeting. Would have been a lot of fucking paperwork to fill out."

Chapter 13

Four hours later, David was so deep in oil, he felt like one of those ducks they used to show on TV after the *Exxon Valdez* destroyed the coast of Alaska. The task Giovanni had assigned—via Harriet, of course, who actually smiled as she dropped the offending material into the in-box that had miraculously appeared on the desk in his cubicle while he was at home recovering from his appendix bomb—was fascinating in theory. David had to calculate what the potential risk to the oil market in general—and the NYMEX in particular—would be if a short but successful revolution ever took place in Iran. But given David's lack of knowledge of the industry, and his even more pathetic grasp of what really went on down on the trading floor, he was forced to start at the basics and work his way up. Four hours of Internet research and visits to the Merc library, and still he felt like a third-grader trying to write a college term paper.

After a fifteenth attempt at putting his thoughts together, he let his pencil clatter against the desk and rubbed his hands against his eyes. He had a feeling that Giovanni had assigned the task as an introduction by fire—and David was beginning to feel a little more than singed. He realized that he was going to need help.

He could really think of only one option. He grabbed a notepad from the drawer in his desk and strolled across the fifteenth floor toward an office to the left of the elevators. He was about to knock when the door swung inward with a creak of mechanical gears.

David stood in the open doorway, his closed fist still in the air.

"Isn't that cool? I had a guy install it after I saw it in a movie. Gives me an edge, right from the get-go. And it's really fun to see the looks on people's faces. Although in your case, it's a real improvement, considering the last time I saw you, you had a mouthful of carpet."

Still seated behind a desk nearly twenty feet away, Mendelson waved David into his office. As soon as David started to move, Mendelson hit a button on the underside of the desk, and the door slammed shut—nearly taking David's heels off in the process.

Mendelson's office wasn't as large or expensively attired as Giovanni's sports museum, but it still had more character than anything David had seen at Merrill Lynch. The dominant theme seemed to be air travel—or more specifically, luxury air travel. Photos and models of private airplanes lined two sets of steel shelves, and the open carpeted area in the center of the picture window–lit room was dominated by a scale model of some sort of futuristic-looking jet with a shiny tubular body, short curved wings, and a streamlined tail that made it look more rocket than plane.

"That's my baby," Mendelson said as David navigated around the model to take a seat on a small leather divan by Mendelson's desk. "She's the most beautiful girl I've ever met, and she can do New York to Paris in five hours."

"Sounds like you're in love," David said.

"You don't know the half of it. I left my second wife for that plane. Or more accurately, my second wife left me when I put seventy million dollars more into my baby than I had into my wife's wedding ring."

David laughed, then realized Mendelson was serious. *Seventy million dollars*. The number was staggering. He remembered what Reston had told him—that Mendelson had been one of the biggest traders around. Obviously, David had come to the right place for information about the trading floor.

"Mr. Mendelson, I need a crash course in trading."

Mendelson smiled. "From what I hear, you've already got the basics down. Pick out the biggest guy on the floor, insult the fuck out of him, then get out of the way."

David grinned. "If that was all there was to it, I'd be down there decking meatheads all afternoon."

"Hah. No, that's not all there is to it. Because those meatheads are actually pretty impressive, when you think about 'em. Not one of them is making less than five hundred thousand dollars a year. A few are bringing down millions, and an even smaller few are bringing down tens of millions."

David whistled. It was hard to imagine a guy like Vitzi making that kind of money. David knew the basics of trading—buy low, sell high, and the reverse—but when it came to oil in all its forms, he was a neophyte. How did you judge supply and demand? How did you factor in all the variables, from the weather to wars in the Middle East to drunk captains driving oil freighters into the Alaskan shoreline?

"It's like that scene in *The Matrix* where all the numbers are floating down the screen," Mendelson said, leaning back in his chair and lifting his bare feet up onto his desk. "At first, it seems like noise, none of it makes sense. It takes time to adapt to what's going on. And one day, suddenly, those numbers have meaning."

There's a method to the madness, he continued to explain, as David furiously filled his notepad. The chaos downstairs was actually a choreographed market system: the traders in the brightly colored jackets reacting to the shifting prices of the different categories of oil derivatives, buying and selling based on the supply and demand of the outside world. The traders were speculators

trying to guess which direction the price of crude oil was going to go and buying or selling future contracts—in blocks of a
thousand barrels per contract—to take advantage of their educated guesses. Some acted on instinct, some on various sources
of information—and some were pure gamblers. Some worked
in groups—like Gallo's zebra-striped jackets—because groups
of traders could keep tabs on one another and make sure each
member was reacting to the volatility of the market as efficiently
as possible. Others were lone wolves playing the market as their
fathers, and their fathers' fathers, had taught them.

"Whatever the method, the root of making money as a trader
is actually all math," Mendelson finally summed it up, and David
tapped his pencil against the notepad.

"You mean to tell me those meatheads are math geniuses?"
Guys who'd never gone to college, who grew up playing stickball
and stealing hubcaps from Camaros?

"Genius is a strong word," Mendelson said. "They're more
like savants. They know numbers the same way a gambler knows
cards—instinctively. And more importantly, they've got balls.
You have to know the math, and you have to be a scrapper. You
have to know how to fight."

David liked the sound of that, because nobody had ever ac-
cused him of not being able to hold his own in a fight. He had
never been the biggest guy on the playground, but he'd been the
one willing to keep getting up, no matter how bloody he got. He
realized what Mendelson was really telling him—to understand
trading, he needed to understand the traders, to know what made
them tick. He already had the basics, because he came from the
same place they did. But he needed to get to know how they used
that background day to day.

"The key to getting close to the traders is what happens
after the closing bell," Mendelson said. "There are three types of
people who trade the Merc. At two forty-five in the afternoon,
after the market's done and the papers have been filed, one third
of them are on the first train back to their wives and kids. An-

other third—guys like me—are on their way back to the office to start preparing for the next opening bell."

"And the last third?" David asked.

"The last third," Mendelson said with a grin, "are already on their way to the nearest bar."

Chapter 14

David grimaced as he kicked sawdust off his only pair of good leather shoes and lowered himself onto what looked like an over-turned wooden barrel. The table in front of him was supposed to be some sort of wagon wheel, but the wooden spokes were marred, warped and so heavily shellacked that the thing looked more like some sort of enormous circular fungus sprouting right up from the sawdust-covered floor.

To call this place a dive bar would have been an insult to the form; it was really more of a cowboy-themed cave, tucked into the shadows of a narrow alley two blocks from the exchange. The place was dingy, dark, and smelled of old beer and new sweat; even though it was barely three in the afternoon, the place was crowded—wall-to-wall men in their twenties and thirties, most of them in brightly colored jackets.

It hadn't been hard to track down the most popular NYMEX hangout in the area; all David had had to do was wait for the closing bell, then follow the stream of colored jackets as they traveled the short distance from the eighteenth-floor bar to the cowboy cave two blocks away. The place was called the Roadhouse, but it may have well been a raucous extension of the trading floor. The only real difference David could see from his perch near the back of the bar were the massive pitchers of cheap beer. And the waitresses of course—cute girls in jeans shorts and tied-off tank tops, probably NYU students from the looks of them, who had been lured to this armpit on the southern tip of the city by the promise of huge tips in the middle of the afternoon. It was either this or a strip club, and even Scores didn't do business like this at three in the afternoon.

The party had already been in full swing when David arrived. He had spotted Vitzi and the rest the minute he passed through the heavy double doors, but he had quickly taken his place at the table as far away from the action as possible. Still, he knew they had seen him come in. A few traders had looked up when he first arrived, using elbows and gestures to communicate the news to the other meatheads. David had done his best not to look directly at them. He was just there on a break from work, having a drink to blow off steam—he was just one of the boys.

It was a game, and David knew the rules—because he had played this game before. When he had first arrived at Oxford, he was the ultimate outsider—a brutish Yank at the most uptight bastion of English education. He had been an interloper, un-wanted, ignored. So he had engaged in the old schoolyard game. He had kept quiet and just followed the other students around from pub to pub until they were forced finally to acknowledge him. And slowly they had grown to accept his presence. Eventu-ally, that acceptance had turned into real friendships. The bumps in the road—a few black eyes, a few near-arrests—were all water under the bridge. Along the way, he had learned to drink like a Londoner, something that he knew was going to come in handy with this bunch as well.

He ordered a beer from one of the passing waitresses. When she returned with a glass the size of a vase, he tried not to think about the report he still had to write for Giovanni—or what Serena was going to say when he came home from work in the middle of the night, reeking of Milwaukee's Best. Still, he wasn't planning on spending the whole afternoon in the bar, just enough time to let the traders know he was going to be a fixture in their lives whether they liked it or not. He didn't expect them to approach him—just to accept his presence.

Assuming they would ignore him, he was surprised when a shadow crossed over his table, a dark reflection swimming across the foam of his oversized beer. He looked up—but it wasn't one of the traders. It was a huge man with curly dark hair, a thick beard, and a stained gray sweatshirt with the word SECURITY printed in big block letters across the chest. Of course, the guy hadn't needed the sweatshirt—because he had bouncer written all over him, especially when he put two huge paws on the table and leaned in close over David's beer.

"You got a problem, buddy?"

David stared at the behemoth of a man.

"Do I look like I have a problem?"

The guy's lips turned down at the corners, and he made a gesture toward the door.

"I suggest you get the fuck out of here before I throw you out."

David had been kicked out of bars before, but never for sitting quietly in a corner. He assumed that the traders were behind this. He had to hand it to them, getting him kicked out by a bouncer was going to put a crimp in his plan. He decided instantly that the worst thing he could do was to go quietly.

So instead he stood up from the table and got right in the guy's face.

"Look, dickhead, I'm having a really bad day. So if you want me to leave, it will have to be through the window, because there's no way in hell I'm going out through the door."

The bouncer's eyes widened. David doubted the huge man had ever been talked to like that before. *Probably for good reason.* David was mentally preparing himself for a second visit to the hospital in a single week when suddenly someone was shoving a hundred-dollar bill in the bouncer's meaty hand and leading him away from David's table. Before David could react, Vitzi was standing in front of him, his own meaty hands on his hips. He shook his cherubic head, his hair flopping over his forehead with the motion.

"Man, do you have balls."

David shrugged. His heat was still up, and if he hadn't backed down in front of the monstrous bouncer, he sure as hell wasn't stepping back now.

"They're big and brass, so go ahead and send over a few more bouncers, because I'm not leaving until I finish my goddamn beer."

Vitzi grinned at him.

"Okay, Russo, calm down. We were just fucking with you."

"Yeah, I know. I might have gone to Harvard, but I know how this shit works. My background isn't all that different from yours."

Vitzi crossed his arms against his chest. "I kinda doubt that. Unless your dad is also doing ten years at Rikers for a misunderstanding involving a dozen stolen BMWs. But hey, what do I know, I'm just a goddamn meathead."

David raised his eyebrows, then realized Vitzi was still grinning.

"Okay, my mistake. Maybe I had it a bit easier than you," David said. "So how the hell did you end up trading oil?"

Vitzi shrugged. "Same way most of us got into the Merc. Clawed my fucking way inside. I had a cousin who was clerking for one of Gallo's boys, and he managed to squeeze me in with him. I found out I was pretty good at keeping ten numbers in my head at the same time. Not a skill that means shit on the outside, but at the Merc it meant I had a chance. One in ten clerks become traders; I was lucky enough to be that one in ten. I went from being one of Gallo's shit heels to standing right next to him in the pit. Now I own the house I grew up in, and when I make my millions, I'm going to buy the rest of my fucking block."

David couldn't help but be impressed by Vitzi's story. Doubly amazed that the kid had stayed true to his Brooklyn roots—choosing to settle in the same place he'd grown up, even though he could easily be living in Manhattan, working his way toward Park Avenue. David guessed that was yet another difference between the traders of the Merc and those David had met at Merrill, those who worked on the NYSE. The NYSE boys wore Brooks Brothers suits and lived in apartments on the nicest blocks in New York. The Merc boys wore jeans and sweats and lived in the nicest houses on the shittiest blocks in Brooklyn. *Because that's where they had grown up, that's what they knew.*

"And here I just thought you were another asshole," David finally said. "I had no idea you were an asshole with a dream."

"An asshole *living* the dream," Vitzi corrected. "Now come over to the bar and I'll buy you the next round."

And with that, David suddenly found himself swept up into the crowd of brightly jacketed young men. He was introduced to Vitzi's cohorts: Joey Brunetti, a thick-necked twenty-seven-year-old punk from Staten Island with greasy brown hair and tattoos of pythons running up both arms—who also happened to be an expert in natural gas. And Jim Rosa, who wore a sweat suit every day beneath his trading jacket, was a part owner of a string of strip clubs in Brooklyn that had the most permissive dances on the East Coast, and knew more about trading crude than anyone since Alex Mendelson himself.

Over the next hour, David kept his mouth shut and his ears open; it wasn't a difficult task, because the only thing the meatheads seemed to like more than trading was talking about trading. Like Giovanni had said, these guys lived for their stories. And to David, who was just trying to understand the insanity of the Merc, those stories were gold: Tales of overwhelmed traders carried off the floor on stretchers, right in the middle of trading. Of new traders hazed by veterans, shoved out of the pit or isolated in corners without access to the rest of the floor. Of parties in hotel rooms after particularly profitable days, parties that usually involved strippers and lasted all night—right up until the next opening bell. Of the fierce lifestyles of the more success-ful meatheads, of weekend gambling jaunts to Vegas, of Ferraris parked right on the streets of Brooklyn.

"Yeah," Brunetti explained as he poured the last few ounces of a pitcher into David's glass before Vitzi ordered another round. "Leaving a car like mine on the street where I grew up is a fuck-ing gamble. But there's nothing we love more than a gamble."

"Even when we lose," Rosa said. "I'd rather lose a bet than not make a bet at all."

"Like just three weeks ago," Vitzi chimed in. "Brunetti here was talking shit about how fast he is. How he ran track in junior high or some crap like that—"

"As if this dumb fuck ever made it past eighth grade," Rosa interrupted.

"Hey," Vitzi spat, "let me finish the goddamn story. So Bru-netti says he can beat any one of us in a race, any time. It's like eleven in the morning, right in the middle of trading, and one of the natural gas guys decides to take the bet. We all head outside in our jackets, with our buy tickets still jammed in our pockets, and they go at it. A hundred yards, right along the East River. Brunetti wins by a hair."

David gave the tattooed trader a thumbs-up. "So how much did you win?"

"Something much better than money," Brunetti grinned. "The next day, the other guy's clerk had to show up dressed like a woman. And, man, the kid was really decked out. Tube top, high heels, blond wig, full makeup. He was so cute, I thought Rosa here was going to get his number."

"Fuck you," Rosa said as another pitcher arrived in front of them. Then he shrugged. "I've always been a sucker for a good tube top. Last month we were at the Yankees game—"

"The three of us had a whole box rented out. One of the prime ones, maybe fifty, sixty thousand dollars—"

"And not halfway into the first inning," Rosa continued, "I see this chick walking past the entrance in this silver tube—man, she had some rockets on her—and I went right in for the kill. Okay, maybe I was a little aggressive, but I had no idea she was on her way to the owner's box. Or that she was Steinbrenner's second cousin. Before I know it, I'm getting hauled out of there by five security guards who don't even have the decency to let me take my beer with me."

"Hell, we paid fifty thousand dollars for that beer!" Vitzi shouted. They were getting louder now, but David didn't care. He was in heaven, listening to the stories.

For the next hour, the stories continued—sometimes bawdy, sexual, even disturbing, but always entertaining. Often they involved gambling; the traders would bet on almost anything, from a one-hundred-yard dash down the East River to a push-up contest—right in the middle of the trading floor—to seeing how quickly they could get themselves thrown out of a bar. Just as often, the stories involved excessive drinking and even more excessive womanizing. The young traders obviously lived a wild life, fueled by the money they were making and enabled by the hours they kept. Getting off work at two in the afternoon meant that there was much more time for them to get into trouble—and with the bankrolls they were developing, that trouble often grew to epic proportions. They'd been kicked out of hotels, strip clubs, restaurants, and, of course, bars. And the bigger the story they could retell the next day, the more valued the escapade itself.

Even more than the stories, David found himself truly enjoying the camaraderie as the afternoon progressed and turned into evening. He assumed it was still a temporary warm front—but he had definitely taken the first baby steps. David hoped that if he played his cards right, sooner or later, these crazy, hard-living traders would begin to accept him as one of their own.

DAVID DIDN'T MAKE it back to the fifteenth floor until well after 9:00 P.M. He was flushed and alive in a way he hadn't felt since he'd graduated from business school, and the feeling was only partially due to the numerous pints of beer he'd imbibed over the past six hours. It was late, to be sure, and he had a lot of work still ahead of him. But after a full day in the company of a dozen young traders, David was sure he could give Giovanni something that would make the man proud.

He came out of the elevator at full speed, determined to get right to work. But before he'd made it two steps toward his cubicle, he saw something that made him change direction: Harriet, directly ahead, on her knees in front of her desk, a huge mess of binders open on the carpet in front of her. She was cursing loudly, and even from a distance David could see that tears of frustration were making a mess of her heavy green eye shadow.

David quickly hurried over to her.

"You look like you could use some help," he said, lowering himself to her level.

She angrily dabbed at her eyes with her sleeve.

"It's these fucking reports from the rest of the board members—Giovanni needs them wrapped up and collated first thing in the morning, and the photocopier is on the blink, and I was supposed to be home two hours ago because I come home so late every night my boyfriend thinks I'm cheating on him, and I really wish I was cheating on him instead of locked away in this hellhole—"

"Whoa," David said. It was one hell of a run-on sentence to digest, especially after so many beers. He was surprised to see this side of Harriet—there was nothing about her that seemed even remotely weak-skinned. "Let's just work together on this. I'm sure we can get it done in no time."

David knew he was fucking up his own evening by helping her, but what the hell, he was no stranger to all-nighters. Harriet finally nodded, and together they went to work on the binders. It was the sort of detail-oriented crap that David had gotten good at in his brief stint at Merrill, and by ten they were already moving through the last few files. All the while, Harriet talked and David listened. She told him about her sisters, who were both married with four kids apiece. About her father, a former priest turned scrap-metal salesman, who still lived in the same house he had first moved into when he'd immigrated from Italy. And about her boyfriend, who sounded like a real piece of work. He had failed out of cop school twice and was now a security guard in a bank in Midtown. Harriet stayed with him because she was pushing forty-five, and she didn't really mind being the bigger earner, because Giovanni treated her real well. As he should, considering she'd been with the Merc for fifteen years.

By the time they finished with the last binder, David felt like they were old friends. After putting the stack back on her desk, she leaned forward, gave him a quick kiss on the cheek, and hurried toward the elevators. When the elevator doors opened, she was moving so fast, she nearly ran headlong into Reston. Reston sidestepped her, then saw David still straightening the binders on her desk. He sidled over, arms crossed against his chest.

"Well, look at you. Helping out, way past your bedtime, eh, Harvard boy?"

Reston's Texas accent was really coming out; David smelled whiskey on his breath and assumed he had just come from the lounge upstairs.

"I try to do the right thing," David said. "Once in a while you have to at least pretend to be human."

Reston snorted, about to respond, when muffled drunken voices came out of the elevator behind him. They both turned just in time to see Vitzi and Rosa wrestling to see who could get through the open elevator doors first—the effect being that neither one of them was likely to make it before the doors reclosed on them.

"Hey, David," Vitzi yelled through the few inches of space between the shutting doors. "We came back for you. You still owe us a pitcher."

David quickly thought through the work he had left, then sighed. "Maybe in a few hours, if you're still at the bar. Otherwise, you jackasses are on your own."

Before they could respond, the elevator had shut. David turned and realized Reston was staring at him.

"A few days ago, these guys are calling you my girlfriend and putting enemas in your hospital room. Now they're inviting you out to drink with them?"

David shrugged.

"My report cards always said I make friends easily."

"Maybe you're not as pathetic as I'd thought. You keep getting in good with the meatheads, and I'll get some use out of you yet. Hell, you're going to be my goddamn guinea translator!"

Now David knew Reston was drunk. But to tell the truth, he kind of liked the designation. That's exactly what he was, a guinea translator. One foot in the traders' world, one foot in Reston's.

Then Reston said something that pricked at David's thoughts.

"You know, the time's gonna come when I'm going to have the power to make some real changes around here. Giovanni has tried—but he's got too much to lose to really do things right. But me—I've got nothing to lose. And Giovanni isn't going to be here forever. When he leaves, who do you think is going to be running this place? And if you somehow manage to last long enough to be here when that happens, you might just luck out yourself, Harvard boy. "

David opened his mouth, but couldn't think of anything to say. He wasn't sure if Reston was talking out of his ass or, in his inebriated state, really trying to tell David something.

Either way, it was kind of a scary thought: the most powerful exchange on earth in the hands of a thirty-five-year-old Texan and his Guinea translator.

Chapter 15

If one were to choose a place in which to have an existential dilemma, one could do a lot worse than a two-story penthouse suite in the Burj Al Arab Hotel.

Khaled leaned back against a luxurious leather couch in the center of one of the suite's huge, glass-walled living rooms, while he watched two European men unroll blueprint after blueprint across the raised, circular glass coffee table in front of him. The two men were well dressed—both in tailored blue suits with crisply ironed ties—but their sartorial splendor paled in comparison to the magnificent decor surrounding them. Polished marble floors, multiple flat-screen TVs, Impressionist art on the walls, a redwood bar running the length of the room that would have rivaled the bar in most watering holes in Cambridge—and this was just one of two living rooms in the suite. Khaled had been given a full tour before the meeting began, and he knew that behind the bar a Plexiglas spiral staircase led upward to a second living room that contained a free-standing, smoked-glass wet room, a media center, two Jacuzzis, and a full-scale model of the ever-changing city down below.

Still, the decor of the place was secondary; it was the glass walls and the 360-degree views they provided that justified the thirty-thousand-dollar-a-night rate the hotel was charging the Europeans. The view was fitting, of course, considering the reason the Europeans had invited Khaled to their suite—and the reason he had accepted their invitation on his eighth day of work with the Finance Ministry. Even from his sunken position on the plush leather he could see the forest of cranes, the framework of constant construction clawing upward into the monumental work in progress that was the city's skyline.

Madness. He could think of no other word for it, though of course even that choice of word was not sufficient. Madness had a negative connotation; what was going on around Khaled was not wrong—it was simply *mad.* He could honestly say that the past eight days had negated everything he had ever learned in business school. Because what was going on outside that window, every day, was so unique in human history that no business textbook or lauded professor could possibly hope to explain it.

The Europeans were a case in point. Khaled shifted his gaze from the windows to the closer of the two men. He had introduced himself as Evin Mcdonough; to Khaled, he was a wild-eyed Irishman with a crown of bright red hair and shiny gold rings on all ten of his fingers. At the moment, he was fighting with one of the blueprints, trying to get the corners to stay flat against the glass table.

The second European was leaning over the Irishman's shoulder, watching the battle with a mixture of bemusement and concern. He had called himself Nigel Barrett, but to Khaled he was an officious Englishman with wire-rimmed glasses and a thin, almost lipless smile.

It was a trick Khaled's uncle had taught him: names were never as good labels as images, which is why people often forgot names but never forgot first impressions. Khaled doubted he would ever forget this meeting in the Al Arab's lavish penthouse suite. Because it wasn't just a first impression of the two men he was witnessing, but a first impression of what his new role in life would be.

Thus, the existential dilemma.

He watched, silently, as the wild-eyed Irishman finally got the blueprint to behave, then stood back, a wide smile on his triangular face. The Englishman looked expectantly toward Khaled, waiting for his response.

Khaled simply could not find the words.

It would have been easier to respond if the two men really were mad—but if anyone deserved to be in a suite such as this, it was these two. The wild-eyed Irishman controlled a seven-billion-dollar real estate fund. The lipless Englishman ran one of the biggest architectural engineering firms in the world. Together, they had built many of the world's most impressive hotels, sky-scrapers, museums, and shopping malls. Still, nothing they had ever done before came close to the projects that were represented by the blueprints they had laid out in front of Khaled.

And these blueprints were just the tip of the iceberg. All week long Khaled had been taking meetings like this. Indeed, dealing with this sort of insanity was the bulk of his job at the ministry. Looking out the windows at the cranes that stretched for miles and miles in every direction, what else could he have expected?

Madness. Even though the entire city-state around him had a population of only 1.4 million people, the relative level of construction dwarfed that of the entire Asian continent, China included. By creating an economic free-zone—unique in the re-gion—and vigorously pursuing foreign partners, the great emir had turned the city into the fastest-growing metropolis on earth. But Sheik Maktoum and his brother Muhammed had not been content to build just another Arab city in a remarkably free cor-ner of the Arab world—each construct had to be *remarkable* in its own right.

You couldn't simply build a hotel; it had to be the Burj Al Arab, the tallest hotel in the world, with a huge sail spanning its entire thousand-foot facade.

You couldn't simply build an island: the Palm Islands, when finished, would be the world's largest man-made island structure—built from a staggering billion cubic meters of sand. And even that was not sufficient for the sheiks: plans were already in place to build an even *bigger* set of islands, designed to resemble the entire world when seen from the air.

You couldn't simply build a shopping mall. The planned supermall that was soon to break ground had to be the largest shopping mall in the world. Twelve million square feet, containing fifteen mini-malls, an ice skating rink, an aquarium, and the world's largest Arab souk.

You couldn't simply build a skyscraper. The emir would soon announce the construction of what would become the world's tallest structure—the final height of which would be a closely guarded secret, an indication of his resolve to attain and hold the title for years to come. Estimates that Khaled had seen in the finance minister's office called for a height upward of twenty-five hundred feet.

And the list continued, on and on:

The world's largest indoor ski slope.

The world's largest museum.

The world's largest—and only—underwater hotel. Completely submerged, accessible only by submarine.

And then there was what the two Europeans were now proposing. If Khaled had not been staring at the blueprints with his very own eyes, he would have thought it was some sort of bizarre joke.

"Of course, some of the technology is still in development," the Englishman finally said, to break the silence. "But I assure you by the time we near completion—2010, we believe—it will be fully operational."

Fully operational. Khaled stared at the blueprint, but still could think of nothing to say.

A fully operational space port, where one day tourists would book trips to the stars. Khaled would have laughed out loud—except it wasn't a joke. It was utter madness—but it was all real.

Khaled had been listening to men like the two Europeans all week long—architects, developers, money managers, urban visionaries—and by now his brain was overflowing with images of a country transforming so fast that it simply did not exist in the present tense.

By the year 2010, when this space port would be completed, the emir's goal was to have fifteen million annual tourists—to a country of one and a half million people. A country whose outdoor temperature regularly reached over 120 degrees. A country that happened to be located smack dab in the center of the war-torn Arab world.

A noble, region-changing goal, magnificent and on a scale almost unimaginable. And Khaled was proud to now be a part of the emir's vision. But at the same time he knew that his role as an agent of tourism—even on the scale that the sheiks hoped to achieve—would not ultimately be fulfilling. He believed he was destined for something more.

Khaled had to believe that for him there were more important things ahead than ski slopes and underwater hotels. He knew, from his own studies, that the emir's goal of turning the country into the ultimate tourist destination was more than simply impressive—it was actually a matter of survival. Unlike other sheiks in the region, the emir's source of wealth had an expiration date—because, simply put, unlike other sheiks in the region, he was facing a situation unique in the Arab world: his oil reserves were going to run out—perhaps within the next fifteen years. So he had come up with a plan to use the wealth he had now to create a new source of wealth for the future.

Tourism to replace oil.

But to Khaled—and assuredly to the emir—this was only the beginning. Tourism and oil were very different beasts. To Khaled, raised in part by a sheik whose seemingly limitless fortune and power were based on what the Arab street had long called "the Black Blood of Allah," oil was much more than just a source of wealth. A nation built on oil was not the same as a nation built on tourism. Khaled, and certainly the emir, knew that tourism alone would simply turn the city-state into a curiosity, an amusement park of sorts. *A huge Arab Disney World.*

There had to be more. And Khaled was determined to use all his faculties to find that next, magnificent leap forward—whatever form it took.

"So," said the wild-eyed Irishman, coughing, his fierce energy finally overcoming his patience, "what do you think?"

Khaled took a deep breath, then pressed his hands together, resting his chin against his fingers. "A space port. Very intriguing. Maybe we could also add some layers to the project. Maybe find some prehistoric DNA. Build an amusement park next door, filled with giant dinosaurs."

The Irishman looked at him for a full beat, then rubbed his angled jaw. "I'm not sure that's something we've figured out yet, is it?"

There was a brief pause, and then the Europeans finally realized Khaled was joking. The Englishman let out a little laugh, then took off his glasses and cleaned the lenses with a sleeve. "Seriously, Mr. Aziz, let's get down to business. The space port is just one idea. We've got plenty more." Undeterred, he pulled another blueprint out from behind the coffee table and placed it on top of the space port plan. "Now this is something really cool, a ten-million-square-foot water park that rotates three hundred sixty degrees every six hours. And get this—*the entire thing is actually one hundred feet underground.*"

Somewhere between the man's description of an inverted waterfall that ran up instead of down and the longest man-made lazy river in existence, Khaled's mind began to wander. If he had all the money and power of a sheik, and he really wanted to change the world, where would he look for inspiration?

Chapter 16

I could get used to this," Serena said, and David squeezed her hands through her wool mittens, going in for a little kiss.

"See, I told you window-shopping could be almost as satisfying as the real thing. Who needs stuff anyway? It would just get in the way of our squalor."

Serena laughed, then pulled him along after her to look at the next store display. David nearly dropped his hat—a Russian job, rabbit fur on top and earflaps that made him look like something out of a 1960s cartoon—and had to twist his body to avoid running into a pair of foreign tourists in matching bright blue puffy coats.

"Slow down," he said. "The windows aren't going anywhere."

With his free hand, he pulled his hat down tighter against his head. The air was crisp and cool, and it was one of those bright fall afternoons that smelled and felt and sounded like New York. He and Serena were strolling hand in hand down Fifth Avenue—the crowded blocks right up near the park—people watching, window-shopping, decompressing from what had been a tense few weeks in their lives and their relationship. And for the first time in days they were both smiling; the reflection David had seen dancing across the glass facade outside of Trump Tower had filled him with pure joy. Serena laughing in the white coat with fur trim that he had given her for her last birthday, a brightly colored scarf wrapped around her throat; he chasing after her, in the foolish hat and one of his father's old gray overcoats, the collar turned up and the buttons running all the way down past his knees.

David was almost beginning to feel human again. After an entire month submerged in the world of high-stakes oil, this was the first afternoon he had spent away from the exchange—and he was loving every minute of it. More important, he was beginning to feel like part of a couple again after four weeks of being an invisible man—coming home after Serena was asleep, leaving before she woke up, every phone conversation becoming an argument about how much he was working and how much more of this she thought she could take, the sort of conversations that David could imagine happening all over the New York financial world. The bottom line was, to succeed in David's game, you had to be smart, you had to be determined—and you had to put in the time. You needed someone by your side—and she had to be the most understanding girl on the planet.

Serena was understanding, but certainly no saint; she'd gone after David and his work hours on more than one occasion, to the point where he'd even begun to wonder if he was making sacrifices that could cause a real rift in their relationship. But the more he got inside the inner workings of the Merc, the more he knew that he belonged there, that he had made the right decision that late night after the meeting at Morton's.

The truth was, he had become more Reston's kid than Giovanni's. Sure, Giovanni handed him the odd assignment from time to time, but most of David's days were spent on projects that came directly from Reston's office. The fact that Giovanni was almost never at the Merc—or, for that matter, in the country, as far as David could tell—was part of the reason things seemed to work that way, but David was also beginning to believe that Giovanni had intentionally delegated much of the Merc's business to Reston. It was Reston who came up with the topics for the board meetings. It was Reston who had drafted most of the recent amendments to the exchange's manifesto. And it was Reston who arbitrated the ugly issues that came up from the trading floor— almost on a daily basis, and almost always involving Gallo or his extensive network of influence.

Giovanni was still David's idol, but Reston had become his boss. And the thing was, even after a month, Reston still hadn't warmed to him. No matter how hard David tried, he'd been unable to earn Reston's complete trust. It was driving David crazy.

He had never worked so hard in his life: ten-hour days, seven days a week, learning the ins and outs of the energy exchange, following the traders from the floor to the upstairs lounge to the bars, sometimes to nightclubs and strip joints—just about everywhere. Sometimes those excursions lasted all night—and once in a while even longer. In fact, one party the traders threw at Crowbar, the legendary Manhattan nightclub, had gone on until noon the next day and cost Vitzi and his friends almost a quarter-million dollars. David had been there until the last guest had stumbled away—because every minute he was with the traders was a minute he was learning about the Merc.

He had truly become Reston's guinea translator: every time Reston wanted to know what the traders on the floor would think of a project he was about to implement, he'd come to David—and David would give him the traders' perspective with near-perfect accuracy.

And yet Reston remained detached and even skeptical—and his attitude toward David often bordered on palpable disdain. Sometimes Reston went so far as to have David bring a notepad to work with him; he'd make David follow a few steps behind, taking notes like a secretary. *Write and walk,* he'd tell David as they went, *that's how you learn in this business.*

It was more than just the odd crack about David's schooling

or his lack of energy experience; the Texan simply didn't seem
to believe that David was there for the long haul and acted as
though he knew that, sooner or later, David would decide he'd
had enough—and bolt.

The thought brought David back to the newest story from
the Merc floor—about a kid named Andre Donneli. Donneli had
been trading heating oil for two years, but recently hit a slump.
Then one day just a week ago, he made a particularly bad trade
and lost over six hundred thousand dollars. Story was, he had
walked right off the trading floor, gotten into his car, and just
driven away. Nobody had seen or heard from him since.

David had no idea what it would be like to lose six hundred
thousand dollars in an afternoon. Hell, with his salary and debts,
he was barely going to make it through the Christmas season—
and the way Serena was peering into the window of the Gucci
store a few feet ahead, he wasn't even sure he'd make it through
the rest of his day off. But no matter what happened, he was determined to stick it out at the Merc. Reston be damned—

His thoughts were suddenly interrupted by a dull vibrating
noise coming from somewhere deep in his overcoat. Serena turned
away from the Gucci window long enough to glare at him, but he
just shrugged, digging between the buttons of his coat.

"Serena . . . ," he started to explain, but she just rolled her
eyes and turned back to the window.

He pulled the phone free. Though the display told him it was
an unlisted number, he had more than a feeling that the call was
work-related. The hours he had been keeping had pretty much
chased away most of his friends outside of the Merc, along with
almost all aspects of his social life. His cell phone had become
an extension of that fucking fortress in Lower Manhattan. He
expected the call was from either Harriet or one of the traders;
the only reason he'd taken the afternoon off in the first place was
that Reston was out of the country, speaking alongside Giovanni
at some conference in Europe. David had assumed that an entire
ocean would protect him, at least for a few hours.

"David here," he said, pressing the phone to his ear.

To his surprise, it was indeed Reston. Voice partially muffled by the distance, even though he obviously had an international cell phone. *Damn that fucking technology,* David thought to himself as he took a step away from Serena so she wouldn't have to hear him grovel—in case he felt the need.

"David, I'm really in deep shit here."

David almost dropped the phone as a pair of Japanese women carrying twice their weight in shopping bags bustled past. He had never heard Reston sound so frazzled before, and it could only be bad news for him.

"Where are you?" David asked.

"Amsterdam. I'm here with Giovanni, and I'm giving a keynote speech at some fucking conference at eight A.M. tomorrow morning."

David took a deep breath. He was really afraid of where this was heading, especially as Reston's voice pitched upward an octave on the other end of the line.

"David, I left all my notes on the airplane. I've got nothing. I need you to write a new speech for me."

David's eyes went wide. *And on the Sunday before Thanksgiving, his one day off from work.*

"On what subject?" he finally asked.

"The North Sea crude market. I know, it's fucking arcane, but that's what the conference is about. I need ten pages, stat. And don't forget, it's six hours ahead here—David, can I count on you?"

David could hear it in Reston's words—the Texan didn't believe that he could. David felt his eyes narrow, his grip on the phone tightening.

"Nick, I'll get it done."

David hung up the phone and shoved it back into his coat. Then he stood there, buffeted by the continued stream of passersby, cursing to himself. *The North Sea crude market?* He didn't know a damn thing about the North Sea, other than it ran along the side of Norway; he certainly didn't know anything about its energy market. Hell, it would take him a few minutes to find the place on a map.

But he wasn't going to let Reston down. He was no Andre Donneli—hell, he didn't even own a car. He wouldn't give the skeptical Texan the satisfaction of being right about him.

He slowly walked back to the Gucci window, where Serena was pretending not to have watched the entire phone conversation. He stood next to her, silently counting the seconds, when finally she turned to face him.

"I know." She sighed. "Go, do what you have to do."

Before he could say anything in response, she grabbed the collar of his overcoat with one hand and pulled him in close. But instead of going for a kiss, she dug into his inside pocket with her free hand and deftly retrieved his wallet.

"But I'm taking your credit card. The longer you take, the more I'm going to spend."

David grinned at her. Then he went in for that kiss—and took off at full speed down Fifth Avenue.

Chapter 17

As David's index finger plunged toward his laptop's keyboard, he felt a rush of adrenaline that was completely out of place in the back corner of a Midtown Starbucks. Of course, the Starbucks itself was at least partially to blame. The Goth chick behind the counter—the one with too much eye shadow and a pierced bottom lip—should certainly have cut him off after his third latte. Instead, she had happily cooked up a fourth—and he was really flying now, every nerve in his body going off in a wondrous symphony of caffeine-fueled bliss. Not only was he hopped up on the finest coffee to ever come out of Seattle; he had just finished what he believed to be the best presentation he had ever written. And at the moment he did not believe there were any words in the English language more beautiful or poetic than the two that now appeared on the computer screen in front of him:

Message Sent

He leaned back from the laptop and stretched his arms above his head. He could hardly believe that he'd done it: fourteen pages, ten accompanying visual slides, and hell, enough information about North Sea crude to get Reston elected to Norway's Board of Trade. It was an amazing accomplishment considering that six hours ago David could not have told Reston what Norway's capital was, or even if Norway *had* any oil exports at all. Turns out it did; in fact, Norway was sitting on more than half of the entire European continent's oil reserves. Most of Norway's economy consisted of oil exportation—but that would soon change. North Sea exports were decreasing at a rapid rate, creating an opportunity for gradual replacement of the crude contract—probably with a different form of crude exported from the Middle East.

And on top of that, Norway's capital was Oslo.

David smiled, rubbing his bloodshot eyes. The lighting in the Starbucks was abysmal; when David had first chosen the little table in the back corner of the crowded coffee shop, there had been plenty of sunlight streaming in through the glass picture windows at the front of the building. But the sun had vanished hours ago, along with most of the other customers. Anyone foolish enough to crave Starbucks after nine at night was either trading Japanese futures or researching Norwegian crude—in short, desperate for free Internet access and the strength to stay up all night if need be.

But the project Reston had assigned David had come together much faster than he had expected, and now he wasn't going to have to stay up all night after all. Really, it had been like an assignment one would get at Harvard Business School—only at HBS David had been forced to deal with overachieving "study partners," because at business school there really was no "I" in "Team." In the real world, David had discovered, teams were all "I"—and little else. Reston didn't want them to work together on the speech—he wanted David to deliver it, lock, stock, and smoking PowerPoint slides.

David shut his laptop with a flourish and rose from his seat. There were muscle spasms going off in both of his calves, and his heart felt like it was trying to tango up his esophagus—but

he'd delivered all right, and with plenty of time to spare. Nine
P.M. in New York, which meant that it was three in the morning
in Amsterdam. Reston was probably still sleeping off whatever
volume of scotch he'd managed to consume since they'd last spoken. Despite the time, David doubted he himself would have the
luxury of any sleep, considering how much caffeine was in his
system, but at least Serena would get to see him for a few more
hours before another week at the Merc began—and the invisible
man returned.

To DAVID'S SURPRISE, even a near-lethal dose of caffeine had
been no match for the collected exhaustion of a month of seventy-
hour weeks. In fact, he'd only lasted a few minutes longer than
Serena, falling into a deep sleep while her head was still resting
on his chest, sometime around midnight. A sleep so deep, he'd
have probably slept right through the incessant braying of his cell
phone had Serena not yanked the pillow out from under his head
to cover her own ears against the sound.

"Will you please do something about that?" she said as she
curled herself into a ball on the bed next to him. He blinked
rapidly, trying to scare the sleep from his eyes. Then he pulled
himself to a sitting position. His cell phone stopped for a second—then started up again, its polyphonic wail cutting through
the dark bedroom. David searched for the digital clock on the
small table by his bed. Four A.M. Not even his mother would call
him at 4:00 A.M. unless it was an emergency—and that was saying something.

He grimaced as he slipped out from under the comforter and
padded across the cold hardwood floor. He found his jeans by the
closet door and clumsily searched the pockets for his phone.

"What is wrong with these people?" Serena mumbled as David
finally yanked the phone free. "Don't they ever sleep?"

David grunted a response. "Yeah, in caves. Hanging from the
ceiling. I promise to keep this short."

He angrily pressed the receive button and jammed the phone against his ear.

"Yes?" he said, refusing to try to find more appropriate words at four in the morning. This time he wasn't surprised to hear Reston's voice on the other end of the line.

"David, it's Nick. I'm on an airplane, on my way back to New York. Giovanni's with me, and we've got about five minutes before takeoff."

David fought the urge to chuck the phone against the wall.

"That's great, Nick. Be sure to enjoy the in-flight movie."

"Shut up, kid. Listen, I'm going to ask you a question, and I'll know right away if you're lying."

David sighed. He didn't know what game Reston was up to now, but he had no choice but to play along.

"Okay. Go ahead."

"Did you copy that speech from somewhere?"

This time David really did come inches away from chucking the phone.

"Fuck you, Nick."

"Seriously, kid. I'm asking you a question."

David clenched his teeth and lowered his voice. "No, I did not copy that speech."

There was a long pause on the other end of the line. When Reston finally came back on, his tone had changed in a way that David had never heard before.

"I've been underestimating you, kid."

David could tell that, for once, Reston was entirely sincere. Despite the hour, despite his anger at having been awakened by the phone call, David felt a thrill move through him. He realized, with a start, that it was the most meaningful compliment he'd received since leaving business school.

"Tomorrow afternoon," Reston continued, in that same respectful tone, "keep your schedule free. We have something important to discuss."

With that, the phone went dead. David placed it carefully on the nearby dresser and padded back across the hardwood floor to his bed. He didn't get under the comforter; instead he sat on the edge, thinking about the phone call. Then he smiled.

Finally, he had broken through Reston's skepticism. He couldn't be sure, but from the Texan's tone, he had a pretty good feeling that from now on things were going to be different.

It wasn't until the next afternoon that David realized just *how* different. In fact, the next afternoon David discovered that his life was about to change—in ways he could never have imagined.

Chapter 18

David should have seen the bombshell coming the minute Harriet led him into the vacant office on the fifteenth floor, then quickly took her leave, mumbling something under her breath about coffee and doughnuts and a going-away party. Instead, David simply stood there like an idiot, in the middle of the empty fifteen-by-fifteen space, staring at the bare walls and the pair of floor-to-ceiling windows, wondering why the hell Reston had wanted to meet in an empty room rather than in his own office, which was right next door.

When Reston finally arrived, David never had a chance to ask that question—because right behind Reston was Giovanni, and right behind Giovanni were two men in overalls carrying an oversized wooden desk.

"Somebody moving in here?" David asked as Giovanni checked out the view and Reston directed the two men toward a corner.

"Yeah," Giovanni answered. "You."

David stared at him. Giovanni pointed through the glass, toward a spot off to the left.

"Hey, you can see the Brooklyn Bridge. Might even be better than your view, Nicky."

David cleared his throat.

"Excuse me, Mr. Giovanni, I think I misunderstood—"

"David," Reston interrupted, as the two moving men finished with the desk and headed out of the room, "shut up and listen."

He shut the door behind the men, then crossed his arms against his chest. Giovanni turned away from the window and aimed his handsome smile at David.

"I told you that this place is changing—well, turns out it's changing a bit faster than even I predicted. David, tomorrow I'm giving my notice. I've chosen not to run for reelection as chairman of the board. I'm leaving the Merc."

The announcement was like a gunshot to David's chest. He exhaled, leaning back against a stark white wall. Giovanni was the whole reason he had come to the energy exchange. And now, barely a month later, Giovanni was leaving? Why? It didn't make sense. Giovanni seemed to love his job—and he certainly loved the Merc. He was the most loyal and proud leader one could want. Why would he leave?

Or was it entirely his choice? Could he have been pushed out by Gallo and the old-school traders, with whom he seemed so much at odds? David glanced at Reston, trying to read the Texan's face. He could see a mixture of emotions there: sadness, apprehension—but also anticipation. *Exhilaration.*

Maybe David was thinking about this all wrong. Maybe Giovanni really did want to leave—for good reasons. David thought back to the conversation he had had with Reston that evening in the hallway. Reston had said that Giovanni couldn't enact real changes at the Merc—because he had too much to lose. Well, maybe Giovanni was leaving to give Reston a chance to fight those battles head on.

"I don't know what to say," David exhaled, looking from one man to the other, from his idol to his boss. "Mr. Giovanni—why?"

David hadn't meant for the question to come out like that—or even at all. But it was such a shock, he hadn't been able to censor himself.

Giovanni simply laughed.

"Too many reasons. Or maybe not enough reasons. It doesn't matter—my decision is made."

Obviously, Giovanni wasn't going to tell David any more than that. Hell, maybe Giovanni simply didn't want to be there anymore. He was incredibly wealthy, after all. He owned a number of companies and could spend his life in any city in the world. He could even go after one of the New York sports franchises if he so desired.

The fact was, he was going.

And who did that leave in charge?

Giovanni stepped away from the window, crossed the room, and put his arm around Reston's wide shoulders.

"We're bringing in a new chairman in a few months, but for the moment, unofficially, you're looking at the new head of the New York Mercantile Exchange."

Christ. When Reston had first floated the idea a month ago— that he could one day be running the place—David had been naive enough to think it might be possible. But over the past few weeks he'd realized how insane an idea like that really was. Reston was in his midthirties. He was an outsider, a Texan with Irish blood. To go up against Gallo and his ilk, without Giovanni there to back him up—it seemed insane. Reston was going to get eaten alive.

David stifled those thoughts for the moment and held out his hand.

"Congratulations, Nick."

Reston grinned as he shook David's hand. Then Giovanni dropped an even bigger bombshell.

"And as my final act as chairman, tomorrow I'm making you vice president of strategy. This is your office, and from now on you're Nicky's right-hand man."

David opened his mouth, then closed it again. *Vice president of strategy*. He was twenty-five years old. He'd been at the Merc for less than a month. He'd shown some sparks of ingenuity, sure; he'd befriended the younger traders, had some success with many of Reston's projects, and had written a damn good speech on Norwegian crude. But there had to be dozens of other people who were more qualified. This seemed impossible. Ridiculous. This was happening too fast.

He realized there had to be a deeper reason why Giovanni would make him a vice president of the exchange. Once before he had felt like a pawn in a game between Gallo and Giovanni. Maybe he really was a pawn—and now Giovanni was striking back at Gallo and his kind by putting one of his kids in an office on the fifteenth floor. The truth was, David hadn't yet really proved himself. He hadn't yet had that chance. No doubt, this move would create a shit-storm downstairs; sure, some of the traders liked David, but would they accept him as a figure of any sort of authority?

"I'm stunned," David finally managed. Truthfully, he was way more than stunned. He was a range of emotions that ran from terrified all the way to skeptical. He knew he was being given this promotion for reasons other than his own performance—and that scared him. He also knew he would be put in a precarious position with the board and the traders—which made him even more nervous. But still, it wasn't something he was going to turn down, that was for sure. How many twenty-five-year-olds got the chance to be vice president of anything? Even if it was just a title, he was going to try to enjoy the moment.

Instead of a response, Giovanni reached out and gave him a full embrace. Then he headed for the door, Reston right behind him.

"You keep your head down and do whatever the fuck Nicky tells you to do," Giovanni said as he exited the room. "And, David, don't ever forget: there's a lot more to be scared of around here than bears."

With that, David was left alone in his office.

Windows, walls, and a door.
His own goddamn office.

THE REST OF the day went by so fast, David didn't even mind the fact that he was still boxing up his cubicle when Harriet passed by on her way home—a sure sign that he was the last one left standing, aside from the security guards and an odd janitor or two. He was so engulfed in the boxes and his own thoughts that it took him a moment to realize Harriet had paused behind him, looking over his shoulders at his piles of crap and multiple binders of unfinished projects. Then she shook her head.

"I feel like my little boy's moving away to college or something," she said, offering a sad smile. "I kind of liked having you out here. Now you'll have a door that you can close, and I won't have anyone to bitch at when I'm PMS-ing."

David grinned at her. As far as he could tell, Harriet was the only one Reston and Giovanni had told about the change that was coming tomorrow—although she'd only mentioned it once to David during the day, when he'd caught her tearing up on her way back from lunch. Giovanni's leaving had been a huge blow to her, since she'd been working for him for such a long time. But she seemed genuinely proud that David was moving up so fast—and she seemed at worst neutral on Reston's temporary ascension to the Merc's highest office.

"You know my door is always open to you," David responded, still in disbelief that he'd have an actual door, let alone one that he could close. "And I could use a good bitching-out once or twice a week, just to keep me grounded."

Harriet gave him a little hug, then started back toward the elevators.

"Try not to stay all night again," she said as she disappeared from view. "It's after ten already. If this keeps up, my boyfriend is going to run away with your girlfriend, and then where will we be? Stuck with each other for good?"

David laughed and went back to boxing up his things. The job was taking longer than it should have because he was having trouble concentrating. He was boiling up inside with his good news—and dying to tell someone, especially Serena and his parents. He hadn't yet informed them of his good news because he didn't think it was the sort of thing you announced over the phone. And since Giovanni and Reston weren't making any noise about it until tomorrow, he figured it was best to keep things quiet while he was still in the building. With all the security the place had, God only knew who was listening.

Ten minutes later, he finally gave up on trying to sort through the files stacked next to his desk and simply jammed them all into the last available cardboard box. Then he grabbed his jacket off his chair and headed toward the elevator.

The fifteenth floor was like a ghost town; Harriet had obviously hit the main lights on her way out, and only a few errant lamps kept the place even remotely aglow.

David reached the elevator and hit the button for the lobby, then yanked his coat on over his shoulders. The lights above the elevator doors indicated that it was on its way down from the lounge upstairs, only a few floors away. David had just begun to straighten his lapels when the elevator doors slid open—and he suddenly found himself face to face with Dominick Gallo.

The Don twirled his still smoldering cigar, then stepped to one side, making room.

"On your way home, Mr. Vice President of Strategy?"

Christ. David considered taking the stairs. But he knew he had no choice now; Gallo wasn't going to let him off that easy. He gritted his teeth and stepped into the metal box, a bare few feet from the old trader. The air inside the elevator was heavy with a noxious mixed scent of cigar, whiskey, and aftershave. David tried to breathe shallow as the elevator doors slid shut in front of him—leaving him truly alone with Gallo for the first time since he'd arrived at the Merc.

"You must be pretty excited," Gallo said, putting the cigar back in his mouth.

David glanced at him, realizing for the first time that he was a good head taller than the old man—even counting the three inches of wiry silver hair sprouting up from Gallo's head. Still, the Don was such a presence, it felt like there was barely room for both of them in the elevator.

"I guess even secrets travel fast around here," David responded, returning his gaze to the elevator doors. He was counting seconds in his head, wishing that the damn box could go a little faster.

"Nothing goes on here without me knowing about it."

Gallo was facing him head-on now, that cigar pumping up and down. Even by way of his peripheral vision, David could tell that the man was fuming. His deep-set eyes had narrowed in their concentric pockets of blackened skin, and his yellowed teeth were visible all the way to the gums.

"Like your little excursions with some of the younger floor traders. You've made quite an impression on my boys, kid. Some of them even think of you as one of 'em. But I know better."

David shrugged his shoulders.

"I'm not trying to cause any problems, sir. Just making friends and trying to learn about the business."

Gallo cocked his head to the side, then took his cigar out of his mouth and pointed it at David.

"You really want to learn something about this business?"

David glanced at the old man. Part of him wanted to crawl right up through the ceiling panels of the elevator and shimmy up the cable to freedom—but another side of him couldn't help but take the bait. Maybe, somehow, he could get Gallo to warm to him. Or maybe, at the very least, he could find out why Gallo seemed to hate—and if Giovanni was right, fear—David so much. Anyway, David had never shied away from a challenge in his life. It wasn't in his personality.

"I'm not here for the morning coffee and bagels."

"Then let's go for a little ride," Gallo responded as the elevator slowed to a stop in the lobby and the doors slid open—and David's pulse thundered through his veins. "My limo is waiting out front."

THE TWENTY-MINUTE RIDE from the Merc deep into the heart of Bensonhurst, Brooklyn, had been the most awkward, uncomfortable trip David had ever taken. Gallo had spent the entire time with his ear to his BlackBerry and had only broken away from whatever business he was conducting to gesture at David twice: first, when they were halfway across the Brooklyn Bridge, to point out the view of the Merc from even lower than Lower Manhattan; and then again, when they turned off Eighteenth Avenue and onto a side street, to let David know that they were nearing their destination.

"I grew up one hundred yards from here," Gallo grunted, slipping his phone back into his overcoat and finally relighting his cigar. "I still own the house where my grandfather washed dishes to pay for a little space in the attic, after he came through Ellis Island. 'Course, I don't live there anymore. But it stays in the family."

David nodded, pretending he understood. He watched as the colored awnings and tapered row houses flashed by, taking in the cement stoops, brick-walled storefronts, and dimly lit alleys that lined either side of the narrow avenue. He wasn't sure exactly where on Eighteenth they had turned off, but he guessed they were just a few blocks north of the Bay Ridge Parkway. Right in the heart of the Italian section of the borough. The most heavily populated Italian neighborhood in the country, it was a community of more than fifty thousand—at least twenty thousand of whom still spoke Italian day to day instead of English.

"My father's family probably knew yours," David said. "They might have come over on the same boat."

Gallo grunted again, then suddenly leaned forward and tapped on the divider in front of him, signaling his driver to stop the car.

Then, without another word, he gestured with his cigar toward the door.

David crawled across the backseat, pushed the door open, and stepped out onto the sidewalk. The street ahead of him was dark and fairly deserted; he wasn't sure what time it was anymore. He felt a chill that had little to do with the temperature as he watched Gallo come out of the limo behind him. Then Gallo pointed toward a storefront directly ahead of them, a place with smoked-glass windows and a slanted, bright green awning. Through the glass David could see huge slabs of meat hanging from hooks. Flanks of beef, twists of Italian sausages, prime cuts of sirloin and pork—

A butcher shop. Gallo had dragged him deep into Brooklyn to see a butcher shop.

David turned to ask what the hell he was doing there—but Gallo just strolled past him and reached for the milked-glass door beneath the awning.

To David's surprise, the door was unlocked. Gallo stepped inside, leaving David outside on the sidewalk. David glanced back at the limo—then up and down the deserted street. He knew he could probably find a cab back on Eighteenth—but hell, he hadn't come all this way to turn back now. Maybe Gallo was psychotic, but he was also a multimillionaire, and a powerful player at the Merc. David couldn't risk angering the man even more than he somehow already had.

He took a deep breath and followed Gallo into the butcher shop.

The first thing that hit him was the smell: the scent of raw meat was so thick, it nearly made him gag. The shop was deserted and small, barely ten feet across, with refrigerated shelves on two sides loaded down with various cuts of beef and pork. Directly across from David was a low counter with a cash register, a pair of stainless steel scales, and a large wooden chopping block. Gallo was to the right of the block, leaning back against the counter. His cigar was still in his mouth, but his hands weren't empty: he was holding a wooden baseball bat. Not a miniature slugger, like in Giovanni's office, but the real thing, the heavy wood stained by age and possibly use.

David stood there, staring at the bat, as Gallo looked up at him.

"My grandfather swept the floors here when he was twelve years old. He came to this country, and he swept blood and meat and bone so that he could make enough money to buy food for his brothers and sisters. For six years, he swept this fucking floor."

Gallo's wrinkled arms strained as he lifted the bat a few inches into the air.

"Two days before his eighteenth birthday, the owner of the shop took a delivery of thirty milk crates from a cousin in the dairy business; he couldn't move the crates, so he asked my grandfather to take care of it. My grandfather took the milk to the trading exchange across the river. There he discovered a new life for himself. And he gave that life to my father. And my father gave that life to me."

David shifted his weight from foot to foot, trying to think of something to say. He wasn't sure what Gallo was trying to tell him—but he had a feeling it had little to do with him specifically and more to do with Giovanni, Reston, and what they represented. *Gallo had brought him to Brooklyn to make a point.*

Before David could come up with any words, Gallo raised the bat again.

"You know what this is?"

David swallowed. Gallo grinned at him from behind his cigar.

"I'm not going to hit you, kid. I'm just asking you a question. Do you know what this is?"

David shrugged.

"I think so."

"No, you don't know a fucking thing."

He tapped the baseball bat against the floor, then stared right at David.

"This is Bensonhurst. This is Brooklyn. This says that you don't walk into *my* neighborhood and try to take what's *mine*."

Gallo opened his gnarled hand and let the baseball bat clatter to the floor. Then he took a step forward, straightening the lapels of his overcoat. David instinctively took a small step back. For the first time, he understood exactly why Gallo hated him so much. Like this butcher shop, the Merc was Gallo's neighborhood. Reston and Giovanni were trying to take that neighborhood away from him. Automating the exchange, internationalizing the trade of oil—any steps toward modernization were a direct threat to Gallo and what his family had built. Gallo truly was a dinosaur. He probably couldn't even turn on a computer, much less use it to trade oil. Reston—and by extension, David—was threatening Gallo's way of life. *His neighborhood.*

David knew he needed to defuse the situation—quickly. He repeated what he'd said earlier in the elevator.

"I'm not here to cause any problems—"

"Bullshit," Gallo interrupted. "Giovanni and that rat Mick of his, Reston, they've got you spying on my boys. But that don't make any difference to me. My blood has been running through that exchange for more than a hundred years. And don't you ever forget—no matter who's sitting up there in the corner office, I run the Merc."

Even from across the butcher shop, David could feel the man's breath against his skin. David wanted to get the hell out of there—but he wasn't going to turn his back on the old man. Instead, he shrugged again, clasping his hands behind his back.

"I'm sure you're right. I'm just trying to get by, like everyone else."

Gallo choked out a laugh. With his right hand, he reached into his overcoat and pulled out a thin manila envelope. Then he looked right at David.

"I hope, for your sake, that's true. I really do. Because I don't think you know who you're dealing with. See, I keep an eye on my traders—and anyone who gets close to them."

He suddenly held the envelope up in front of David's face.

"Which means I'm keeping an eye on you too, Harvard boy.

And I don't care what position they give you, you're still Giovanni's little shit to me. So watch your toes, little shit. You can bet I'm watching 'em. Every fucking day."

Gallo let the envelope fall to the floor in front of David. Then he walked right past him, heading for the door.

David waited until Gallo was gone, the door swinging shut behind him, before he bent down to pick up the envelope. His stomach churned as he undid the clasp and removed a single black-and-white photograph. A sheen of sweat broke out across the back of his neck as he turned it over in his hands.

The photo had been taken by some sort of telescopic lens, from a distance that had to have been at least a hundred feet, maybe even more. Still, David had no problem making out the image—because it was as crisp and clear as the day on which it had been taken.

A mane of cascading curls. A hand resting gently beneath the crook of a chin, a Harvard ring clearly visible on one finger.

It was a picture of him and Serena, kissing outside the Gucci store on Fifth Avenue.

Chapter 19

NOVEMBER 25, 2002

For the third time in ten minutes, Khaled's life flashed before him.

Eyes wide with fear, screams lost in the fierce sand-tipped wind whipping across his face, he felt himself go completely airborne, his body suddenly contorting as he struggled vainly to keep his grip on the searing hot vinyl seat beneath him. There was a moment of complete weightlessness—and then he felt a hand catch him by the wrist and, with almost inhuman strength, yank him back down.

He crashed against the passenger side of the open-topped jeep and wrapped both arms around the flailing twist of rope that passed for a seatbelt. Then he turned to stare at the man who'd just saved his life—not coincidently, the same man who was continuing to endanger it as well.

The Pakistani was hunched over the jeep's steering wheel, one hand on the gear shift between them, the other adjusting a pair of overly large driving goggles. Most of the man's dark face was obscured by the goggles and a bright yellow, turtle-shell-shaped construction hat that had been pulled down low over his thick black hair, but beneath a thick, bushy, brown mustache, he was grinning like a madman, his teeth abnormally white in the glare from the midday desert sun.

"That was a good one," the Pakistani shouted over the wind. "I think we got five feet into the air. You should really hold on to that seatbelt, young sir. As you can see, the path can be quite treacherous."

Khaled turned back to the mud-spattered windshield, peering out at the brown scar of mud and sand that supposedly counted as a "path." *Treacherous* was the understatement of the century. And it certainly didn't help that the jeep was traveling at close to seventy miles per hour, or that the Pakistani seemed to be purposefully aiming at the errant dunes that intermittently marred the way.

Still, it had been Khaled's choice to take the tour, and he had known from the minute he met the Pakistani manager at the complex's main helipad that the man was a character. Dressed in dirty white overalls, with that yellow construction helmet and that same maniacal smile, the man had first introduced himself as Saumya Das, an old friend of Khaled's uncle, and then had proceeded to tell Khaled a story about the sheik and a party in London that involved a cricket bat thrown through a second-story window and a pair of Slovakian models taking turns behind the wheel of the sheik's Lamborghini—resulting in the car being driven into a ditch, the Slovakians hitchhiking back to the hotel, and the car being lost for three weeks. Khaled hadn't doubted the accuracy of the story—he knew there were many similar stories involving his uncle, as the public sheik was extremely different from the one Khaled knew in private—but he'd had trouble picturing the sheik hanging out with the five-foot-four, mud-spattered Pakistani. Still, he'd been grateful that the man volunteered to show him around, especially considering that Khaled's expedition to the neighboring country of Qatar had been so last-minute and that he'd arrived at the fairly remote location in the middle of the small country without any real notice other than a single phone call from his office at the

Ministry of Finance. Without any real hesitation, he'd gladly accepted the jeep tour of the Pakistani's complex. Of course, that was before he'd witnessed the man's questionable driving skills.

Now that they were circling the Dukhan oil field for the second time, Khaled wished that he had opted for a video tour in the man's air-conditioned office instead. At the moment, Khaled felt like he'd just stepped off the front line of a war. His hair was sticking straight up from his head, and his clothes were soaked in sweat. There was sand lodged in every possible crevice, and his skin burned where it had made contact with the jeep's seats and the metal roll bar above his head. The desert sun was high in the sky, and the temperature had to be more than 120 degrees. The steady blasts of wind did nothing to cool the air around him, and if it wasn't for the thin scarf that Khaled had wrapped around his mouth, he doubted he'd have been able to breathe at all. And from the looks of things, he was certain he'd be trapped in the jeep with the crazed Pakistani for some time to come.

It had taken an entire hour to get around the massive complex the first time, and the Pakistani was obviously trying for a better time in their second pass. Perhaps it was one of the ways the men who worked in the desert oil field passed the time—or maybe the Pakistani really was insane, a product of days spent laboring in the searing heat of the Qatar desert and nights dreaming about parties staffed with sheiks and Slovakian prostitutes.

Well, Khaled thought to himself as the jeep took another hairpin turn and he held on to the "seatbelt" for dear life, *you wanted inspiration. If this place doesn't inspire you, you might already be dead.*

The truth was, up close and in person, the scale of the Dukhan oil field was truly amazing. From the air, it was a yellow and brown yawn of earth that stretched for eighty kilometers, a twisting mass of steel tubing, grated catwalks, and skyscraping, fire-belching smoke spires that almost defied description. But here on the ground, it was ten times as monstrous—like some sort of alien construct that had been dropped right down into the middle of the desert, a churning perpetual motion machine of levers and gears and pipes and stacks, spitting dark smoke and flame from every conceivable angle.

"Bigger than you expected?" the Pakistani asked as he yanked the steering wheel to the right to avoid a pothole that would surely have swallowed the jeep entirely. "That's usually how people feel when they see Dukhan up close. It's the largest oil field in the region by a factor of five. And one of the top three in the world."

Khaled nodded, squinting through the windshield at the twists and turns of the piping that disappeared like great straws into the very earth. He knew from his own research that the oil field had brought Qatar—and its sheiks—almost unbelievable wealth. Millions of dollars a day in fact, which was even more spectacular considering the entire country was barely the size of Rhode Island—and yet largely because of Dukhan, it had one of the largest GNPs in the region.

And like most of the nations in the Middle East, Qatar had only one export.

"Nearly three hundred and thirty-five thousand barrels every day," the Pakistani shouted. "We're now capable of over one hundred and twenty million barrels a year. From a mother lode that's estimated at nine billion barrels, maybe more. It's quite staggering, isn't it?"

Khaled exhaled, now barely noticing the sand and wind whipping at his teeth. He had traveled to Dukhan for inspiration—because in his mind, if he truly wanted to know how to properly spend a sheik's fortune, he needed to know what it was to be a sheik. There was the religious component, of course, and the political implications. But the very definition of sheikdom was power—and power, in the Middle East, had only one real source. Dukhan had therefore been the obvious choice, because of its size and proximity to Khaled's new home—and also, more importantly, because Dukhan had been feeding the region and its sheiks since the 1940s. The birth of this belching monstrosity in the desert coincided with the birth of the modern Middle East, and the two were distinctly intertwined.

"And what happens to the oil after you pull it up from the ground?" Khaled asked.

"It goes through the pipeline to the refinery at Mesaleed."

"And then?"

"Well, to the market, of course," the Pakistani said, guiding the jeep through a patch of swirling sand. "We are partnered with a dozen international firms, which ship the refined and unrefined barrels across the oceans. Our oil goes all over the world. What is pulled up from the sand today, a week from now is in the tank of a Volvo in some parking lot in a mall in Nebraska."

Khaled felt a smile fighting the stiff wind that battered his face. Without realizing it, the Pakistani had summed it all up in that one sentence, beginning in the desert in Qatar and ending in a place in the middle of the United States, a place that most on the Arab street could not even imagine—and certainly could not understand. And yet, from the Pakistani's vantage point as one who lived and breathed oil—sometimes literally—that was the way the world seemed: different parts of the same sentence.

This is an answer, Khaled realized. If not *the* answer, certainly one of a possible many.

He turned from the Pakistani back to the monstrous oil fields, then to the great and swirling desert that surrounded them.

Khaled knew in his heart that the Black Blood of Allah was not simply a source of power. Oil was also a river that flowed from east to west.

Perhaps there was a way to turn that river around.

To turn a source of power into a source of peace. . . .

Chapter 20

Look at the bright side, kid. At least they weren't dirty pictures."

David leaned back in his seat, watching Reston dig into the massive tower of tortilla chips that took up most of the table between them. David's fingers had gone numb against the glass of his frozen margarita, but he didn't care—the rest of his body had been pretty much numb since the moment Gallo had confronted him in the butcher shop with the photograph of the kiss in front of the Gucci window.

"And at least it was your girlfriend," Reston continued, washing the tortillas down with a deep sip from his own frozen drink. "Can't blackmail someone with pictures of him kissing his own girlfriend."

David forced a laugh, though he didn't really see the humor in the situation. And it certainly didn't help that they were sitting in some dingy faux cantina three blocks from the exchange, complete with rattan tables and chairs, not to mention waiters wearing mini-sombreros and plastic bandoliers.

The place was called Little Tijuana, and it was obviously a

favorite of Reston's—not for the decor, but because the margaritas came in glasses the size of fishbowls, with little umbrellas and enough salt on the rim to de-ice the FDR Drive. Likewise, the tequila shots came by the tray—and even though it was four in the afternoon on the day before Thanksgiving, there was already one tray of a half-dozen shots hidden somewhere on the table, deep in the shadows between the great tortilla tower and its accompanying bucket of salsa.

"I don't think he was trying to blackmail me," David responded. He'd gone over the moment in his head a dozen times, but it still made him nauseous to think about it. He hadn't mentioned the confrontation to anyone other than Reston—not Serena, not his parents—because he knew they'd react badly. Hell, *he* was reacting badly. After he'd left the butcher shop, he'd wandered the streets of Bensonhurst for nearly an hour before he'd stumbled upon a taxi willing to take him back to Midtown. By the next morning, he could hardly believe that the episode had even happened—it seemed so completely monstrous. Certainly, the whole thing put an ominous spin on his recent promotion to vice president of strategy, and he no longer felt much like celebrating.

"Of course it wasn't blackmail," Reston said. "The Don was just beating his chest, letting you know where you stand. A little over the top, yes. But surprising, no. I mean, how did you expect him to react to Giovanni's little bombshell? You have to understand the stakes here. The trading floor is Gallo's fiefdom. He sees us as the enemy, literally trying to take away his life's work. Giovanni was a pain in his ass—but in a way, he was almost as old school as Gallo. Me? I'm so far in the future, I'm a fucking space alien as far as he's concerned. He's afraid I'm going to bulldoze his trading floor and replace it with a bucket of iPods. To him, I'm the fucking comet that killed the dinosaurs. And you—you're some punk kid who he suddenly can't ignore, because now you're a vice president—which pisses him off, to say the least."

David took a drink from his margarita, shivering as his tongue touched the icy, spiked slush. The truth was, it wasn't just Gallo;

the reaction from the rest of the board had been almost as ugly. Giovanni's announcement that he was retiring had nearly been overshadowed by the news about David's promotion. It had all gone down during an impromptu board meeting the day before: when Giovanni told them about David's ascension, the proclamation was met with utter silence—followed by numerous complaints, calls for explanations, and even a few insults. Nobody seemed happy to have a twenty-five-year-old made vice president of the exchange, especially when the president and acting head of the Merc was barely ten years his senior.

"Look," Reston said, seeking out one of the shots of tequila and holding it in the air between them, "nobody reacts well to change. You and I are a frightening combination."

"I think it's more than that."

"We're going to push this place into the modern world," Reston continued, pretty much ignoring David, "whether they like it or not. I'm talking about expanding. I'm talking about automation. I'm talking about taking the place international. Pretty much everything Gallo and the old-world traders fear—but really, after a while they'll understand that it's for the good of the Merc. If the Merc doesn't grow and modernize, it will be overtaken by other exchanges and lose its power. In the end, that would be a lot worse for everyone."

David wasn't really sure what any of that meant. Truthfully, he just wanted to get Gallo off his back and then figure out a way to win over the rest of the board. He wanted to prove himself, earn the respect his promotion had bypassed.

"At the moment," he said, his honest feelings coming out, "I feel like I'm about to get run out of town."

"Funny you should mention that," Reston responded.

David didn't like the look in the Texan's eye.

"What do you mean?"

Reston drained the tequila shot and slapped the glass down on the table. Then he chased it with a long suckle of margarita.

"David, what do you know about Dubai?"

David squinted into his own margarita. *Dubai?* The country?

"Well, I've heard of it of course. Part of the United Arab Emirates, in the Middle East, right? There were a couple of kids whose parents worked there in my class at Williams. Supposedly the place is very rich, very cutting-edge. Every now and then there's some crazy story on the news about the construction of some huge hotel, or an indoor ski slope. And then there's that man-made island, right? The huge one in the shape of a palm tree that you can supposedly see from space?"

Reston suddenly downed another one of the tequilas, then followed it up with another sip of his margarita. He nearly nailed himself in the eye with the umbrella in the process.

"I'm not sure that's true, but yes, that's the place. Dubai, in the U.A.E. Turns out that at the moment it's pretty much the fastest-growing economy in the world. Sixteen percent growth in GDP last year, which is six times that of China. It's an impressive story."

David was having trouble pretending that he gave a shit about some country in the Middle East, but he did his best to stay focused on what Reston was saying. Dubai? What the hell did he care about Dubai? The Don had obviously paid some private eye to take pictures of him on his day off. Didn't he have more important things to think about than some social studies topic?

"Yeah, impressive. Oil-rich and getting richer—"

"Actually, no. Dubai has very little oil compared to the rest of the Middle East. They had a windfall back in the fifties, but it's been dwindling ever since. At the moment, oil makes up just six percent of their economy. Turns out, all their growth is coming from real estate development, banking, and tourism."

David raised his eyebrows, the tiniest bit more interested.

"Tourism? In the Middle East?"

Reston laughed. "Sounds crazy, right? Turns out, Dubai sees more tourists every year than all of India. And makes more money off of real estate than most of the countries in Europe. And it's just getting started. The shit they're building—it's really hard to believe. We're talking shopping malls the size of cities. Apartment complexes based on chessboards. Revolving sky-scrapers and underground racetracks. Dubai is rapidly turning into one of the real wonders of the modern world."

That was surprising, but still, David wondered, what did it have to do with them?

"Well, what the hell does the Merc care about a tourist trap?" Reston shrugged.

"Absolutely nothing."

Then he leaned forward over the table, lowering his voice.

"The thing is, before he left, Anthony forwarded me this strange little invite from the kingdom of Dubai to come check the place out. Three nights, all expenses paid, all of it first-class. I'm not even entirely sure where the invitation came from, but the letterhead is from the Ministry of Finance, and it's signed by both Sheik Maktoum and Sheik Muhammed."

"Sheik Maktoum and Sheik Muhammed," David repeated. This was beginning to sound like some sort of practical joke. Sure, they were involved in the business of oil, but the closest the board of the Merc Exchange ever came to dealing with sheiks was when they were trying to predict who the U.S. might invade next—and what the ramifications would be on the price of crude.

"Here's the thing," Reston continued. "We can't simply ig-nore this invitation, because it's got two sheiks' signatures on the bottom of the page. And these aren't just any sheiks. These sheiks—they're pretty fucking powerful. Not just multibillion-aires—the Maktoum family is considered one of the biggest forces of change in that entire part of the world. The family is worth almost thirty billion dollars. The brothers were educated in England and have a liberal, cosmopolitan worldview that's pretty unique for rulers of an Arab country. Sheik Muhammed, the younger brother, started Emirates Airlines with ten million bucks and two planes. Now it's one of the most successful, pres-tigious airlines serving the Eastern world. They've had similar successes with real estate, tourism, horse racing—building some of the most profitable businesses in the region. True innovators. Even so, I don't want to go—hell, with the mess that Giovanni's left me, flying halfway around the world isn't even an option. So on Anthony's recommendation, I've made my first executive decision: I'm sending you to Dubai the day after tomorrow. It will take some of the heat off your being made vice president, and it will give you a chance to report to the board about something interesting—even if it's just a nice story about revolving ski slopes and giant shopping malls."

David stared at him. Finally, he put the margarita down and clasped his numb fingers together.

"You're sending me to Dubai the day after Thanksgiving because you don't want to be rude. To the two sheiks."

Reston grinned.

"That's about the size of it."

David looked at him for a full beat, then realized that there wasn't going to be a punch line. Reston wasn't kidding—and that meant, the day after tomorrow, David was going to Dubai.

"Well, shit," he said finally. "I think we're gonna need another tray of tequila."

DAVID'S HEAD WAS still spinning as he stepped out of the taxi in front of his apartment building in Midtown—and the cerebral motion was only partially due to the tequila in his system. He'd expected that his first few days as the newest vice president of the Merc Exchange would be chaotic—but he'd never guessed he'd be hopping a plane in forty-eight hours, bound for the center of the most tumultuous region in the world. Furthermore, he hadn't told Reston the whole story: David had his own personal reasons to feel conflicted about the upcoming trip. Of course, every American—and certainly every New Yorker—had his own preconceived notions of the Arab world, but David had thought more about the region than most men his age. The truth was, he'd been forced to confront his feelings about the Middle East on many occasions over the past year—and now Reston had thrown all of it right back in his face, with the invitation David really couldn't refuse.

David sat down on the steps that led up to his apartment building and took a deep breath, letting the brisk air slow the rotations in his skull. He knew he had no choice but to put his personal feelings aside and look at this for what it was—an assignment.

In a lot of ways, it would be the classic consulting situation. He'd spend twenty-four hours studying up on the place, then another fourteen hours on the plane going through his notes. He'd hit the ground running, meet a few people, find out what the hell the two sheiks wanted from a bunch of Italian sons of garbagemen—and then get his ass back to New York. Dubai was an Arab country in the Middle East, but it was also an international center of business, and David would be there in a business capacity.

Ten minutes alone on the stoop, and David had nearly convinced himself that it was going to be fine, just a wonderful opportunity to see a part of the world he'd never thought he'd see. Then he remembered that convincing himself was only one part of the equation.

He reluctantly pulled his cell phone out of his pocket and dialed the number. She answered on the second ring.

"Hey, Mom."

Even before his mother responded, David could hear many voices in the background—his extended family had obviously already arrived for the Thanksgiving holiday, and he could picture the house on its way toward pure chaos: his mother in an apron in the kitchen, wielding a wooden spoon like a sword, as uncles and aunts and cousins bounced back and forth from one room to another. His father, hiding out in his study, trying to stay out of the maelstrom as long as was humanly possible. And soon, David and Serena would be thrown into the mix. Reston's bombshell about Dubai would only aggravate what was already the most aggravating of situations.

"David!" his mother exclaimed. "When are you getting here?"

"Tomorrow morning, like I told you yesterday."

"That's right. Well, your aunt Maria knitted you the nicest sweater, and your cousin Joey is in from City College, and everyone is very excited to hear about your promotion—"

David decided to get it right out in the open, before his mother drowned him in family gossip.

"Mom, guess what? I'm going to Dubai on Friday. For work."

"Where? Detroit?"

"No, Mom. Dubai. It's a country."

There was a brief pause on the other end of the line, the phone muffled as his mother said something to someone behind her. Then she came back on: "Well, okay, David, that's nice. Make sure you give me your flight information. And we'll see you and Serena tomorrow. Don't be late—you know how your father gets when you're late."

There was a click as she hung up the phone, and David was left in the darkness of his stoop, wondering how the hell it had gone so well. Had she heard him right? He'd repeated it twice, hadn't he? He suddenly found himself smiling. Maybe he'd underestimated his mother. Maybe he was making a bigger deal of it than it needed to be—

His thoughts were interrupted by a loud buzzing as the phone in his hand suddenly sprang back to life. He looked at the number on the screen—and his smile disintegrated as quickly as it had come.

He put the phone back to his ear and hit the receive button.

To his surprise, this time it was his father.

"David, your mother just fainted."

David's throat tightened up.

"What?"

"She looked up Dubai on a map. Turns out it's in the Middle East."

David coughed.

"I know, Dad."

"Well, now your mother is lying on the kitchen floor."

The phone went dead, and David lowered his head to his knees.

Yes, it was going to be one hell of an interesting Thanksgiving.

Chapter 21

How long do you think we could stay in here before they sent out a search party to find us?"

David grinned at Serena in the mirror as she reapplied her lipstick. There was barely enough room for both of them in the small downstairs bathroom of his parents' cozy two-story home—but David was just thankful that for a brief moment there was a door between them and the three dozen refugees from central casting who made up his extended Italian family.

"I think they're fun," Serena said, finishing her lips and moving on to her hair. David thought she looked great: her black skirt and matching roll-neck sweater brought out the dark pools of her eyes, and her understated makeup highlighted her rising cheekbones and smooth, porcelain skin. It was almost a travesty that his current reflection was sharing the backlit mirror: his mother had forced him to don the bright orange sweater his aunt had knitted for him as an early Christmas present—even though the arms were different lengths and the collar was so high it was doing battle with the cleft on his chin.

"Of course you do." He grimaced. "That's because they aren't related to you, so they pretty much leave you alone."

Serena came from a small family, and most of her relatives still lived in her native Colombia, so she and David saw them only on rare occasions. The few dinners David had shared with Serena's clan had been sedate, classy affairs. Nothing like Thanksgiving at the Russo home in Staten Island—where it was every gavone for himself.

"They're psychotic." He sighed, shaking his head. "Maybe we should just make a run for it. I'm not sure how much more of the third degree I can handle."

They were barely halfway through dinner, and David had already endured three hours of intense questioning—about his job, his relationship, and his future plans. If he heard one more uncle ask him why he hadn't gone to law school or med school, he was going to stick his head through a window. And if one more aunt asked him when he and Serena were going to get married, he was going to use a candle from one of his mother's elaborate center-pieces to light the house on fire.

The only good news so far was that nobody had mentioned Dubai yet—a small miracle considering that his father hadn't been exaggerating when he'd told David that his mother hit the kitchen floor on hearing the news. She still had a bright red mark on her forehead where she'd bumped the counter on the way down.

David didn't blame her really. This was a woman who'd never been out of the country, never been on an airplane—hell, David wasn't even certain whether she'd ever been out of New York. The idea that her only son—the pride of Staten Island, in her eyes—was flying into the middle of the place she'd only seen on the TV news, well, it was almost heartbreaking.

David sighed as Serena finished with the mirror and started for the bathroom door. He'd just have to keep praying that there were already enough issues for the family to continue torturing him about to make it through to dessert, without Dubai being brought up. But even as Serena led him by the hand back into the crowded dining room, David knew his prayers were futile. He could tell by the way everyone was looking at him as he found his seat—jammed between his uncle Joseph, a skinny, mustachioed forty-five-year-old who ran an undertaking business in northern New Jersey, and his cousin Jimmy, who was a frighteningly obese freshman at City College—that his luck was about to run out.

He pretended not to notice the attention as he reached for one of the half-dozen trays of turkey on the enormous main table that bisected the dining room. The table had been borrowed with the help of a neighbor who worked at the local high school, along with most of the chairs, but David's mother had done a pretty good job dressing up the institutional-style furniture with home-made seat coverings, matching tablecloths, and no less than five centerpieces—conflagrations of brightly colored flowers, candles, and the odd party balloon—that made the room seem more crowded, if that was even possible. The fact that more than thirty Russos—a good half of them weighing well over two hundred pounds each—could fit in any one home in Staten Island was amazing, but having them all jam into one dining room for Thanksgiving dinner was a true feat of physics.

What this meant, in practice, was that the minute David took his seat, he was pretty much trapped, and now that Serena was five relatives over, in the prime position between David's mom and his great-aunt Velma—direct from Sicily, no less—he had no-where to run when the question finally erupted from his dad's oldest brother, good old Uncle Morty, who owned a shoe store in Newark.

"So your mother tells us you're going to Dubai."

David nodded, then quickly jammed a spoonful of cranberry sauce into his mouth. Maybe they'd let him just eat for once. *Yeah, right.*

"Where is that, in England?" one of the cousins asked from farther down the table. David couldn't be sure which cousin, as he was too busy concentrating on getting a fork loaded with tur-key in alongside the cranberry sauce.

"No, it's near Egypt, isn't it?" his mother's youngest sister, Aunt Tina, whose family lived two doors down, chimed in. "Or am I thinking of China? Is it near China?"

Uncle Morty rolled his eyes at the rest of the family, then pointed a finger toward David.

"The Middle East, right? Dubai's in the center of the Middle East. Right, David? That's where you're going?"

David continued chewing, nodding. Uncle Morty leaned back in his chair, crossing his meaty arms against his utterly inflated belly.

"So tell me again why you didn't want to be a doctor?"

David groaned inwardly, instinctively searching for the nearest window. On the way, he matched eyes with his dad, who was sitting at the far end of the table. To his surprise, his dad gave him a little wink, as if to tell him that he understood David's pain. The wink was followed by a subtle gesture toward the door that led to his father's study—a signal that he had something to talk to David about, if and when he survived the Russo onslaught. David nodded, then glanced wistfully at the window—and went back to chewing his turkey.

IT WAS ALMOST two hours later by the time David made his way into his father's study, which was actually little more than a converted pantry located down a short flight of stairs. His father was already there when David arrived. Once a bear of a man, with thick dark hair and oversized features, his dad was now somewhat whittled down by the years and the aftereffects of the accident, but still amazingly vibrant, reclining on his patched-up old La-Z-Boy, the back of the chair leaning against the cluttered bookshelf that took up most of the office's far wall. David was glad his dad was already in his chair; he hated watching his father struggle to force himself down the stairs, no matter how important the doctors believed the exercise was. He knew that the basement office—once a comforting refuge, a place where his dad went to think—was now actually part of the older Russo's therapy. David knew that the very fact that his father could get down those steps, and then calmly carry on a conversation in a place so small and confined, was major progress. But that didn't make the situation any less painful for him to accept. In many ways, visible, physical scars would have been easier to deal with. As it was, David could only hope that one day he'd be able to look at his dad without thinking about the hell the man had been through.

"You're still in one piece," his dad said, smiling, as David took a seat on a workbench across from him. "Study" was really a poor description of the little room, considering that a good half of it was more wood shop than homebound accountant's lair. David's dad had paid his way through accounting school by doing carpentry part-time, and most of David's childhood neighbors had a set of shelves, or a screened porch, or a bed frame that had been built by his dad. It had always made David proud, when he played at one of his friends' houses, to see the results of his dad's work making their homes that much better.

"Barely," David responded, running a hand through his hair. "I think this sweater has magical powers. It glows even brighter every time someone brings up law school or med school."

David's father laughed. "Your aunts and uncles mean well. They're just trying to find some common ground. None of us really understands what the hell it is that you do."

"Well, sometimes I don't even really know," David said truthfully. "But it can be fascinating. And the excitement—Dad, you have no idea what that trading floor is like. I feel like I'm part of something huge."

His dad nodded. There was a slight flicker of something familiar at the corners of his eyes, but David tried not to notice; he knew from talking to his dad's doctors that, on some level, the panic was something his father was going to have to live with, every day. Even when the emotional scars appeared to be healed, your mind never completely got over an accident like that.

"David," his father said when the flicker was gone, "I know I've been tough on you, like the rest of the family. Maybe I wanted you to be a lawyer or a doctor too. But I need you to understand something."

He leaned a few inches closer to David.

"When I realized that plane was coming right toward the building, I thought about one thing. *You.* When the plane flies through your window, David, I don't want you to have any regrets."

David's throat went dry, and he shifted uncomfortably against the wooden bench. Even after a year, it was hard for him to talk out loud about the accident. And the truth was, he had never really discussed it with his father or mother before. They had all simply dealt with it, silently, every day since it happened.

"If you think what you're doing is important," his father continued, dead serious, "you keep doing what you're doing. And if it's not important, you go out and try to *make* it important."

His father wasn't trying to be profound. He was just attempting to get the message across. *You might think you have a whole life to make a difference in the world—but the truth is, you never know when that airplane might come crashing through your office window.* That was a lesson every New Yorker had learned—though maybe not as firsthand as David's dad—and taken to heart.

"I'll do my best, Dad."

As David said the words, he knew that he meant them. He didn't know how, and he didn't know when—but he was going to find a way to make his father's emotional scars worth something. He was going to do his best to make his father proud.

Chapter 22

Now *this* was the way to travel.

David was wearing silk pajamas and lying flat on his back, his head against a pillow that had to be stuffed with down feathers, his feet warm beneath a blanket that felt like it was made out of cashmere. A nineteen-inch television screen telescoped out from the wall in front of him, a brightly colored movie flashing by, subtitled in three different languages—none of which he could read, two of which he couldn't even identify. To his right there was a small desk with an air-phone, an Internet connection, and even a fax machine. The remains of his dinner sat on a tray to his left—though there really wasn't much remaining of the pheasant and pasta combination, as it had been one of the best meals David had eaten in months, and he could only imagine that there was a five-star chef strapped in some overhead compartment, cooking up such meals as they thundered across the Atlantic.

David smiled at the image, then grabbed the glass of champagne from next to the tray and took a sip. Cristal, of course; if you were thirty thousand feet in the air, yet lying flat in your own little compartment, it had to be Cristal.

David grinned as he placed the champagne glass back on its roost—an elbow of rounded plastic sticking right out of the wall, as if it had been designed specifically for such a task. Truly, the compartment was nicer than his cubicle back at Merrill. If Emirates Air was any indication, David was going to have to quickly reset his perspective on the Middle East. Already, from everything he'd learned in the past few hours from the crash course he'd given himself on Dubai—through the Internet, the many guidebooks he'd purchased before boarding the flight, and the phone calls he'd made to consulates and tourist bureaus—he had a feeling that any preconceived notions about third-world conditions in the Middle East were going to be sorely off base.

Although the trip to Dubai had seemed to him and Reston like it had come out of left field, the truth was, according to David's research, the tiny emirate of Dubai was going through a fascinating social, economic, and cultural upheaval—and on such a unique and massive scale that it was well worth the interest of any forward-looking institution, including the Merc. Maybe especially the Merc, since in some ways Dubai's growth paralleled the trading exchange's expansion from a little dairy and potato market to a world-leading oil player—except that Dubai was going through it all at hyperspeed. In barely twenty years, Dubai had gone from an insignificant desert-port trading outpost that nobody had ever heard of to a fully modern, futuristic first-world city. In effect, the sheiks who ruled Dubai had compressed what had taken the rest of the world two hundred years into twenty, using dwindling oil resources and sheer ambition to turn sand dunes into skyscrapers—almost overnight.

One of the seven emirates—or kingdoms—that made up the United Arab Emirates, Dubai was a sandy curve of beachfront desert bordering the Persian Gulf. As Reston had commented, unlike the rest of the U.A.E., Dubai's oil reserves made up only about 6 percent of its GDP; the rest came from tourism, real estate endeavors, banking, and other forms of business speculation. Even more startling for a nation in the usually conservative—and

Islamic—Middle East, Dubai's current population was predominantly expat; in fact, U.A.E. citizens made up fewer than one-eighth of the emirates' total population. Europeans, Southeast Asians, Russians, even Americans—Dubai was a city of transplanted foreigners. Trying to juxtapose this fact with the history of a place that began as a little fishing, pearling, and trading settlement founded by Bedouins who had literally ridden camels out of the desert was mind-boggling. The more David read about the city's distant past, the more unbelievable its current state seemed.

Initially populated in 1830 by a nomadic tribe led by the Maktoum family—who still ruled today in the persons of the current Sheik Maktoum and his brother Muhammed—the city had subsisted for more than a hundred years by becoming an outpost for trading pearls, sheep, and goats. Independent until 1971, when the U.A.E. was formed, Dubai entered the oil age in the late sixties and early seventies—but even then the ruling sheik knew that oil wasn't going to sustain the kingdom forever. He had thus set out to employ those oil profits brilliantly to turn the city into the ultimate expat business and tourist destination. What resulted was a crazy juxtaposition of old and new, of traditional desert culture and staggering modern wealth.

After David's crash course on what sounded like a truly complex and magical place, he was thrilled to get the chance to visit and see how much of what he'd read was real and how much was exaggeration. To begin with, Emirates Air was by far the nicest airline he'd ever traveled, its first-class service from JFK unparalleled.

His thoughts were interrupted by a quiet knock on the door to his minicabin. He sat up, flicking the switch that unlocked the plastic door. The door slid open, and one of the three flight attendants who staffed the first-class section of the 747 stepped into David's compartment. She was tall and elegant, with long dark hair pulled into a tight ponytail and sharp, vaguely Icelandic features. She efficiently gathered up his food tray, then looked at him from the doorway.

"Is there anything else I can help you with? We'll be landing in two hours, and it's been a pleasure serving you, Mr. Russo."

David thanked her, maybe a little too obsequiously, and she smiled at him.

"Your first trip to Dubai, sir?"

David raised his eyebrows.

"How could you tell?"

"You mean aside from the guidebooks?" she responded, pointing to the stack of paperbacks on the desk by the fax machine. "Actually, it wasn't hard to figure out from the look on your face when you boarded the plane. We get it all the time on this flight. The Europeans have already discovered Dubai, but America is just barely opening its eyes. It's like watching someone discover a Picasso at a yard sale. All of your expectations are thrown right out the window."

"Is it really that amazing?" David asked.

"You'll see for yourself. There's a reason many people around the world refer to Dubai as the City of Gold. I promise you this— by the time you go back to New York, your eyes will certainly be opened. Nothing in those guidebooks can prepare you for what you're about to see."

She gave him a little bow, then exited the compartment, sliding the door shut behind her. David lay back on the bed, his arms behind his head. *A Picasso at a yard sale.* Even the flight attendants were poetic.

David had a feeling that the woman was right; hell, his eyes were already open pretty wide, and he hadn't even landed yet.

Chapter 23

The minute he slung his carry-on bag over his shoulder, stepped out of the jetway, and walked into the ultramodern airport, David knew it wasn't just hyperbole: this place was going to blow his mind. Any grogginess left over from the fourteen-hour flight immediately disintegrated as he moved into the bright, high-ceilinged terminal. He wasn't sure what time it was, but the eye-watering glow from the enormous windows and glass-paneled domed roof made it feel like high noon on the surface of the sun. And the sun, from the looks of things, was immaculate, forged of equally shiny metal, steel, and stone and furnished by space aliens by way of some futuristic interpretation of Ikea.

And the people, David thought, *my God, the people.* It seemed like every ethnicity, nation, and sartorial preference was accounted for: Persian-looking men in tailored suits walked next to women in brightly colored burkas; African men in tribal outfits traded business cards with Asian women wearing Christian Dior; a trio of young Arab men, in flowing white robes with colored sashes at the collar, smiled at the Americans and Europeans streaming out of the jetway—

And then suddenly David realized that one of the three Arabs was holding a cardboard sign with a name written in calligraphy across the front: DAVID RUSSO, NEW YORK MERCANTILE EXCHANGE.

David nearly dropped his carry-on bag. He had assumed that someone would be meeting him at the airport, but he had figured it would be by baggage claim—and he had certainly not expected to be greeted by three men in robes who looked like they had stepped right out of a Hollywood movie. He felt an irrational burst of fear as the men spotted him—the one with the card waving, smiling, and pointing—and quickly chided himself for the stupid, unwarranted emotion. He knew, to some extent, that he had been brainwashed over the past year by the TV news; any American since 9/11 who pretended not to have preconceived notions about what young Arab men in robes thought of the U.S. was lying to himself. But there was no reason to think these three particular Arabs had anything but the best intentions. This was Dubai, not Afghanistan. And from everything David had read over the past couple of days, it was just plain racist to confuse the two.

He hurried over to the three men and held out his hand.

"David Russo. Great to meet you."

One of the men took his carry-on bag, despite his protests, and the other two ushered him forward through the terminal. All three looked to be barely out of their teens. Two spoke with fairly heavy Arabic accents, but the third—who seemed to be in charge—spoke perfect English. He introduced himself as Anwar al Sheman and explained that he was a senior at Dubai University, in the midst of an internship with the Ministry of Finance. He intended to go into business when he graduated, he told David with a grin, because, well, in Dubai there really wasn't any other choice.

"It's all business in Dubai," he said as he led David out of the terminal and into an even more crowded hall with moving walkways and huge security doors running the length of the far wall. There were a dozen armed security guards at the doors and seven huge lines of Europeans and Americans stretched all the way from one end of the great room to the other; David recognized signs that explained, in English, that this was customs, and he dug into his pocket for his passport—when Anwar patted his shoulder.

"Not necessary, Mr. Russo. You are an honored guest of the emir."

Anwar and the two other men in robes led David around the long lines of Europeans and Americans, straight to the security doors. As they approached, Anwar pulled a plastic card covered in Arabic writing out of his robes and waved it at the nearest security guards. The doors were immediately buzzed open.

David felt like some sort of rock star as he strolled through the doors with his escort of robed young men. He had to admit, he loved the attention he was getting from the other travelers, who watched in awe as he moved right through customs without even showing his passport.

After customs, the men led him straight to baggage claim. Again, he was struck by how modern and clean the airport was.

"We've just completed a six-hundred-million-dollar expansion," Anwar explained. "Last year we had fifteen million visitors. In the next three years, we expect to double that."

The two unnamed Arabs in robes retrieved David's bag, and then his small group was on the move again. Anwar led them down a short escalator to a pair of sliding glass doors. As they stepped through, Anwar grinned at him.

"You're very lucky to be here in November. We can actually park in the outdoor driveway rather than in the air-conditioned basement garage. It's quite a treat here to be able to step outside without bursting into flames."

David laughed and followed the young man outside. It was actually quite warm—not unpleasant, maybe ninety degrees, but thankfully not unbearably humid. David had read in one of the guidebooks that in the summer months Dubai reached temperatures of 130 degrees—a number that was almost impossible to comprehend. He was glad to be visiting when he was—as he doubted he'd ever be back. Hell, on his own, he'd have barely been able to afford the cab ride to JFK, let alone the seat on Emirates Air.

"Ah, here we go," Anwar said, pointing toward the curb. "The driver is right on schedule."

David's eyes opened another inch as he took in the silver stretch BMW limousine with tinted black windows that was parked right at the curb. David hadn't even known that BMW made limousines; the thing was simply beautiful, its silver curves positively glowing in the bright sun.

"Wow" was all David managed.

"Yes," Anwar said, holding the door open for him. "Wow."

David climbed inside, breathing deep the smell of expensive leather. He took a seat by the window, facing forward, and the three robed Arabs climbed in after him. Anwar shut the door behind them, and the car glided away from the curb. Anwar offered him a bottle of water from a miniature fridge, but David declined, his focus captured by the view through the tinted window.

In a matter of minutes, the elegant, modern airport had disappeared behind them, and they were now traveling down a freshly paved, four-lane highway that seemed to stretch on forever; on either side he saw desert and sweeping mountains of sand shifting in the breeze, broken only by the errant palm tree. There were other cars on the road, mostly expensive models—Porsches, Lexuses, even the odd Ferrari—but the silver BMW weaved around them with expert ease, like some sort of exotic snake stalking a midday meal. David couldn't tell for sure, because the ride was so damn smooth, but he had a feeling they were moving fast, maybe more than ninety miles per hour. Still, the speed didn't bother him; in fact, it felt perfectly natural—the infinite desert that stretched around them on all sides seemed somehow to negate the laws of physics.

"Have you ever been to the Middle East before?" Anwar asked.

David shook his head. Anwar grinned.

"Well, you'll find that Dubai represents the best of the Middle East the same way Manhattan represents the best of the U.S. You can find a little bit of every region here—but the sum is so much more than the parts. And the change that is going on all around—well, you'll see for yourself. It's like nowhere else in the world."

David began to notice buildings in the distance, sprouting up from the sand like shimmering mirages of glass and steel. He was about to ask Anwar how much farther the city proper was from the airport when suddenly the BMW slithered over a paved sand dune—and an immense skyline exploded into view, so abrupt and impressive that it literally took David's breath away.

"Christ," he whispered. All three Arabs laughed, but David didn't turn away from the tinted window. It was the most amazing sight he'd ever seen. Like Manhattan, but more modern, sleeker, and so much denser, all the skyscrapers jammed close together as if huddling for safety against the vastness of the desert that surrounded them. What made it even more spectacular was the thought that just twenty years ago he would have been staring at nothing but desert. And the scale of it was just incredible: in the distance he could see the huge hotel, the Burj Al Arab, with the billowing white sail that ran up one side; the two massive glass and steel Emirate Towers, which housed many of the government and corporate offices; the spectacular Gate, surrounded by more giant skyscrapers that the guidebooks hadn't named—because they didn't have names yet. Everything was so damn sparkling new—in fact, even newer than new, as most of the place seemed like it was still under construction. In less than a minute, David counted seventeen different humongous skyscrapers being built—*at the same time*. There were maybe ten times that many cranes—literally hundreds of them, spires playing tricks with the sun, casting crisscrossing shadows that turned the road ahead into a spider's web of fresh pavement.

"And it gets bigger as we get closer," Anwar joked. David was beginning to enjoy his host's sense of humor. Despite his robes, he did not seem all that different than the kids David had gone to college with. "And I hope you like cranes. We have a lot of them. Eighty percent of the world's tall cranes, in fact. Most of the rest are in China. But one day we'll probably have those here too. The emir has many more things he'd like to build."

They were rolling right up into the city now, the silver BMW limo dwarfed by the buildings on either side. The driver took a sharp turn—tires screeching, as if he couldn't be bothered by the brake pedal—and then they were in a circular driveway beneath one of the twin Emirate Towers. David's eyes widened even more.

"This is where I'm staying?"

"We apologize that the Burj Al Arab wasn't available. There's a golf exhibition going on at the moment, and the top players have booked most of the hotel. But I'm sure you'll find the Towers very comfortable."

The BMW came to a stop, and Anwar crawled out first, then held the door for David. Once outside, David peered up the facade of the building, marveling at the way the sunlight cascaded across the glass. Anwar handed David's things off to a bellhop in an immaculate blue uniform, then held out his hand.

"It was a pleasure meeting you, Mr. Russo. I will be escorting you to your meeting with the minister of finance later this afternoon. In the meantime, I hope you enjoy your time in the City of Gold. Salaam Alekhem."

David shook the young man's hand. He had read the proper Arabic response in the guidebook, but had already forgotten the words. He figured a smile and a nod would have to do. Then he turned and followed his meager luggage through the gold-rimmed, glass revolving doors that led into the lobby of the hotel.

He hadn't even fully revolved out the other side when he found himself face to face with a staggeringly pretty woman in a stiff, tailored white suit, holding a small blue envelope.

"Mr. Russo, welcome. It's an honor to have you at our hotel."

David blinked; it was a lot to take in at once. Not just the beautiful woman, who was looking him right in the eyes, but the lobby, the polished black marble floors, pillars, and walls, the glass picture windows overlooking glowing, brightly colored fountains, the eucalyptus and palm trees sprouting up in various corners of the cavernous middle atrium. In some ways, it reminded David of the lobby of the Bellagio in Las Vegas, which he had walked through once back when he was a college senior. Except this wasn't a casino—this was a hotel in the Middle East, and the gorgeous woman standing in front of him already knew his name.

"Thank you," David gamely responded. "I'm glad to be here."

The woman handed him the blue envelope, then gracefully gestured toward a bank of gilded elevators on the other side of the atrium. "You'll find your magnetic key in the envelope, as well as some information about our hotel and your schedule. I believe you have a meeting at four P.M. with the Ministry of Finance, which is located in our twin tower, a short, air-conditioned walk away. Will you be needing a reminder call from the front desk?"

"Um, yes, I guess that would be great."

The woman nodded, and David nodded back. Then he headed for the elevators. He'd already lost sight of the porters and his luggage—which was probably a good thing, considering he had no idea how much one was supposed to tip in a place that was detailed in marble and gold.

The elevator seemed even more air-conditioned than the lobby, and by the time David reached his floor he was shivering beneath his clothes. He was looking forward to a quick shower and a brief nap before the meeting. Even on a flat bed, flying halfway around the world was moderately exhausting.

The hotel's hallway was as elegant as its lobby: plush carpeting, ornate wooden doors, detailed ceilings, expensive lighting—again, he felt like he was in one of the better resorts in Las Vegas.

Sad that he lived in Manhattan, but his only framework for lavishness was Vegas. But then, the New York that equated to this place was far beyond his means and would probably remain that way for many years to come.

He reached the end of the hallway and found a door beneath a gilded number that corresponded with the number on the blue envelope. Then he opened the envelope's clasp and pulled out a plastic wand-shaped key. He realized, as he looked from the wand to the door, that there was no actual keyhole—just a small, square, brightly lit plate, right beneath the doorknob. David shrugged and did the only thing that made sense: he waved the wand in front of the plate, and there were a series of clicks from inside. He put his hand on the door and pushed.

As he stepped inside, he immediately realized that there had been some sort of mistake. The hotel room—if you could call it that—was bigger than his apartment in New York. Thick carpeting, marble walls, a raised kitchen area, two large-screen TVs, a sunken Jacuzzi right beneath the massive picture windows—it was utterly ridiculous. Even more ridiculous, off to the left David saw a glass spiral staircase that led up to a second floor. From his angle, he could barely make out another living room upstairs, as well as a doorway that led to a bedroom.

David shook his head. This wasn't right at all. There had definitely been a mistake. If Reston could have seen this room, he'd probably have fired David on the spot. The Merc would never have paid for something like this, and they wouldn't have expected anyone else to either. And certainly, this had to cost a fortune. David took a small step into the room, then quickly found a cordless phone resting on a chrome pedestal by what appeared to be a fully functioning wet bar.

The front desk answered on the first ring.

"Yes, Mr. Russo? How may we help you? Is there a problem with your room?"

Did everyone in the country know his name already? David cleared his throat.

"I think there's been some sort of mistake. I'm probably supposed to be in a much smaller room."

The woman on the other end of the line seemed amused. "No, Mr. Russo, we have you in one of our executive suites. You're an honored guest of the Ministry of Finance, and the upgrade was the least we could do. Your bags are on their way up as we speak. Is there anything else I can get for you?"

David declined an offer of champagne and caviar and delicately hung up the phone. He moved a little farther into the incredible two-floor suite. Then he shook his head.

An honored guest of the Ministry of Finance. Cristal on the airplane. A silver stretch BMW waiting for him at the curb. And a hotel room right out of Donald Trump's fantasies. David wasn't sure who these people were or what they wanted—but they sure as hell had gotten his attention.

Chapter 24

From the very moment David lowered himself into his seat at the postmodern, black-glass conference table in the huge, brightly lit penthouse office on top of the second Emirates Tower, he realized that he was way out of his element. And it didn't help that the walls of the room were entirely made of milky-white transparent glass, making it feel like the meeting was taking place on top of a cloud; the view from the top of the world was staggering, but also dizzying and maybe even a little nauseating. Worse yet, the way the rotund minister of finance was peering at him from across the table—his doughy brown face seeming to melt right off the bones, his sausagelike lips bent into a palpable frown—David felt like he had already made some grievous cultural error, and he hadn't even said anything yet.

He told himself he was just being stupid; that was probably just the way the man's face always looked. Certainly, Minister Hakim Al Wazali was, to put it mildly, a *generous* man; rolls of fat leaked out of the collar of his tailored blue suit, and his fingers, laced together beneath his chin, looked like raw hot dogs that had just been yanked from their packaging. The minister was in his midfifties, and it was obvious from his bearing, and from the way the younger, equally well-dressed man to the minister's right deferred to him, that the portly man was very powerful.

"So you are the vice president of strategy for the New York Mercantile Exchange," the minister said, after the view had been duly appreciated, introductions had been officially made, and everyone had taken their seats. David nodded. His gray suit felt stiff after having made the long journey in his cheap luggage; it had taken him a good hour to figure out the high-tech ironing system in his hotel room, and he had only just finished work on the jacket when Anwar arrived to take him to the meeting. He noticed, with a little jealousy, that both of the men on the other side of the table were wearing much more expensive suits—three buttons each, with vests, and both were in gray as well. Still, he was glad they weren't wearing robes; that would have made him even more uneasy than he already was.

"That's right," David responded. "And it's a great honor to meet you, sir. Your country is beautiful—"

"And nobody else saw fit to make the trip with you?" the minister interrupted, waving one of his meaty paws.

David swallowed and nodded again. So that was the reason for the man's expression. In the eyes of this minister, the Merc had answered Dubai's invitation by sending a kid. Maybe Hakim had been expecting Reston, or one of the more powerful board members—certainly not a twenty-five-year-old who'd recently been made VP by the departing chairman. David realized he had to put the man at ease, as soon as possible.

"I'm the president's right-hand man," David said. "I'm reporting directly back to him. I have his full authority on matters of the New York Mercantile Exchange."

The last part was a complete fabrication, but David felt he had to add something because, really, Hakim was right—David had been sent because nobody else wanted to make the trip. Giovanni was gone, Reston was too busy, and the rest of the board would have laughed at the idea of spending fourteen hours on a plane to visit the Middle East. What the hell was the minister expecting anyway? David wasn't even sure what *he* was doing there. Dubai was fascinating, but what did it have to do with the NYMEX? There wasn't even much oil in Dubai. And even if this had been Saudi Arabia, with black gold coming out of the bathroom faucets, the Merc wouldn't have had any real business here: the Merc was an exchange. Oil contracts were traded on its floor, but that's where the relationship really ended.

The young man to the right of the minister cleared his throat.

"The minister and I are very pleased that you have elected to meet with us," he said quietly. "And maybe in the future your superiors will have a chance to see our wonderful city for themselves."

David turned his attention from Hakim to the younger man. He had introduced himself as Khaled Abdul-Aziz; he was a good-looking kid, with high cheekbones and piercing dark eyes. He was also a few inches taller than David and had ridiculously good posture—which made him seem almost towering as he sat next to the squat minister of finance. David couldn't be sure, but Khaled was probably around the same age as he was, though from the looks of his clothes and the polished nature of his mannerisms, he was from a much wealthier background. Maybe he had grown up in this futuristic place. It was impossible to place his background from his voice: his English was slightly accented, but David couldn't quite place the accent. His diction was perfect and precise and made David wonder if the kid had taken acting lessons somewhere in his past. In short, he was extremely well spoken, and he seemed to choose his words very carefully.

"Dubai is growing quickly," he continued, looking right at David. "And more people are discovering our city every day. There are enormous opportunities all around us."

David could see many of those opportunities through the milky glass walls: skyscrapers, amusement parks, shopping malls—billion-dollar projects sprouting right up out of the desert. But what did any of it have to do with him?

Before he could ask the question, the minister abruptly rose to his feet, then nodded to Khaled and to David.

"I apologize, Mr. Russo, it was a pleasure meeting you. I have other business to attend to at this time. My associate will continue the meeting—as he has full authority on matters of the Ministry of Finance."

David blushed as his own words were thrown right back at him. He quickly stood, shook the minister's hand, and watched him wobble right out of the conference room. When the door had shut behind him, David turned back to the younger man, who was already back in his seat.

"Why am I here?" David asked, a bit flustered. "I don't think the minister has any interest in talking to me."

To his surprise, Khaled smiled.

"The minister didn't invite you, Mr. Russo. I did."

Now it was David's turn to be surprised. He lowered himself back into his seat. This kid across the table had invited a representative of the Merc to make a first-class trip all the way to Dubai? On a letter from the Ministry of Finance, with two sheiks' signatures across the bottom?

No wonder the minister had acted as though the entire meeting was a waste of his time: he had obviously been there as a favor to his young charge. Obviously, Khaled had some impressive pull in the Dubai government. But he was young, and from the way the minister had hightailed it out of the room, probably no more powerful in the greater scheme of things than David was at the Merc.

"Why?" David finally asked.

"I wanted to pick your brain, Mr. Russo. You see, I've spent the past month meeting with various interests, discussing potential projects—real estate, commercial, whatever—for the continually changing landscape of our city. These projects represent trillions of dollars of foreign investment, much of it from this region of the world, but also from Europe and, more recently, your country."

David listened patiently as Khaled spoke. There was something almost musical about the young man's tone; he was smart, that was obvious, but he was also very controlled—almost as though he was holding himself back. He clearly wanted something from David, but the more Khaled told him about his job, the less likely it seemed that David had anything worthwhile to give him.

"Some of these projects will cost the ministry billions of dollars. And when finished, they will be quite spectacular."

"I imagine so," David said. "What you've done already is, well, spectacular."

"Mr. Russo, I'm not interested in spectacular. I feel that Dubai is in a unique situation. We've got a ruler who has made it his prime purpose in life to make Dubai the greatest city on earth. We've got money and, more importantly, the attention of Europe and America. I want to find a way to use these things to change the entire region. To change the world."

David stared at the kid. He could tell that the words were not just hyperbole—Khaled meant exactly what he'd said. And he was being completely honest. David doubted that he'd have opened up like this if the minister had still been in the room. Maybe he'd also have held back his feelings if Reston or one of the older members of the board had been there. But for some reason, he had let David in on his grand intentions. Maybe it was simply the fact that they were similar in age. Or maybe, somehow, he knew that David was the type of person who would respond to such intellectual grandeur—even if it was obviously going nowhere, because how the hell could a twenty-five-year-old Arab kid who couldn't keep his boss in the room ten minutes hope to change the world?

"Cool," David finally responded. He knew it was a pathetic response, but he wasn't sure what else to say.

"Yes. And that's why I sent the letter to your exchange. You see, I've been reading up on your business—and I think there might be a way for us to partner on a project here in Dubai."

David raised his eyebrows.

"Partner? Who, the Merc Exchange? And Dubai?"

David had no idea where this kid was heading. His own personal hesitations toward the Arab world aside—hell, what American didn't have personal hesitations toward the Arab world?—he couldn't think of a bigger mismatch than the Merc's board of old-world Italians and Jews and what he'd seen so far of Dubai.

"That's correct. I believe that a partnership with your oil exchange is exactly the sort of endeavor that could change the way people view our part of the world. If we could re-create here what you've created in New York, I believe it would be region-changing."

David blinked, then stared at the kid. David wanted to make sure he had heard Khaled correctly.

"You want to build an oil exchange. In Dubai."

The room went silent. Khaled laid his caramel hands out flat against the black-glass table. David coughed, then repeated himself.

"An oil exchange in the Middle East."

Khaled had to be kidding. Even putting aside what most Americans—and especially the sort of men who ran the Merc—thought of the Arab world, it was an insane idea. Stock exchanges existed in places like New York, London, Berlin—first-world cities that were centers of capitalism, with massive, international appeal, particularly with respect to oil and energy: an oil exchange was in itself a center of capitalism, a real-time casino built around the world's most important commodity. An exchange in the Middle East—it was a crazy thought. Other than Israel—and David knew they certainly weren't talking about Israel—the Middle East had no democracies. The place was run by sheiks, for God's sake. Was it even really capitalist? Could capitalism really exist in an Islamic world?

David had thought he was out of his depth before, when he'd first entered the conference room; now he knew he was at the bottom of the Persian Gulf. He didn't want to be rude, but part of him wanted to get the hell out of there. No wonder the minister of finance had left so quickly. Even if this kid was wild-eyed and idealistic enough to think of something so absurd, the minister probably knew better.

"Look, I'm no expert on religion," David said, "but isn't Dubai an Islamic country?"

Khaled nodded. "Of course. But there are caveats. You see, the emir, in his infinite wisdom, has established a number of free zones in the city, where most forms of trade can flourish. The International Financial District, which surrounds us, offers a location particularly attractive to corporations; no corporate or personal income taxes, a top-notch banking system, and a legal code favoring the ownership of property. The free zones are not subject to the application of sharia law."

David had never heard of sharia law—and he was pretty sure the meatheads from Brooklyn and Staten Island hadn't either.

"Okay, but an exchange is, by its nature, international. If you opened an oil exchange here, you'd have to bring in traders and brokers from all over the world. You'd have to create oil contracts with the help of the big players in the local region as well: Saudi Arabia, Iran, Qatar—"

"We would have to navigate around a few obstacles, certainly. But what would be the result?"

David sat back in his chair. An oil exchange in the Middle East? Even if he thought such an idea was remotely possible, was it something he'd want to be involved with? Still, he felt he owed it to Khaled to at least entertain the concept, however absurd he thought it was. After all, this crazy kid had invited him all the way to Dubai. David decided to humor him—to do his best and imagine that somehow he could overcome the prejudices and hatreds, that somehow he could get the board interested enough to move forward, that somehow he could get the rest of the world market involved in building an oil exchange here in the Middle East. What would be the result?

A center of pure capitalism? Maybe. If Dubai really allowed the Merc to re-create what they'd done in New York, bringing in players from all over, resetting the way oil was traded and even priced—hell, there were so many angles, David would need a month to figure it all out. But simply put, Khaled was right about one thing: if such an exchange was successful, it would quite possibly change the entire region. It would be like a revolution of international market forces in the center of the Islamic world. It would certainly put Dubai on the map as a financial center and give it a role in the pricing and trade of oil—in many ways, making it as important as its bigger, oil-rich neighbors in the region.

"Exchanges are living, breathing institutions," David finally said, rewording something that Giovanni and Reston had once told him. "Building one here would be like building a soccer stadium and inviting the whole world to come and play."

Khaled grinned. It seemed exactly what he wanted to hear. If that wasn't changing the region—and by extension the world, because they were talking about the Middle East, the source of so much war, terrorism, and hatred—then nothing else was. David couldn't help but feel the kid's energy, even from across the room. *Christ, the kid really was a dreamer.*

"What about on your side?" Khaled asked. "Would the New York Mercantile Exchange partner with us on such a project?"

David fought back the first answer that popped into his head—a huge, resounding no. He wanted to try to humor the idea a little longer, if only because Khaled's enthusiasm was so damn infectious. But the idea of selling this to the Italians and Jews who ran the Merc—it seemed overwhelming. When kids from Brooklyn pictured Arabs, they saw men in robes riding camels and chopping off heads.

Certainly, Gallo would never go for the project; it would be exactly the sort of change that he dreaded. David could just picture him in that butcher shop with his baseball bat. On the other hand, Reston might be swayed to at least entertain the idea—to think about the ways such a project could benefit the exchange in terms of publicity. And of course, financially, a Dubai exchange could be structured to benefit the Merc immensely: they could create a new set of oil contracts so that they didn't compete with the contracts sold in Manhattan—and in that way open up an entirely parallel oil market. But for Reston to feel strong enough to set out to convince the rest of the board to partner with an Arab country—well, that was unlikely, to say the least.

"I don't know," David finally said, trying to sugarcoat his response. "There are many members of the board who would definitely be against it."

Khaled nodded.

"I do know what you're thinking, Mr. Russo. I understand that there are a lot of misconceptions—on both sides. I know how the West views the Islamic world. I spent time at NYU, then finished my schooling in Cambridge and Geneva. I know what you see on TV."

David shrugged. Was that what was holding him back from taking this idea more seriously? Stereotyping? Racism? Unintentionally, David thought back to his father, unable to step inside an elevator or to take a one-hour flight to watch his only son graduate from business school. The image brought up more dark thoughts—angry thoughts. David quickly pushed them away. In truth, those thoughts embarrassed him. He was not going to be controlled by emotions like those. And besides, it wasn't emotion that made Khaled's idea seem insane—it was the impracticality of it. This was an Arab country. The Merc was a purely Western idea. Oil was the only thing they had in common—but to Khaled's people, oil was "the Black Blood of Allah." To David's people, oil was money, pure and simple.

Luckily, before David needed to respond, Khaled rose from the table, clapping his hands together. Then he gestured for David to follow and suddenly headed toward the door.

"I know you are skeptical, Mr. Russo, but at least do me the favor of keeping an open mind. Give me a day or two to work on you. The only way to truly change one stereotype is to create a new one. That, more than anything, is what Dubai is attempting to do. Maybe you and I will find a way to be a part of this revolution."

As David followed the young Arab out of the conference room, he decided that, at the very least, he could do as Khaled asked and keep an open mind. At the same time, somewhere deep in the back of his mind, he couldn't help but think about the last conversation he'd had with his father.

Khaled's idea seemed impossible—but then again, a center of market capitalism in the middle of the Arab world . . . *if that wasn't something important, then what was?*

Chapter 25

The nightclub was called Kasbah, though it didn't need to be; it was an extravagant, cavernous, three-floor affair dressed up like a sheik's palace, with arched entryways, Persian carpets, palm trees, wicker baskets, and flowing draperies. If it hadn't been for the multicultural, well-heeled crowd and the thundering and thoroughly modern Arab dance music, David would have felt transported right into the pages of an Arabian fairy tale.

"There's something for everyone," Khaled explained as he waved off a waitress in a tube top and a miniskirt attempting to sell them shots of pure oxygen from a yellow tank slung around her waist. "Originally, Dubai's native population had a thriving souk culture, which means that it's a city with a trading heritage. When the emir decided to thrust the nation into the modern era, it was natural to invite in partners from all over the world—and places like this sprung up almost overnight. Now the City of Gold caters not only to foreign investors but to foreigners as well, with a social scene that rivals that of any big city in the world."

Having visited a half-dozen bars, restaurants, and discos before settling into the Kasbah, David could not argue with Khaled's assessment; certainly, the Kasbah matched anything David had seen in New York or London. Even though it was barely eleven at night, the place was packed; every table in the VIP was reserved, and he'd counted more than twenty bottles of champagne gliding past on trays carried by members of the gorgeous waitstaff—all of those bottles in the last twenty minutes.

At first, David had been surprised to find that the club served alcohol. But Khaled had explained that most of the nightclubs, discos, and expat bars existed in a differently regulated part of the city.

"There are really two separate Dubais," he had said as they were led to the VIP table by an Asian hostess wearing harem pants, a midriff-bearing top, and a veil. "One for devout Muslims, and one for the expats—who, by the way, now outnumber the indigenous population almost eight to one."

It was an amazing statistic, but the number wasn't surprising: during the tour Khaled had given him over the past few hours, David had noticed that most of the people they passed were either European or Southeast Asian. Even the Arabs they saw—often young men in large groups dressed in Western style, but occasionally in smaller cliques wearing traditional robes— seemed to be from elsewhere, either tourists or businessmen. And David had also noticed that a large proportion of the people he'd seen were young.

"And it's not just the nightlife," Khaled continued. "The citizens here recognize that many of our visitors come from very different cultures; as long as the respect flows both ways, there are no problems with the many varied lifestyles."

David nodded. Khaled had already explained much of this in the BMW ride over from the Emirates Tower. The conversation had begun when David asked him about something he had seen in the lobby of the building: a woman was showing a marriage certificate to one of the security guards before entering an elevator that led up to her hotel room. Khaled had explained that after a certain hour women and men were allowed into the same room only if they proved that they were husband and wife. It was all very quiet, very reserved—but the rules were there, and this was assuredly a double society. You could drink and play in the clubs, but you didn't flaunt things in public, you didn't walk outside with a beer, and you didn't try to bring a girl back to your hotel.

At the Kasbah, the alcohol flowed and the girls wore miniskirts; outside on the street, women didn't have to wear burkas—though David had indeed seen a few in the hotel lobby and on the sidewalks—but they didn't flaunt their sexuality either. There were codes of behavior, but once you understood that, Dubai seemed as free as anywhere else David had been. And from the looks of the Kasbah, there was certainly room for debauchery.

At the moment, however, David was sticking to Perrier—partially out of respect for Khaled, who did not drink for religious reasons, and partially because he wanted to keep his mind sharp as he surveyed the Dubai scene. Ever since he'd left the conference room, his thoughts had been on overdrive; though he still believed it was an impossible idea—and one that he wasn't even sure he wanted to take part in—he had already begun deconstructing the notion of a Dubai oil exchange analytically, like they'd taught him in business school.

Breaking it down to its simplest form, David realized that to build an oil exchange in Dubai you needed three things: you needed the physical exchange; you needed the personnel who would be willing to go trade there; and you needed the rest of the world to take it seriously.

Considering the amount of money the emir had been pouring into construction, the physical exchange was not an issue. And places like the Kasbah—and the multitude of high-end restaurants, lounges, and dance halls that Khaled had shown him on their tour—went a long way toward solving the second task. It was incredibly important to be able to show traders and brokers that living in Dubai was really no different than living in London or New York—that the comforts they expected were available and there was ample opportunity to spend the money they'd be making.

David stretched his neck to peer over the brass-rimmed balcony toward the dance floor below. Certainly, there were women everywhere—some as beautiful as he'd ever seen walking down Fifth Avenue, and that was saying a lot. In fact, the club seemed disproportionately women—tall, well-dressed, striking women with plenty of makeup, mostly in groups of four or five, writhing to the beat coming from the huge overhead speakers.

Khaled nodded to David. "Although it's not something generally spoken about, our after-hours scene has also flourished with the growth in the expat community. Women from all over Europe—models, royalty, socialites, the party set—have come, following the wealth to its source."

David turned back to his Perrier. Selling the lifestyle of Dubai wouldn't be the hard part, that was for sure. It was the third aspect of building an exchange that would be the nonstarter. How would the trading world take seriously a center of pure capitalism smack-dab in the center of the Middle East? Khaled had been giving him the full-court press—first-class travel, first-class hotel room, a tour of the megaclubs—and still he was having trouble believing that Khaled was entirely serious. He was truly beginning to like the kid, and he respected his intelligence—but what was his angle? Didn't he have to have an angle?

"Khaled, you studied in New York, Cambridge, and Geneva. Now you're working on multibillion-dollar deals with developers, banks, whatever. Why do you want to go after something like this, a twenty-million-dollar project that will probably fail anyway?"

Khaled paused as a pair of young Lebanese men dashed by their table, chasing a pretty blond Russian who was heading for the stairs that led to the dance floor. Then he leaned forward over the table.

"David, I'll be honest with you. I'm not like most of the young men in this city. I am not here chasing wealth. My uncle is one of the richest men in the world. My father—rest his soul—always provided me with the best that life had to offer. I could leave Dubai tomorrow, go live in one of my uncle's many palaces, or enter the party circuit in a dozen cities around the globe—maybe along the way drop my beliefs and pretend I was a secular and free Lebanese like many of the Arabs who visit Dubai on vacation pretend—but none of that interests me."

His high cheeks were flushed, and there was real fire in his dark eyes.

"Dubai, for me, is not about wealth and Western-style debauchery. I believe I was sent here to make a difference."

It was strange to hear something like that, especially in a place like this. David knew that Reston would have laughed his way right down to the dance floor, corralling a waitress or two in the process. But David didn't feel like laughing. Instead, he was again reminded of his father—and about what his thoughts had been when that airplane was heading toward his window. *About doing something important.*

David looked at Khaled, at his dark Arabic features. It was more than irony—it almost seemed like some sort of cosmic joke. That the thing his father spoke of—the important thing that David could do—might come from a kid with those features, in a place like this.

"Khaled," he started, then he stopped himself. Did he really trust this kid enough to tell him what he'd kept inside for more than a year? And why him? Why here?

But David knew the answer. He *wanted* Khaled to know—and respond to—what he carried inside.

"On 9/11," he started again, "my dad was at work on the twenty-seventh floor of the World Trade Center. I was at Harvard Business School at the time, and I was sleeping off an all-night study session in my dorm room. I got a call from the dean's office and rushed over in time to see the buildings collapse on TV. I was so hysterical, they gave me these knockout pills to keep me from hurting myself. By the time I woke up, they'd found my father. He was alive. In fact, he had no physical injuries to speak of, but sometimes the worst kinds of injuries don't show up on X-rays and MRIs."

Khaled's expression softened, but he did not turn away. Nor did he interrupt; he just let David say what he had to say.

"He'd been trapped inside that building, watching people burning and falling to their deaths—and it just broke something inside of him. Two days later, he suffered a serious heart attack. Then, after he'd gotten out of the hospital, the panic attacks and the claustrophobia started."

David blinked away memories he didn't want to talk about: *His father unable to see him graduate because he couldn't get on an airplane. His father calling him, desperate, from the basement of a department store because he couldn't get back into the elevator or find his way upstairs. His father, this big, Italian tough guy, unable to do the most simple fucking things in life, like ride in the back of a taxi or get on a city bus.*

"A couple of weeks after that happened," David finally continued, "I wanted to bomb the whole fucking Middle East. This incredible rage overcame me—to the point where I almost lost myself. It took months for me to realize how stupid I was being—and I'm embarrassed by my own reaction, even today, a year later. I don't think I'm racist, and I don't blame the Arab world for the actions of a handful of terrorists. But I do know, firsthand, the sort of feelings much of the West has for your part of the world."

Khaled lowered his eyes for a brief moment, then shook his head. "Then you also know why we *have* to at least entertain the idea of working together on this. Why this exchange may be the most important thing you ever do." He looked up, his intensity magnified. "David, this might be hard for you to understand, but when 9/11 happened, most Arabs felt the same pain and anger that you did. We wanted to hunt down the men responsible and kill them—not only had they murdered innocent people, but they'd killed a part of our culture too and set us back so many years in our efforts to be respected by the West. But the Arab world is complicated; educated, powerful Arabs like my uncle could not come forward and speak these things—because the Arab street would not have allowed it."

David had heard the term only a few times before: the Arab street, the pictures of the Arab world that Americans saw on TV whenever a terrorist bomb went off or an anti-American rally made the news. In truth, he doubted that the Arab street was as unfamiliar a concept as most Americans probably thought. It was the consensus of the silent mob—the people, the everyday Joes. In America it was akin to the silent majority. The passionate—though often misled and disillusioned—people who populated the cities and towns across the country. In the Arab world the silent majority's voice was heard in the street because in many ways the street was the center of Arab culture.

"My uncle—along with my father before he died—has spent a lifetime quietly finding ways to work *around* the Arab street, to try to fix many of the problems of our region, but also to find ways to unify us with the West. I think you and I have an opportunity to do the same."

David listened to Khaled speak. He had never told anyone other than Serena about the day his father had been ruined by the collapsing building. He could hardly believe that he'd shared the story with Khaled, a total stranger, but somehow it seemed to make sense. And what Khaled was saying—could it also make sense?

David shook his head. He and Khaled were just two kids. Still, deep in his mind, he couldn't help wondering: What if somehow they brought the Merc to the Middle East? What if they built that damn soccer stadium in the middle of the Arab desert?

Would the rest of the world really come and play?

David's thoughts were interrupted as Khaled suddenly rose from his seat. David turned in time to watch a young man approaching across the VIP balcony. If David had had to guess, he would have placed the young man's age somewhere around thirty; European-looking from the way he was dressed—in a sleek, buttoned-down shirt, designer slacks, and a tapered DKNY jacket—he had a confident, polished gait and slicked-back brown hair that reminded David of the rich trust-fund kids he'd known at Williams and Harvard.

The young man was grinning as he reached their table and held out a hand to Khaled.

"Khaled," he said, and his accent immediately pegged him as British. "Never expected to find you here, out slumming with us Eurotrash."

Khaled nodded toward David. "Just entertaining a new friend from the States. David Russo from New York, this is Stephen Seebeck, London. He's with Signature Asset Management out of the U.K. Real estate, banking, what have you. He's also quite a regular in the late-night expat scene."

"There's nothing regular about us," Seebeck said. "In fact, I'm on my way to a wonderful little soiree right now. I don't suppose you chaps would like to tag along? What do you say, Khaled— show our new friend the real Dubai?"

David was beginning to wonder how many "real" Dubais there were. Khaled sighed, patting Seebeck on the shoulder.

"Sadly, I don't believe I can keep up with you and your friends. But I think David should take you up on your offer. He's seen as much of the city as I can show him tonight. My Dubai usually ends where Mr. Seebeck's version begins."

Seebeck winked at David. "What do you say, New York? Ready for a second act?"

Part of David would have been content to stay talking to Khaled, but another part of him figured there wasn't any better way to get to know a city dominated by foreigners than by following a European kid out into the night. He grinned back at the Londoner, then made his good-byes to his new Arab friend. After Khaled had shaken both their hands, Seebeck walked David down a set of stairs to a back entrance behind the VIP balcony. As they pushed past a group of dancing Southeast Asian women, Seebeck leaned in close to David's ear.

"Khaled's a good egg, and piety's a wonderful thing. But—no disrespect intended—why spend your time trying to pray your way into some future paradise when it's right here in front of you?"

They reached a pair of double doors at the back of the club, and Seebeck pushed his way through with an outstretched palm. They burst out into a back street that ran perpendicular to the club. Parked a few feet from the curb was a bright red Porsche 911 convertible: top down, black leather interior, ivory-white dashboard glistening in the low evening light.

With a flourish, Seebeck produced a set of shiny keys and flashed an equally ostentatious smile.

"In Dubai, this is what we call a company car."

A minute later, David was hastily strapping himself into the bucketed passenger seat, his body vibrating as Seebeck revved the RPMs. David took a deep breath—the smell of the leather from the seats mingling with the scent of burning gasoline—as the expat shifted the car into reverse, burned a streak of pitch-black rubber into the pavement, and skidded away from the curb.

Chapter 26

The swimming pool was enormous and shaped like a kidney; curved, tiled in marble, and brightly lit from below by more than a dozen underwater spotlights, its double-ellipsed circumference spanned the entire length of the gated modern condo-complex that rose up, four stories high, above its shimmering aquamarine surface. Surrounding the pool was a vast stone-tiled patio teeming with wicker deck chairs and tables, umbrellas, and potted palm trees. Mingling between the palm fronds and twists of wicker were about fifty people, maybe more—and from the looks of things, the party was just getting started. Throbbing hip-hop music echoed off the stone tiles as model-hot girls in skimpy bikinis cavorted with young men in designer jeans and fitted T-shirts. Waiters in white uniforms carried trays overflowing with Arabic delicacies—stuffed vine leaves, olive cakes, hummus dips, and Syrian bread—while pool boys in pale blue uniforms handed out towels and bathrobes. No matter that it was probably close to midnight; the air was a balmy seventy-five degrees, and the mood seemed as bright as the spotlights at the bottom of the pool.

"My God," David said as Seebeck led him through a gated entrance toward a mildly less crowded section of the patio. "What is this place?"

"A pool party, David. Haven't you ever been to a pool party?"

Seebeck paused to give hugs to a threesome of lithe girls in matching white bikinis, sitting together on a reclined deck chair. Then he continued forward, David rushing to keep up.

"I know it's a pool party. I mean, why here? Who are all these people?"

Seebeck grinned back at him.

"You mean who are all these girls. These condos are owned by Emirates Air. This is where they house their flight attendants. So my friends and I, in our infinite wisdom, have turned this place into the best after-hours scene in Dubai. With the help of some corporate credit cards, of course."

David watched a group of girls in the shallow end of the pool playing a form of volleyball with what looked to be some sort of Middle Eastern melon.

"These girls are all flight attendants?"

"That's right. Australians mostly. That's why they're all so goddamn tall. They grow them like that in Australia. Emirates Air picks and chooses the prettiest of the pretty and puts them all up here. Sometimes as many as seventy girls."

Seebeck slowed his swaggering gait as they approached a group of four well-dressed young men standing beneath a pair of palm trees. The four men all looked to be between David's age and Seebeck's. Actually, David had yet to see anyone over thirty; this could have been a party at any trendy club in downtown New York—except the girls were even prettier and the men were even better dressed. Also, David noticed, nobody seemed to be drinking any alcohol. Three of the four young men in front of him were holding clear bottles of water, and the fourth had a soft drink in a can.

Seebeck made the introductions; two of the young men worked at the same asset management company as Seebeck and were both from the U.K. One of the remaining two was an investment banker from Germany, and the fourth was a real estate consultant from Barcelona. None of them seemed even remotely surprised when David told them where he worked; it was obvious that none of them doubted for a moment that Dubai was becoming the focus of every business—not just real estate, tourism, and banking. And from what he'd seen of Dubai so far, David had to admit that no upwardly mobile young man would need any excuse to want to be there.

"And this is just one of a dozen parties going on tonight," Seebeck said to David as his friends bantered with each other about some soccer league they had started with a group of Indian money managers. "There's another set of condos about four blocks away full of corporate secretaries—mostly Swedish and Swiss—that we may visit if this gets tiresome. Then there are nine or ten after-hours clubs where the Eastern European girls hang out. Mostly prostitutes actually, but they're really nice to look at."

He winked in a way that made David think that he'd done more than look, but then he quickly changed the subject by grabbing a pair of bottled waters off a tray carried by one of the waitstaff.

"I know, it's not exactly vodka and Red Bull, but we have to show some semblance of respect. For the most part, we've traded excess for alcohol. Even so, of course, the emirate doesn't exactly condone these parties. And certainly, Khaled and his bunch don't like the idea of bikini-clad Aussies and Bulgarian prostitutes. But there's sort of an unwritten rule here: you live how you want to live, you just don't flaunt it when you're around the Arabs. You don't stumble down the street drunk, you don't hold hands with a girl in public, and unless you're about to jump into a swimming pool, you don't dress like you're on your way to an orgy. Even if you are."

"Did someone say 'orgy'?" the German banker butted in, and Seebeck gave him a smack across the cheek.

"Focus, Hans. It's way too early for orgies. Our young American friend has only been in Dubai for a few hours. We need to break him in slowly. Or maybe we need to break him in real fast. Real goddamn *fast*."

David assumed Seebeck was kidding about the orgies. But then he noticed that all five of the Euros were grinning at each other and nodding as if they'd just come to some unspoken conclusion.

Seebeck clapped his hands together, then suddenly all five Europeans were heading back toward the gated entrance to the patio. David stared after them—then quickly rushed to catch up.

"We're leaving already? We just got here."

"Change of plans, New York. Just stick close—I promise you're going to like this."

Considering they were leaving a pool party filled with Australian flight attendants, David couldn't even begin to imagine what Seebeck had planned for them next.

CROUCHING AT THE edge of a makeshift parking lot in the middle of the desert, staring at a pitch-black stretch of the Sheik Zayed Highway, his thighs starting to ache and the exhaustion from twenty-four hours of pure culture shock beginning to set in, David was starting to believe that his new expat guide had actually gone insane. They'd left a perfectly good pool party for this? Even though there were a dozen of the nicest luxury sports cars David had ever seen in his life parked behind them, and twice as many expats crouching alongside them, staring out at that blank highway, this was by no means a party. In fact, in the past ten minutes since they'd arrived in Seebeck's Porsche—parking between a BMW 5 series convertible and what looked to be a souped-up Lotus—and taken their position in the sand, nobody had uttered a word. No explanations, no pleasantries, nothing.

Finally, David couldn't handle the silence any longer. He leaned close to Seebeck.

"Man, what the hell are we waiting—"

Seebeck suddenly held up a finger.

"Shh. Here they come."

David stared at him, then turned back toward the highway. He didn't see anything. They were so far from the center of the city, apart from their makeshift parking lot, that there were no signs of civilization. They could have been on the surface of the goddamn moon. So what the hell was Seebeck talking about—

And then David heard it. At first it was just a low rumble, at the very edge of his hearing. Then the sound grew, getting louder and louder, turning from a rumble into a thunderous roar. David's eyes widened—and suddenly, in the far distance, two sets of headlights flashed into view. The headlights were right next to each other, moving straight down the stretch of highway. Except "moving" wasn't the right word. The lights were fucking flying, like two jets screeching along the highway right next to each other—and now the roar really was like jet engines, so loud that David could feel it in his chest.

"Hold on!" Seebeck shouted, and a roar rose up from the gathered, crouching expats.

Barely a second later, the two sets of headlights became two sleek, speeding blurs of metal, fiberglass, and rubber tires. Both cars were low to the ground, curved and polished, and futuristic—except that in that moment David recognized the two beautiful racing beasts from pictures he'd seen in magazines: a two-hundred-thousand-dollar Ferrari Modena, pitch-black with tinted windows, and a three-hundred-grand Lamborghini Diablo, bright green with backward-spinning silver hubcaps. The two cars sped by in a flash of sound and motion, barely inches from each other—and then, just as they'd come, they were gone.

"Holy shit," David said as the crowd of expats roared again.

"Hell, yeah!" Seebeck shouted back. "Riley's definitely taking that one. I think they're doing about one-eighty. Fucking A, that Modena is a sweet ride. Riley's bosses at SwissBank would have a shit fit if they knew how he was using his transportation 'allowance'—to kick all our asses from one end of the Sheik Zayed to the other!"

David shook his head.

"You mean you all do this? Race your cars along this high-way?"

Seebeck smiled, shaking his head. "Hey, not everyone goes for the sports cars. And you can't very well race a fucking Rolls, can you? But most of us have tried a little street race now and then. There's nothing like driving a fast car really fast."

David shook his head again. His adrenaline was really going. It wasn't just the cars—it was everything. On the ride over, Seebeck had described to him the ten-thousand-dollar-a-month apartments the expats were all renting—on company credit, of course. And then, on top of that, there were the girls—*my God,* David thought, *there were so many girls.* Not just the Austra-lian flight attendants; even during the twenty-minute trip to the deserted stretch of highway, Seebeck had managed to introduce David to dozens of girls from so many different backgrounds. There were the staggeringly tall Russian models coming out of an after-hours party that one of Seebeck's banking buddies was throwing two doors down from the Emirates Air condos. Then the half-dozen German and Polish blondes they'd run into out-side of a falafel hut on their way to the drag strip.

And now that the first race of the evening seemed to be over, the girls had started to arrive even here—a makeshift desert park-ing lot in the middle of fucking nowhere. Interspaced between the Porsches and BMWs and Ferraris, David counted at least twenty more girls who must have just arrived in the past few minutes, all of them model-beautiful and elegant, European, Eastern Euro-pean, and Southeast Asian, mingling and flirting with the young men. In New York, girls like that would be around only if there were twenty bottles of Cristal lined up in the sand, but here the girls didn't need champagne to light their way to the money. The very nature of this place seemed to be about money—and where there was money, there were always girls.

"This is pretty amazing," David said, watching a group of Italians in silk skirts who could easily have passed for swimsuit models chatting up a pair of bankers in suits. "It's like New York or London—but times ten."

"Actually," Seebeck responded, brushing sand off his slacks, "you'll find this place is pretty unique. Not just the quality of the girls—which I'm sure you've noticed by now—but the way they behave."

He flicked a hand toward a group of seven more girls, stepping one at a time out of an oversize stretch limo that had just pulled into the parking lot. David noticed that the girls were all wearing long trench coats—which they quickly removed, revealing more miniskirts and tiny lace designer tops.

"That about sums it up right there," Seebeck continued. "In Khaled's Dubai, those birds would keep themselves wrapped up and proper, but here in our Dubai it's a very different story."

David watched as two of the girls grabbed one of the bankers—who couldn't have been older than twenty-three, a skinny kid with glasses and slicked-back blond hair—and dragged him back toward the limo. The three of them landed on the backseat in a laughing heap, and as they shut the door behind them, David caught a quick glimpse of connected lips and intertwined limbs.

"Are they—"

"Hookers? No, actually. In this town, the hookers are much more refined. Those girls are tourists. I swear, this place is becoming more and more like Ibiza every week. Hard to believe you're in the Middle East, isn't it?"

It was hard to believe this existed anywhere—let alone the Middle East. David stretched his legs as Seebeck and his friends started back toward their hundred-thousand-dollar cars. In his head, he was mulling over what he had seen—from the moment he'd arrived in the Dubai airport to the moment he'd watched those two maniacs race down the Sheik Zayed Highway.

And somewhere in the midst of all that sat Khaled's intriguing proposal. To open a branch of the Merc, here, in this crazy desert kingdom full of parties, expats, and race cars. To try to bring a truly Western, capitalistic market to a place of such juxtapositions, such dichotomies. Old and new, Arab and expat, religion and excess.

Was David crazy enough to try to make Khaled's proposal a reality? Because really, he'd have to be crazy to think that he and Khaled could pull off such a thing.

Then again, listening to the dwindling roar of the Ferrari and the Lamborghini, watching the young Euros mingling together with the models and the hookers and the flight attendants, David wondered: when you're standing in the middle of an asylum, aren't you supposed to go a little crazy?

Chapter 27

It wasn't until David was sitting in the first-class lounge in the Emirates Airline terminal twenty-four hours later, waiting to board his return flight, that he finally came to a decision on Khaled's proposal. Although David's resolve had been building throughout the past day—ever since Seebeck had brought him home from the final after-hours party at five in the morning—it wasn't until he was sitting in a leather chair in the lavish airport lounge, sipping orange juice out of a crystal glass, that he saw the final sign—and it was something he simply could not ignore.

"David fucking Russo. Now what the hell are you doing here?"

A friendly hand came down on his shoulder, and David nearly dropped his orange juice. He looked up—and it took him a good minute to recognize the skinny kid in the pinstripe suit who was standing in the airport lounge next to him. The kid had thick glasses, pointy ears, and a really bad haircut, but he was smiling like he owned the world—and that smile was what gave him away.

"Irwin Cutler," David said, surprised. Then he stood and

shook the kid's hand. Cutler had been one of the top students who graduated with him at HBS; the son of a carpet king from St. Louis, Cutler was a double Crimson, having spent four years as a Harvard undergrad before entering the B-School. A bit of a geek, he was also one of the sharpest kids David had shared classes with—and now here he was, standing there in the first-class lounge, wearing a suit that looked like it cost as much as David's rent.

"I could ask you the same question," David continued, after they both sat back down. "What are you doing in Dubai?"

"Mckinsey, baby. Actually, this is my third trip. And I saw Smitty last night, at Tangerine. He's here full-time now. This place is ridiculous, isn't it? Off the hook."

David raised his eyebrows. Smitty—Walter Smith Jr.—was Cutler's roommate at HBS. If David was not mistaken, Smitty was an analyst at UBS, where his father was a partner. And he had moved to Dubai? Tangerine sounded familiar—but then, David had seen so much in the past twenty-four hours that some of his memories were already beginning to run together. His last day in Dubai had been amazing—but also a total whirlwind. After being woken up by the ubiquitous Arabic call to prayer that floated in through his hotel room's open patio door, he'd toured a dozen construction sites in the rapidly growing International Financial Center. Lunch had been at the Dubai Four Seasons, and dinner at a nearby Thai place, followed by another night at another disco—this one a spectacularly modern complex with a laser light show on the ceiling and a fountain in the middle of the dance floor made to look like an active volcano, spitting plumes of fiery red liquid ten feet into the air.

And from there things had gotten even wilder. Khaled had once again handed him off to Seebeck, who had taken him to three more after-hours parties. At about four in the morning, when David finally suggested that it was time to head back to the hotel, Seebeck had grinned and told him there was just one more stop to make.

David had been surprised when Seebeck pulled his Porsche to a stop in front of what looked like a quiet oceanside mansion a few miles from the center of town. The place was too quiet for an after-hours party, and the austere front facade—marble pillars, wide front steps, detailed heavy wooden doors—didn't look like the entrance to any club David had ever seen before. It wasn't until Seebeck had slipped a shiny black plastic card into a slot by one of the pillars and the great wooden doors had swung inward that David realized what sort of place this was.

The front hall of the mansion had been designed to look like some sort of Arabian oasis: a shimmering, egg-shaped wading pool took up most of the area, surrounded by a gold-tiled foyer decorated with palm trees, ivory-white benches, and woven, free-standing hammocks and swinglike chairs. Scattered about the foyer, David counted at least fifteen staggeringly beautiful women of varying ethnicities, dressed in elegant silk robes. Some were lounging on the hammocks, benches, and swings; others were standing around the wading pool, hands on hips, long bare legs extending out from beneath the swaths of silk.

David had stared at the women in the opulent lobby—and it had slowly dawned on him what this mansion by the ocean was. Then he had turned to Seebeck, shaking his head. As tempting as the scene was, he knew instinctively that it was not for him.

"I'm sorry, man. I think I really should be getting back to the hotel."

Seebeck had only shrugged. He had waved at the girls in the lobby, then led David back toward the car. The huge wooden doors shut behind them, and as Seebeck slid behind the steering wheel next to David, he offered a simple explanation.

"Khaled asked me to show you everything, David—even the Dubai he doesn't need to know about."

And David had understood. There were so many layers to this city; Dubai was truly unique, and in two days he had only scratched the surface. Khaled had arranged for Seebeck to take him around—although at first it had seemed a serendipitous arrangement—because he'd wanted David to understand: there was a good reason why Dubai was the fastest-growing city in the world, why businesses from all over were flocking there, why the expat community was thriving to such a degree.

But it wasn't the mansion on the ocean or the discos or the restaurants or the beautiful girls trawling the streets and shopping malls that had sealed the deal for David; it was the geeky kid in the pinstripe suit sitting next to him in the first-class lounge— what he had already said and especially the bombshell he dropped next.

"In two months," Cutler added, grinning from pointy ear to pointy ear, "I'm also going to be living here full-time. Mckinsey is bringing over fifteen of us. Got us sweet apartments right by the beach."

And just like that, David's decision was made. The smartest kid from his graduating class was moving to Dubai—sent by the top financial consulting firm in the world. And Cutler's roommate, an HBS legacy whose father was a major player at the biggest bank in New York, was already living there.

David knew exactly what that meant. Khaled could tell him stories about billion-dollar projects and economic free zones all he wanted—but the real evidence that the place was about to explode was right here in this first-class lounge.

When the smart young kids start showing up, then it's time to open your eyes.

Dubai was happening. And David was right there, in the middle of it.

"Well, you might be seeing a lot more of me," David said, and Cutler grinned back at him.

The decision had been made. Now all David had to do was head back to New York and somehow sell the idea of an oil exchange in the Middle East to a boardroom full of Italians and Jews.

Chapter 28

At that very moment, ten miles away, Khaled closed his eyes as the soft tones of a classical guitar ballad filled his brightly lit office. The music had been a gift from a classmate in Geneva, an Egyptian girl whose parents had worked for one of the studios that produced a few of the earlier films of Khaled's father. Though Khaled was hardly a fan of Egyptian pop music, he had always found this particular CD soothing, especially the complicated guitar ballads at the end; it had become a habit of his to play this particular song over and over whenever he truly needed to think. As he did so, he tried not to dwell on the irony that his relationship with the CD had far outlasted his relationship with the Egyptian girl. Ironic—but not surprising considering that he'd never had a girlfriend, or even a real friendship, that had lasted more than a few months.

Perhaps it was yet another symptom of his nomadic upbringing; you didn't make friends on movie sets, and you had brief liaisons that almost always ended when the director yelled "Cut!" for the final time. And you didn't keep girlfriends for very long when you moved from boarding school to boarding school, country to country, at the whim of a billionaire sheik. But you did learn how to read people—because you often had to make quick judgments if you were going to have any sort of relationships at all.

Khaled opened his eyes and looked down at the photos and typewritten notes that were spread out across his glass desk. He had compiled the dossier over the past forty-eight hours—beginning even before David Russo had first boarded the plane in New York. He had similar dossiers on Nick Reston, Anthony Giovanni, and many of the other major players in the New York Mercantile Exchange, but Russo's file was the only one that seemed important at the moment. Because at the moment it seemed that the success of Khaled's idea lay in the hands of the fresh-faced young man.

Khaled knew that his fantasy of a Dubai exchange was audacious; in fact, it had taken enormous effort just to convince the minister to let him invite a representative from the Merc to Dubai. And although the emir himself had tacitly allowed Khaled to continue forward—after Khaled had submitted a thirty-page proposal explaining why he felt such an exchange would benefit Dubai, to the continued glory of the ruling family—he knew his charge was tenuous at best. The river of distrust ran both ways, and there were stereotypes and emotions to overcome on both sides. Still, Khaled knew, with a certainty that grew every day, that the project was important—and indeed possible. But not without the Merc—and thus not without David Russo.

Certainly, Khaled and the Ministry of Finance could attempt to open an energy exchange without the help of the Americans. They could throw money into the project until it grew roots. They could build a beautiful building with a state-of-the-art trading floor, bribe traders from London and even New York to come play—but Khaled had no doubt that such an exchange would end up a failure, no more significant than an indoor ski slope or a shopping mall. Because without the legitimacy that the Merc would bring to the Dubai exchange, the rest of the world would not take it seriously. Like so many other things in Dubai, it would be viewed as a curiosity—another of the emir's whimsical creations.

Khaled gravitated toward one of the photos on his desk, one of David Russo in an Oxford crew sweatshirt that, like most of the other photos, Khaled had pulled off the Internet. Originally, it had been printed in the Oxford school newspaper, after Russo's crew team won some long-forgotten race.

Russo was grinning in the picture, his square jaw and wavy brown hair having captured the attention of the photographer as much as the expression of pure joy on his face. Looking at the picture, Khaled was reminded of a story from his second year at Cambridge about an American from Oxford who had punched out the captain of the Cambridge crew after a particularly nasty race. Khaled had no doubt he was looking at the same American; he could see it in his eyes, the competitive heat, the determination. This kid was a fighter.

And he was also smart. Over the past twenty-four hours, Khaled had been both surprised and impressed by how fast Russo had caught on to what Dubai was all about. He'd understood, almost instinctively, what Khaled was hoping to achieve by bringing an exchange to the Middle East: Dubai would benefit in so many ways by being a part of the pricing of oil—and the entire region would move forward in the wake of such a venture. When Russo had first told Khaled about his father and the emotional injuries he'd sustained on 9/11, he hadn't been searching for sympathy; he had been letting Khaled know that the obstacles they would face had nothing to do with money. The obstacles they would have to overcome had to do with people, beliefs, ideas, and emotions.

Khaled felt his hands ball into fists. Of all the projects he'd been pitched since coming to Dubai, only the exchange took aim at truly making Dubai the representative of a new, worldly Middle East. The very obstacles he and Russo would face—people, beliefs, ideas, and emotions—were the things that needed to change if Islam and the West were ever to truly become two parts of a whole.

David Russo understood, and he was a fighter—but he was also young, and he didn't have a billionaire sheik as an uncle.

By his bloodline, Khaled had the ear of the minister of finance and enormous resources at his fingertips. David Russo would be fighting his side of the battle on his own. And though David had not been specific, he had said that there were powers at the Merc who would certainly try to stand in his way.

Khaled paused for a moment, letting the vibrations of the guitar strings clear a path for his thoughts. Then he reached for his phone.

It took him a full ten seconds to dial the fifteen digits from memory; the call was now encrypted, as secure as modern technology allowed. After a series of metallic clicks, Khaled heard a familiar voice on the other end of the line:

"Khaled, this is indeed unexpected. You've caught me with my pants down—quite literally. I was about to change into a wet suit because your uncle has decided to go for a swim."

Khaled smiled, trying to picture the sheik's enormous Lebanese bodyguard in a bathing suit. Agha must have been quite a sight, his bulging muscles rippling beneath the overstretched rubber. Among other things, Ali Agha was an expert diver; before the sheik went in the water, Agha always surveyed what would be swimming beneath him. Agha was thoroughly professional—which was exactly what Khaled needed.

"I'm glad to hear my uncle is out enjoying the sun," Khaled responded.

"We're off the coast of Corsica at the moment. The girls are taking turns waterskiing off your uncle's new cigarette boat. It's quite a scene."

This Khaled chose not to picture. He paused, collecting his thoughts, then spoke quietly into the phone.

"Ali, I have a favor to ask."

"Anything, young sir."

Khaled quickly told Agha what he needed—down to the very last detail. If Agha was surprised by the request—and most certainly he had to be, since Khaled had never asked him for anything like this before—he did not let it show in his voice.

"I can put together a team," Agha finally responded. "With your uncle's approval, of course. It shouldn't be too difficult, from what you've described."

Khaled nodded. He was not concerned about his uncle's approval; his uncle would understand, since the project was exactly the sort of thing he was born to support. Khaled was much more concerned that the favor he was requesting be executed with the utmost discretion.

"I will personally get involved," Agha continued, putting Khaled at ease. "If your uncle approves, I can even go to New York myself."

"Thank you, Ali," Khaled said, completely confident in Agha's professionalism. "I doubt that will be necessary, but thank you. I will send you all the information I have right away."

After more pleasantries were exchanged, Khaled hung up the phone and began to gather the photos and notes from across his desk. He'd messenger the entire package to Agha—and then the thing would be put into motion. Khaled had no doubt that the Lebanese bodyguard was entirely up to the task.

David Russo would still be fighting the battle on his own, but if the battle turned ugly, Khaled—and Agha's team of professionals—would do what was necessary to help out.

Chapter 29

JANUARY 15, 2003

You have three minutes. Don't embarrass yourself."

It wasn't exactly Caesar inspiring his troops to battle, but David took what he could get. He tried to hide the fact that his hands were shaking as he moved toward the front of the board-room, clutching a bound copy of his proposal against his chest. He could see that Harriet had already done a thorough job of circulating the proposal to all of the board members; he counted at least twenty bound copies on the table, interspersed between plates of half-eaten bagels and steaming Styrofoam cups of coffee. Although the proposals had been handed out earlier in the day, David could tell from the bindings on the copies on the table that very few had yet been disturbed; hopefully, after he spoke, that would change. He had put a whole lot of sweat into those pages.

Two hundred pages to be exact. David could see, as he reached the front of the room, that many of the board members were eyeing the bound tomes with a mixture of awe and fear—not unlike what David would have expected if he had shown up at the board meeting with a box full of poisonous snakes. He knew he was taking a risk with the massive compilations; most presentations to the board ran less than ten pages. But David had always been thorough. And considering how controversial his proposal was, he could not have approached the task half-assed.

The two-hundred-page manuscript represented nothing less than the past two months of David's life: fifteen-hour days, seven days a week. Some of that time had been spent in the Merc library, compiling economic graphs and predictive matrixes, using information that already existed. Some of that time had been spent on the phone with Khaled, who had been an invaluable source of knowledge on everything to do with the Middle East, oil production, and the like. Some of that time had been spent agonizing over the plan itself: What steps did he need to take to convince the board to let him at least feel such a project out? How could he convince these men who'd grown up thinking one thing about the Arab world that a partnership could indeed work, that the Merc could benefit by taking such a huge first plunge into such unknown waters? And some of that time, unfortunately, had been spent arguing with Serena about the direction their relationship was taking—and about when David might turn back into the human being she had fallen in love with back in Boston. He had tried to explain that if he had gone into investment banking or consulting he'd have kept much the same hours, but that hardly changed the fact that their happy relationship was one of the temporary sacrifices he had chosen to make in his quest to bring this project to the board.

That Reston was even letting him make the presentation was a sign of David's perseverance. When he had first returned from Dubai and told Reston about the idea, the Texan had reacted with pure skepticism. *An exchange in the Middle East?* What were they going to trade, camel contracts? And who was going to do the trading? Some nut job in a turban spinning a scimitar over his head?

It had taken David about a week to convince Reston that he was serious; at the same time, he had been convincing himself,

letting Reston represent his own inner reservations at following through with what he'd decided in Dubai. By the end of the
week, he had convinced himself that the project had immense
merit, that Dubai was the next big thing, and that they'd be
crazy not to jump at this opportunity. Reston hadn't acquiesced so easily: he'd conceded that the Merc could make a fortune by partnering with Dubai and launching new oil contracts
that wouldn't compete with what was being traded in New
York but instead would bolster trade in both places. And he'd
understood that, as in New York, the Merc would get a cut
from every trade, buy, or sell. Reston had also instinctively understood how Khaled had been able to convince his own people
to attempt the project: Dubai would benefit by becoming the
most important energy player in the entire Eastern world. It
would thrust the entire region forward, forging relationships
with every aspect of the global financial market. In short, Reston had seen that, on paper, purely from a financial and strate-
gic perspective, the idea was entirely win-win—but in reality, in
Reston's words, that didn't mean shit. Because the reality was,
no matter how much money the Merc could make, no matter
how wonderful it would be to play nice with the Arab world,
selling this idea to the board and to the worldwide energy community was going to take more than chutzpah. It was going to
take an act of God.

"You don't have a shot in hell," Reston had finally conceded.
"But I'll give you a forum at the first board meeting after the New
Year. Be ready by then."

David was fairly certain that Reston had given him his one
shot simply to get him to stop bothering him. Reston had assumed—
probably rightly so—that David would be shot down within the
first thirty seconds of his appeal and that would be that. But
David didn't care about his odds; he had been given a brief green
light, and thus a marathon two months had begun. With nights
running into mornings running into afternoons, he pondered his
strategy—both in getting the board to let him move forward and

in deciding what steps he would take if he somehow got that second green light.

Now it all came down to three minutes—180 seconds—to convince this group of middle-aged men, many of whom had never been out of New York City, of the importance of building an oil exchange in Dubai.

If ever a moment had existed when David needed to straddle the two worlds he had come from—Brooklyn and Harvard—this was it.

He reached the front of the room and waited for the place to go silent. He could see that Reston hadn't taken his usual seat at the head of the table; instead he was standing by the door, arms crossed, like a determined substitute teacher, making sure that the board members were all giving David the floor—at least for his three minutes. He could also see that Gallo was indeed in his customary place—straight ahead on the other side of the long table, his pitted eyes narrowed into slits. David quickly looked away. When the room finally was as quiet as it was going to get, Reston nodded at him, and David began.

"Gentlemen, by now you've all gotten a copy of a proposal I've put together, on a very unique project that I think is something the NYMEX should seriously consider. Simply put, we've been offered a chance to partner with the Ministry of Finance of Dubai to open an energy exchange in that country."

Well, there it was, out of his mouth and into the boardroom. David paused for a moment, half-expecting someone to stand up and walk out, but nobody moved, not even Gallo. The board members were all waiting for him to continue.

"I've been to many places in my life," he said, gaining confidence, "but I've never felt an energy like I have in Dubai. The amount of money pouring into the place is staggering. Their infrastructure is first-rate, and they are serious about this idea at the highest levels. Regardless of what we decide to do, Dubai is going to be a strong player in energy. I believe we should take this opportunity to get involved."

He placed his proposal down onto the table, with the minimum of flourish, catching a glance at his watch on the way down. One hundred and twenty seconds—a minute to spare. Short and sweet, but hopefully he'd covered all the bases. He looked up at the board members—and to his surprise, saw that nobody was looking at him. In fact, the board members were making a point to avoid catching his gaze. His stomach churned. He had expected questions, a conversation, an argument—hell, he had expected something. But this was even worse than an argument. They were actually ignoring him. Even Mendelson, usually a supportive face, was concentrating on a spot on the wall behind David.

In fact, the only one who wasn't treating him like Serena's invisible man was Gallo. Quite the opposite—Gallo was boring holes in his skull with those dark, deep-set eyes.

"Is this a fucking joke?" Gallo muttered under his breath, his cigar jerking up and down in his lips.

Although the question hadn't exactly been aimed at David, he realized he had less than a minute to salvage the Dubai exchange. The project was crumbling right in front of him—and he knew he had to act fast. He had to make them acknowledge him. He had to break the fucking silence.

Swallowing the fear that was dancing up his esophagus, he stared right back at Gallo, matching eye to eye for the first time since he'd met the man.

"Do you have something you'd like to ask, Mr. Gallo?"

The words hit the room like a leather strap yanked tight. Now the board members were looking up, most with shocked expressions on their faces; it was one thing for Reston or Giovanni to go head to head with Gallo, but for a twenty-five-year-old kid to call the Don out like he was an uppity kindergartener—it was nearly blasphemy. But David didn't care. He had worked too hard over the past two months to throw this moment away so easily. It wasn't even about the exchange at the moment—it was personal. He wasn't going to back down before he even started. That wasn't his personality. Fuck it, he knew he was young—but he was also a vice president of the Merc. He deserved at least a modicum of respect.

Then he saw the color in Gallo's face darken and those eyes narrow into venomous slits—and his resolve nearly ran right out of his body, along with all feeling in his lower extremities. He gripped the edge of the table, just to stay standing, as Gallo half-rose out of his chair, his voice almost guttural with fury.

"Yeah, I got something to fucking ask, you goddamn piece of shit! Where the hell do you think you are? Fifty fucking yards from the hole in the ground where those ragheads crashed two airplanes, and you want us to partner with *them*? Dubai? What the fuck is Dubai? You can stick your goddamn two hundred pages up your ass if you think any one of my traders is going to squat in a fucking desert next to those bastards."

David swallowed, his face turning red. Out of the corner of his eye, he could see Reston mouth the word "careful," but he wasn't going to step down. The truth was, he'd secretly hoped Gallo would react like this; in fact, if he was going to get the board behind him, he'd actually needed Gallo's explosion. Because Gallo was only saying what many of them were thinking—and the ugliness had to get right out there, in the open, if David was going to have any real chance.

"I know exactly where we are, Mr. Gallo," David said, keeping his voice completely calm. "We're in the boardroom of an exchange so important that barely one day after those planes hit, this place was up and running; your traders were moving oil just like they'd done two days before, because both as a symbol and as a market, this exchange is at the heart of our free economy. And now we have an opportunity to bring this unique, powerful market to a part of the world that is moving forward just as we're moving forward."

David glanced around the table at the board members, who were watching both him and Gallo. Amazingly, they actually seemed to be listening to what he was saying. Perhaps it was Gallo's bigoted language, or the fact that David hadn't immediately backed down to the Don—but David hadn't lost them yet, as far as he could tell. At least he was still in the room.

"What the hell do the Arabs know about trading oil?" Gallo grunted angrily.

David noticed that the Don had backed away from the derogatory language; maybe he'd realized that his outburst had done him more harm than good with the board. Nobody likes to have their own prejudices thrown in front of them—and there was nothing uglier than a shared sense of bigotry. David knew that he had an opening—and it was time to go in for the kill.

"Absolutely nothing. This will be a partnership from the ground up. Your traders will never have to set foot in the desert; if all goes well, we'll get international traders to do the work for us. And over time, it will be immensely profitable for both sides."

David knew his time was nearly out. For the moment, he felt he had made his case as well as three minutes would allow.

"In any event, I'm not asking for a decision from the board—just for the chance to investigate this opportunity, to see where such a partnership might lead. As crazy as the idea of a Merc in Dubai might seem, it would be even crazier just to walk away without at least giving the idea a chance."

David cut himself short before Gallo could respond again, thanked the board, and took a step back from the table. Thankfully, he watched as Gallo finally lowered himself back into his seat. The color was gone from the old man's cheeks, but his eyes were still slits, and his cigar was hanging so precipitously from his lips, it looked like it was suspended by nothing more than saliva and sheer force of will.

As for the rest of the gathered board members—well, they had gone right back to ignoring David. David's stomach flip-flopped again as he searched for even the slightest sign that he had gotten through, but it was like trying to decipher Stonehenge—a useless endeavor. David had thought he'd made his point, but from the reaction of the room, it certainly didn't feel like a victory.

Reston gestured at him to take his customary seat in the corner of the room. He thanked the board one more time, then quickly took his place.

"Okay," Reston said as he moved toward the front of the room, "on to other business. Let's go over the minutes from our last meeting. . . ."

And just like that, David's moment was over. He tried to ignore the sweat pooling beneath his shirt as he listened to Reston drone on about end-of-the-year margins and tax calculations. He also tried to keep his head down and his attention away from the table—but at one point deep into the meeting he couldn't help himself. He looked up—and saw only one set of eyes aimed back in his direction.

Deep-set, slitted eyes.

Well, at least I made an impression on one of them, he thought to himself. Then he quickly lowered his gaze.

FORTY UNBEARABLE MINUTES later, David watched as the last board member filed out of the room—and still nobody had glanced in his direction, not even for a second. He waited until Reston had shut the door, leaving them alone in the vacuumlike atmosphere, before he slowly pulled himself off his chair.

"I guess that's that," he said glumly. "Looks like I got turned down."

Reston turned, and David realized suddenly that Reston was grinning at him.

"No. If they had turned you down, you'd know it. That was a tacit yes. No one is willing to go on record either way—because they don't know what's at stake. And the way you went at Gallo—that was fucking brilliant. No better way to get the board behind you than to make it look like you're sticking it to the Don."

Reston tapped his hands against the table. "Two hundred fucking pages of notes—and don't think for a minute that they didn't scan at least the first few chapters. You convinced them that Dubai is a player—and nobody wants to go down on paper as ruining our chances of being a part of what's going on there. Especially since the Merc can make a ton of money by opening a new trading center—and as long as we don't compete with ourselves, everyone's gonna benefit. And none of the board is going to go on record siding with the guy who just called the whole Arab world a bunch of ragheads. So at the moment you've been given the go-ahead. A subtle authority to proceed."

David stared at him, shocked. He couldn't believe what Reston was saying. The Texan walked over to him and put an arm around his shoulder, then led him toward the door.

"Here's my advice as you go forward with this. Keep your fucking mouth shut. Don't mention the project again until it's too late for anyone to stop it from happening. The longer you can go before anyone knows what you're up to, the better."

David nodded. His entire body was trembling. He couldn't wait to tell Khaled, and then Serena—though after their last argument, he wasn't sure if she'd celebrate with him or dump his belongings out onto the curb. Because David knew that this was only the first step. A huge first step—but still, just the beginning of the work that lay ahead.

"Now, you get on a fucking plane right away," Reston said, putting David's thoughts into words, "and start building the relationships you'll need to make this happen. Your first step is probably London. You'll need to get our friends at the trading floor there on board right away. Then a few other hot spots in Europe to get the international energy community on track. Then the brokers in Houston—fuck, you're the one who wrote a fucking book on this project, why am I telling you what to do? Just get on a goddamn plane before anyone tries to stop you."

Right before David stepped out the door, Reston swung him around, then gave him a friendly slap on the cheek.

"You did good, Harvard boy. But I still think this is gonna be a miracle if it works out."

David smiled back at him.

"At the very least, I'll get a few frequent flier miles out of it."

His mind was already whirling ahead—to the places he was going to go, the people he needed to meet.

But first there was one more thing he needed to do.

Chapter 30

The trading floor was in full swing as David stepped through the double doors. It was only 11:00 A.M., but from the frenetic motion coming from the trading pits, it was obvious the day was going to be even more chaotic than usual. David, of course, knew the reason for the tumult: a few days earlier, the National Weather Service had predicted a warmer than normal winter for the Northeast—which meant that the demand for heating oil would wane. The report would be devastating to some traders and a boon to others—but to David, at the moment, the shouts, screams, and shoving were simply background noise. At the moment, he was on a mission.

It took him less than a minute to spot Vitzi and his bright orange and red jacket, leaping up and down a few feet deep into the main trading pit. He was obviously trying to unload some crude position—and just as obviously failing to get the price he wanted. But David knew it was a temporary loss for the big kid; Vitzi was fast becoming one of the most successful meatheads in the game, and David was glad for their burgeoning friendship. Even more so, at the moment, considering that Vitzi was also the perfect vessel for what he had in mind.

David reached the edge of the pit and waited for Vitzi to finish unloading his crude position. When Vitzi finally turned and spotted him for the first time, David waved the thick-shouldered kid over. Vitzi grinned, shoving a pair of smaller traders out of the way, and gave David a big bear hug.

"Back from the Middle East with your head still intact? I guess a goombah like you isn't even worth kidnapping, eh?"

David laughed, then wriggled out of Vitzi's grip.

"Man, I wouldn't mind getting kidnapped if it meant an extra day in Dubai."

"What do you mean?" Vitzi asked.

Without pause, David launched into the most graphic—and only partly fictitious—story about Dubai's all-night party culture, from the Australian flight attendants and their all-night pool parties to the Russian models who trawled the streets to the Arabian princesses who staffed the hotels; from the massive discos where everything was available to the street racing on the Sheik Zayed to the back alleys where you could find the most perverse pleasures imaginable to the members-only oceanside brothel that Seebeck had shown him. As Vitzi's eyes grew wide, David wrapped it all up with a bullshit story about three blondes he'd met in a communal hot tub at some crazy outdoor beach party and graphically described what they were doing to each other as David floated nearby.

As he spoke, David snuck a glance past Vitzi, toward a group of young traders about twenty yards away, huddled around a bank of broker-connected telephones. They were easy to spot: their black-and-white zebra jackets made them stand out in the room full of color. David smiled inwardly, then went back to his story, which he finished on a high note—something about an Emirates Air flight attendant and a bathtub full of frozen daiquiris—good enough to evoke a full high-five from the widely grinning trader.

"You fuckin' animal" was all Vitzi said. Then he gave David a thumbs-up and headed back into the pit.

David turned, his work on the trading floor finished. He tried to keep his cool as he rushed back into the elevator—but inside he was doing cartwheels. His plan was now in motion.

David knew that his inflated, sex-fueled stories would sweep around the trading floor in a matter of hours; as he'd been reminded by everyone he'd met at the Merc, that was the nature of the place. Vitzi would tell Rosa and Brunetti, and from there the tales would move from pit to pit until everyone was talking about the hookers in Dubai, the mega-clubs, and the all-night parties. Eventually, the stories would reach the zebra-striped traders, who in turn would parrot the information to Gallo. *Exactly as David had planned.*

Even before their confrontation in the boardroom, David had known that Gallo was his main threat as he moved forward with the project. After what had happened, there was no way Gallo was going to sit back as David pursued something that seemed so dangerously new. *Unless, somehow, David gave him the idea that the exchange wasn't the real reason he was interested in Dubai.*

David grinned at his reflection in the elevator doors. Once he heard the stories from Vitzi—via his own zebra-jacketed traders—Gallo would assume that the real reason David was pushing the Dubai exchange was because it gave him free rein to party in the world's newest city of sin. Gallo would think he'd figured out David's angle, and his concerns would be somewhat allayed—allayed enough at least to buy David some time.

At the moment, time was David's most crucial resource. Reston was right: to pull this off, Khaled and David would need a miracle. *More accurately, a series of miracles.*

Well, what better place to look for miracles than a magical little sheikdom in the center of the Middle East?

Chapter 31

It's kind of like chess. The key is always to think six steps ahead of the other guy."

David nearly fell off his stool as he dodged the rail-thin arm that shot past him toward the miniature conveyor belt. At least his reflexes were still intact; jetlag combined with eight marathon hours of meetings had taken its toll on his vision, appearance, and certainly his hair—which, he could see from his reflection in the glass that partially covered the conveyer belt in front of him, was sticking up from his head in disobedient, curly twists of brown— but not his reaction time. A good thing, because it appeared he'd need every ounce of his athleticism to survive the emaciated Brit's lesson on the finer points of eating Kaiten-zushi.

When the Brit had first suggested that they try the conveyer sushi place on top of the famous Harvey Nichols building in Knightsbridge, David had loved the idea. He'd read about the popular Japanese restaurant fad in the British Airways magazine on the flight over—which seemed like so long ago, even though he'd been in London for less than ten hours. But as soon as the Brit had ushered them to seats at the circular counter—right in front of a tight curve in the long moving belt that wound through the upscale hip restaurant—David knew they were in for an interesting meal.

"That's why I love this place," the Brit enthused, waving a newly captured bright yellow plate in the air in front of David's face. "It's like an analogy to the business world. Eating as a form of war. And you mustn't ever underestimate the competition—or you're certain to go home hungry. That bastard simply has no idea who he's dealing with."

The Brit made an obscene gesture at another diner on the other side of the circular counter—a middle-aged man in a tweed jacket–pants combination—who quickly looked away. Then the Brit grinned, placing his new conquest next to a pile of similar yellow plates, and went to work on his freshly won dish—strange, brightly colored twists of raw fish.

David cracked a smile, then glanced past the Brit to Khaled. He could see that his Arabic friend was equally amused by the antics of their evening's tour guide. Then again, even if the man had taken them to the most conservative pub in London—rather than this mousetrap of a restaurant where colored plates wound past the customers at varying speeds, tempting them to make snap decisions or forfeit choice pieces of sushi to those with more pressing appetites—he'd still elicit amusement simply from his bizarre appearance. Gaunt as a stick figure, with a shock of bright orange hair, thick plastic glasses, and a dark pinstriped suit that hung off his skeletal limbs like some sort of Bond Street kimono, Marvin Hatfield was quite a sight for jetlagged eyes.

Certainly he didn't look like a senior vice president of one of the most powerful companies in the U.K.—actually, one of the most profitable corporations in the entire world. But as it turned out, the orange-haired Brit was the director of new projects for UK Petrol, the third-largest producer of crude oil in the United States and the seventeenth-largest producer of crude overall. UKP also happened to be one of England's largest industrial companies—and inarguably one of the biggest players in the oil business.

David had been shocked that he and Khaled managed to get a meeting with Hatfield and his team at UKP, but it had turned out that the combined influences of the Dubai Ministry of Finance and the New York Mercantile Exchange opened some pretty heavy doors.

The meeting itself had taken place two hours ago, at one of UKP's main offices in London's financial district. It had been David and Khaled's last meeting of the day; that day had started forty minutes after their hired car picked them up at Heathrow and dropped them off for a breakfast with the heads of London's energy exchange. They'd gone from that breakfast to lunch with a handful of gasoline fund managers who were heavy hitters on the London exchange, followed by afternoon tea with a team of consultants who had offered to help them navigate deeper into the European trading community—then a second helping of tea in the company of a pair of real estate developers whom Khaled had chosen as the most likely candidates should they ever actually be prepared to break physical ground in Dubai.

But of all the long day's meetings, there was no doubt in David's mind that the sit-down with BP had been the most important. If, somehow, they managed to convince UKP to get behind their efforts—even if only philosophically—it would give them leverage over the entire European oil community. So when he and Khaled had first walked into the sterile conference room at the UKP office building and the skeletal, orange-haired Brit had taken one look at them and exclaimed, "What is this, kiddie hour? You lads look like you've just taken your A-levels!" David had nearly vomited right down the front of his brand-new Zegna suit. Still, he and Khaled had plowed ahead with their presentation, taking turns summarizing the reasons why an exchange in Dubai was so important, what it would do for the region, and how it could become profitable and a major international player in a very short time. It had been hard to gauge Hatfield's opinion of their presentation from his decidedly British lack of expression—so when the orange-haired, freakish VP had suddenly ended the meeting by inviting them to dinner à la conveyer belt, they had gleefully accepted.

Now, an hour into a meal that seemed more a sporting event than anything else, David was no more certain of their situation with UKP—but a lot more skilled at collaring moving platefuls of raw fish.

"Now that's a good one," Hatfield applauded as David grabbed what looked to be a dish filled with unagi off the belt. "I think the Yank's getting the hang of it."

Hatfield grinned at Khaled, who raised a thumb in appreciation. Hatfield grinned even harder, then leaned back and suddenly slapped both of them on the back.

"You chums are good sports," he said, "even though I think you're both completely bonkers."

David raised his eyebrows. He wasn't an expert on U.K. slang, but he was pretty sure the orange-haired muppet was calling them crazy. Ironic, to say the least.

"An oil exchange in Dubai," Hatfield continued, chewing thoughtfully on a piece of blood-red salmon. "A free market cornerstone in an Islamic sheikdom."

"I know it seems improbable," David started, and the Brit nearly coughed up his fish.

"Improbable? You're talking about a center for trading derivatives in a country largely ruled by sharia law."

David nodded. After first hearing the term from Khaled in Dubai, he had spent some time over the past couple of months researching sharia law and how it applied to what they were attempting. Basically, sharia law was a system of rules derived from Islamic principles of jurisprudence—political, economic, and social order as dictated by a sometimes modern, sometimes ancient interpretation of the Koran, the Muslim holy book.

And Hatfield was right: under strict sharia law, the trading of derivatives would be *haraam,* forbidden. But according to Khaled, in practice as it applied to Dubai, sharia law was whatever the religious and political leaders in Saudi Arabia decided it was. When it came to matters of business in Dubai, Saudi Arabia was the eight-hundred-pound gorilla in the room, because of its level of investment in the region and its power over the sheiks themselves. In many ways, Saudi Arabia pulled the strings that made the entire Middle East work. Its massive wealth gave it tacit veto power in the region, and for something as important as a Dubai exchange to succeed, Saudi Arabia would have to be on board. At the moment, David and Khaled had no clear idea how the Saudis were going to react to their project, but Khaled had explained that it was a subject they would deal with when the proper time emerged.

For the moment, Khaled simply waved a chopstick gently through the air. "The ministry believes that the concept of the free zone covers the trade of derivatives."

David glanced at him, wondering if it was the ministry talking or just Khaled. Over the past few months, Khaled had often made grandiose statements like that—and David could never be sure what was really behind his young counterpart's confidence. Khaled never seemed truly concerned about what his boss might think; David wondered if Khaled's attitude was simply the product of his privileged upbringing or if he really *was* that powerful.

Hatfield swallowed his salmon, then crossed his marionette arms against his chest.

"Okay, putting that issue to one side, do you really think this can happen? David, will your traders in New York—and our traders here in London—accept an Arab exchange?"

David knew where Hatfield was heading. It was the same question he had been asking himself for months. The more he read about the divisions between the Eastern Islamic world and the West, the more depressed he became. Since 9/11, you didn't have to look far to find evidence of how bad things were. Every newspaper and every television news show spent twenty minutes on the subject every day.

"This division between us," Hatfield continued, mostly addressing Khaled, "these feelings we have toward each other—in London you see evidence of it every day. Protests over immigration, counterprotests, etc., etc. The Arab street hates the West, the West fears and despises the Arab street. Can people really change?"

Khaled paused long enough for the middle-aged man in tweed across the counter to get two yellow plates ahead of Hatfield, before answering with a shrug.

"If they have the right incentive. Hate is a very expensive emotion, Mr. Hatfield. People only choose hate when there's no other acceptable option."

David hadn't been able to tell if Hatfield liked the answer or not; the Brit had simply turned his attention back to the conveyer belt, his snakelike arms striking forward, leaving Khaled and David to try to prophesize answers from his growing collection of colored plates.

IT WASN'T UNTIL they were outside on the street that Hatfield finally gave them his decision. They were about to put him into a cab when he turned and ran the back of a hand across his salmon-red lips.

"I'm sorry, lads. I really can't give you the clean answer you're looking for. It's just too controversial an idea for us to openly get involved."

David's chest fell as he heard the words. He could tell that Khaled was equally disheartened from the way his friend's shoulders suddenly sloped inward. But then Hatfield threw them the tiniest of bones.

"But I will say this. If somehow, some way, you do actually get this thing up and running, I'll work my hardest to convince the folks at UKP to take part in your exchange. Sorry to say, that's the best I can do."

And just like that, in a flash of red hair and spindly limbs, he was into the cab and off, leaving David and Khaled standing on the curb. It was David who finally broke the silence, with words more air than voice.

"Well, it wasn't a total failure."

"No." Khaled sighed. "A total failure would have involved humiliating laughter and maybe some finger pointing. He basically told us that he thought we were crazy, but if we succeed, he'd be right there to celebrate with us."

"It's better than nothing." David shrugged. "In fact, fuck it, I'd call it a victory. He didn't say he wouldn't support us—just that he couldn't support us right now."

Despite their shared sense of frustration, Khaled grinned at him. "How very American of you. Silver lining and all. Are we supposed to celebrate the fact that he didn't spit in our faces?"

"Damn straight!" David joked, grabbing his new friend in a fake, Vitzi-style hug. Khaled laughed, then hastily fought his way free.

"You're going to scare the tourists. They'll think you're subduing a terrorist."

David was surprised by the joke, which made him laugh even harder. They both needed to laugh, considering that it was beginning to look like their trip to London wasn't exactly ending in success. When he had regained his breath, he jerked a thumb in the direction of their hotel—which happened to be right across the street.

"Should we 'celebrate' at the hotel bar? I know you don't drink, but the Mandarin Oriental's Perrier is first-rate."

David wasn't exaggerating: considering how lavish the hotel was, it probably had its Perrier shipped by private jet straight from the source. Even from across the street, the spotlit facade of the grand old twelve-story hotel dominated their view. David would never have stayed in a place like that himself—and the Merc certainly would never have paid for such luxury—but Khaled had insisted on setting the whole thing up, via the Ministry of Finance. David had halfheartedly argued with him about the expense—then had acquiesced when Khaled had assured him it was completely within his budget. David had done his research—and he wouldn't even try to calculate what sort of budget Dubai would give the nephew of a multibillionaire sheik.

To his surprise, Khaled was already hailing a second taxicab.

"Before we celebrate, I want to show you something."

"Another nightclub with a laser show? Maybe some girls dancing in cages?"

Khaled didn't answer. Instead, he slid into the cab and ushered David to follow.

FORTY MINUTES AND about an equal number of pounds later, the taxi turned onto a quiet, well-lit suburban street and pulled to a stop next to the curb. David squinted out through the window: narrow two- and three-story walkups squatted next to each other on either side of the newly paved road, and he couldn't help thinking that the area reminded him a little bit of the Brooklyn of his childhood. That is, until his gaze settled on a domed, four-story building directly ahead of the taxi: the complex seemed newly refinished, with freshly painted walls, arched windows, and carefully designed Eastern touches such as two mock minarets rising from the roof and, of course, the dome—gilded in shiny gold leaf.

It was the sort of place David would have expected to see in Dubai—not somewhere east of London.

"Where the hell are we?" he asked.

"We're in a predominantly Muslim suburb in East London," Khaled responded. "That building is an Islamic school. It services grades kindergarten through high school. And there are night classes open to everyone in the community, Muslim or not. They study Koran—also history, government, and business."

As he spoke, two young Arabic-looking men came out the front door of the school. They were both wearing sweatshirts and jeans, with books under their arms. They could easily have fit in with the college kids strolling around Union Square in New York—except for their long, traditional beards.

"It's very nice," David said, wondering why Khaled had taken him there. Then he had a thought. "Did Dubai pay for this school? It looks brand new."

Khaled shook his head.

"Not Dubai. My uncle sponsored this . . . reclamation."

He took a long breath, then turned toward David.

"My uncle put two million dollars into this community. His generosity gave this place a chance. This neighborhood was desperate, starving—if things had continued on that path, it could have gone in an entirely different direction. Maybe a dangerous direction."

"But how do you know, a few years down the line, that the community won't degrade again? Do you have to keep infusing money?"

Khaled turned back toward the window. He touched the glass with his brown fingers.

"This is a school—not some statue or swimming pool or amusement park. You build infrastructure like this, and you give a community a future."

Now David knew why Khaled had taken him to this Muslim suburb outside of London. This school represented exactly what Khaled was trying to do with the oil exchange in Dubai. This was the answer Hatfield had been looking for at dinner.

"If only we could have made Hatfield understand. You change people's minds by giving them a future," David said.

Khaled tapped the divider that separated them from the driver, signaling the taxi to take them back to the hotel.

"A future," Khaled said as they started back toward the city, "is something the Middle East has never had before."

DAVID'S JETLAG HAD begun to kick in full force by the time they found seats at the sparsely crowded Lucite and marble bar on the first floor of the Mandarin Oriental. The cab ride back through the pitch-dark, windy suburban streets surrounding London hadn't helped matters, nor did the knowledge that they were going to be heading back to Heathrow in less than seven hours to catch a short flight to Geneva for the next—hopefully more successful—leg of their European tour. But David assumed that the bright lighting of the surprisingly modern hotel bar would keep him awake long enough to finish at least one Perrier.

To his surprise, it wasn't the fluorescent bulbs on the ceiling that gave his adrenaline a kick as he and Khaled launched into a conversation detailing the events of the day—it was the view from the opposite side of the bar. The second David took his first swig from the green bottle of carbonated water, he had spotted her—and nearly choked as the bubbles caught in his throat.

Christ, she was beautiful. A brunette, like Serena, but with shiny, jet-black hair ironed so straight that you could see every strand; ivory, almost jarringly perfect facial features that seemed to have been chiseled out of the purest, blue-tinged ice; and full, teasingly plump lips with a hint of white teeth peeking out between them.

And the view below the neck only got better. David hastily turned his attention back to Khaled—but not before he'd followed her long, pale neck to the open collar of her designer, black-velvet corset top and the high, rounded bulge of her exquisite decolletage.

"She's quite something, isn't she?" Khaled suddenly asked, and David realized his friend was grinning at him. David grinned back.

"So you spotted her too?"

"I'm Muslim, not dead."

David laughed. He took another sip of his Perrier, trying to play it cool in front of Khaled.

"So why don't you go over and talk to her?"

Khaled shook his head.

"I don't usually find girls who share my—ah, interests—in bars. But why don't you go buy her a drink?"

David caught himself sighing. He quickly forced the sigh to transform into a cough.

"Because I've got a girlfriend back in New York."

David wasn't sure if he was explaining the situation to Khaled or vocally reminding himself—but either way, the fact was a fact. Serena, the girl he was assuredly in love with, was back in his apartment in Midtown, probably watching TV while wearing one of his oversize college sweatshirts. She certainly wasn't out at some bar, staring at unbelievably high cheekbones, gazing down a long, arched slice of neck, floating across curves that seemed so lickably soft—

Khaled tapped the bar with his fingertips, bringing David back into focus.

"And do you look at your girlfriend back in New York that same way?"

David stared at Khaled, exasperated. But to be honest, he wasn't sure. Definitely not recently; though he and Serena had patched things up as much as possible before he'd left for London, his job had certainly taken a major toll on their relationship. He tried to picture Serena as he had last seen her—curled up in the bed, watching him pack, a look of frustration on her pretty, puckered lips.

Damn it, David thought to himself. Then he held up his palms, the universal sign of surrender.

"She's a girl in a bar," he said finally.

Khaled seemed to understand and dropped a twenty-pound note on the open check in front of them, taking care of the Perriers.

"Then let's call it a night. We've got another big day ahead of us."

David nodded. He took one last quick look at the brunette— then he rose from his seat, finished his drink, and with a cough that was really a sigh, followed Khaled toward the elevators.

Chapter 32

If ever there was a moment that seemed to justify the decisions David had made over the past six months of his life, this was it.

Legs furiously pumping as a crisp, clean breeze splashed against his cheeks and tugged at the wool hat he'd pulled down low above his eyes; the sound of crushed snow crunching beneath his sneakers, harmonizing perfectly with the rhythm of his heart pumping in his chest; and the warm swirl of blood beneath his skin, heating him from within, forced his mind to become wonderfully clear as he focused on the path winding through the closely packed trees ahead of him, though his eyes caught glimpses between the snowy branches of the scenery beyond—the powerful Rhone River rushing by, churning waves glistening in the wintry moonlight, and of course the great Alps rising up above, massive but never menacing, a sloping, fertile brand of magnificence that spoke of rolling meadows, sloping vineyards, postcard villages, and picturesque fields.

It was hard to believe that just six months ago David had been trapped in a cubicle at Merrill Lynch, looking forward to a lengthy incarceration trudging away on the bottom rungs of the financial world's massive, mechanized pyramid. Now here he was, jogging along a river in Geneva, burning off the adrenaline rush of an evening spent addressing four hundred of the top energy players in all of Europe.

It was amazing how his life had changed so quickly: from a chance meeting at the National Italian American Heritage Institute gala to a strange invite from the heads of a country he'd barely even heard of, to a friendship formed by way of all-night bull sessions, world travel, and shared ambition—to this, a moment when things cautiously seemed to be coming together, when the impossible was slowly starting to feel, well, at the very least, slightly less impossible.

Three hours ago, when David had first taken the podium next to Khaled in the imposing main lecture hall at the University of Geneva, he had half-expected the two of them to be laughed right off the elegant, snowbound campus. At the very least, he had expected to be met by the same level of skepticism they'd encountered with Hatfield. The five-hundred-seat circular amphitheater had been nearly full, the audience a veritable who's who of the European energy community. Representatives from the big oil companies, analysts from the major international banks, energy academics from all over the world, journalists from more than a dozen European business media outlets—nearly all facets of the energy world were gathered together for a five-day post–New Year's conference on the state of oil as it pertained to the European community. David and Khaled could not have asked for a better place to publicly float the notion of a Dubai exchange, but for David's part, he would have wished that the opportunity had come further down the line, not bare weeks after he'd first pitched the idea to the board of the Merc. No doubt, to be shot down in Europe by such a prestigious audience would mean certain doom.

But somehow, by the end of their forty-minute presentation, David realized that the gathered experts weren't going to shoot down their idea; more than anything, the assembled crowd was simply curious about the partnership that he and Khaled were attempting to put forward. The enthusiasm of the crowd's questions during the brief Q&A was heartening—that was, until one high-level executive from one of the Swiss banking conglomerates asked if the Merc's board was truly going to green-light a boisterous, American-style trading exchange in a place so close to Saudi Arabia, where foreigners were literally flogged on the street for wearing shorts. David had expected their entire presentation to unravel right there and then, but somehow Khaled had talked their way out of the situation, explaining that Dubai, though often shadowed under the Saudis' gentle wing, was a very different bird. Or something poetic like that—David couldn't remember the exact words. In any event, by the end of the presentation the audience seemed to be at least moderately on their side.

If they weren't moving forward by leaps and bounds, at least they didn't seem to be moving in reverse. They were raising awareness of their project, and sooner or later pieces would begin to fall into place. At least, that was what David hoped. At the thought, he felt a new burst of adrenaline and launched himself at full speed over a frozen tree root. He kept up the intense pace for a few more minutes as he followed the jogging path through a series of sharp turns. The river, a glowing ribbon of water so close David could feel the icy moisture against his skin, was fully visible now.

Breathing hard, David finally slowed to a walk and checked his watch. He wasn't sure how far he'd gone, but it was definitely time to get back to the hotel. He had no doubt that Khaled had already written up a veritable tome of notes for him to go over for the meetings of the next few days, and he'd be lucky to get six hours of sleep before they headed back to the airport for the next leg of their journey.

It took him a good thirty minutes to wind his way back to the hotel, and by the time he stepped into the subdued, art deco lobby of the Mandarin Oriental Du Rhone, his Oxford crew sweatshirt was drenched with sweat. He quickly navigated past the sunken

couches and bucket loveseats, glad that the place was fairly deserted for ten at night. He still felt out of place in these bastions
of affluence and half-expected some Swiss security guard to come
after him with a hose and a bar of soap; maybe on their next trip
he'd convince Khaled to let him pick the hotels. Nobody had
ever felt self-conscious sweating his way through the lobby of a
Courtyard by Marriott.

Thankfully, David reached the elevator without incident. After
hitting the button with a damp palm, he was carefully wiping the
damn thing dry with the sleeve of his sweatshirt when the gilded
doors slid open. Without looking up, he stepped forward—and
nearly crashed headlong into a woman on her way out.

"Excuse me," he started, and then his eyes widened and he
froze.

She was wearing a black turtleneck sweater and dark jeans,
ankle-high leather boots, and a white cashmere scarf wrapped
around her long, angled neck. Her jet-black hair was pulled back
in a ponytail, and her high, almost elvish cheekbones glowed in
the light from the lobby's chandeliers. Her dark cat eyes peered
out at him from behind anime-length eyelashes, and her eyebrows
crooked upward as her full red lips pulled into an amused smile,
revealing more of her startlingly white teeth.

"Are you going to let me out of the elevator, or are we going
to stand here all night?"

David blinked. Her accent was unexpected—decidedly French,
though her vocabulary seemed perfect—and she was much taller
than she'd looked the night before. Then again, the night before
she'd been seated at the bar—and now she was standing right in
front of him, arms crossed, impatiently tapping a leather heel.

"Are you following me?" David croaked, feeling foolish the
minute he'd said the words.

The girl's eyebrows moved up another notch—and then recog-
nition flashed across her chiseled features.

"You were in the bar in London. Sitting with a young Arab
gentleman. You were drinking Perrier."

David exhaled and took a step back, letting her out of the elevator before the doors slid shut.

"So you are following me," he joked, realizing it was obviously just a coincidence—an amazing, terrifying, wonderful, horrible coincidence. "Keeping tabs on what I'm drinking and who I'm hanging out with."

The girl laughed, a beautiful, high-pitched sound.

"Yep, you caught me. I'm the worst spy in the business. I was hiding in the elevator when you pushed the button."

She paused, then held out a thin hand.

"I think we're just on the same travel schedule. My name's Jasmine Cross. I work for the Mandarin Oriental Hotel Group—so if you're one of our frequent guests, this probably won't be the last time you'll run into me."

David tried to ignore the sparks running up his spine as he shook her hand. She looked to be about his age, maybe a year or two older. And even through the thick sweater, her curves were torture on his peripheral vision; it took most of his concentration to keep his attention above her turtleneck.

"David Russo," he said, introducing himself. "No wonder my friend raves about this hotel chain. And here I thought he was just happy about the Toblerone in the minibars."

Jasmine laughed, then cocked her head to one side.

"Actually, the way you were looking at me in London, I should be suspicious of you. Although any stalker who can afford to stay at our hotels is probably worth the risk of a restraining order."

David coughed, suddenly aware that she was looking him over—and even more aware that he was wearing sweats and mud-stained sneakers.

"I'm not stalking you, but I am bringing down the property value of your beautiful lobby. I need to go upstairs and get cleaned up. But it was a pleasure meeting you, Ms. Cross."

He hit the button for the elevator again, and thankfully the doors slid right open. As he stepped inside, he felt her light touch against his arm.

"How about after your shower you come back down here and take a walk with me. There's nothing quite like Lake Geneva at night."

David swallowed, momentarily unable to answer, as a battle raged inside his conscience. There wasn't anything explicitly seductive about the invitation—except, of course, that when a girl was this hot, anything she said was by its nature an act of seduction. And when David looked into her eyes—mainly to keep from looking anywhere else—he saw what he interpreted as a hint of loneliness in the darkness of her pupils; maybe she'd seen something similar in him, or maybe she was reaching out because they were two travelers who'd somehow found themselves in the same unlikely orbit. Or maybe she was just bored. Or maybe—fuck it, David was tired of trying to think of maybes.

Jasmine shrugged, stepping away from the elevator.

"Unless you're too tired from your jog."

David stopped the closing elevator doors with both hands.

"I'll be down in five minutes," he said.

He cursed to himself the whole way up to his room. He cursed his way through a lightning-fast shower. He cursed his way all the way back down to the lobby. By the time he caught sight of her again, standing outside on the cobbled sidewalk, her long sable ponytail swaying in the breeze, her dancer's legs and perfect ass struggling against the tight material of her jeans—he'd completely run out of curses.

DAVID WASN'T REALLY sure how it happened, or whose fault it was. After the fact, he couldn't have even re-created it in his mind, because the moment changed so damn fast it defied any sense of time or place—it simply *was*. One minute he and Jasmine were walking along the snowy banks of the great lake, talking about their lives and their hopes and their dreams, sharing stories of two very different cultures and worlds, trading jokes and gentle barbs—and then the next minute they were kissing, first gently and cautiously, then with a fierceness and a passion that seemed to erupt out of nowhere.

And at first David's mind tried to fight back. *Christ,* he screamed at himself, *this is a huge mistake, this is not what I'm here for, this is not who I am.* This girl was not Serena—she was a stranger in a strange place, and no excuse of time and location would make this right. But even so, whether it was the thrill of the unexpected, or the crisp alpine air, or the way the lake seemed to shimmer in front of them, for a brief moment, as David's hands moved beneath her sweater and up the holy curves of her body, as her bare flesh burned against the tips of his fingers, he wasn't thinking about Serena or Dubai or even oil. For that brief moment, right and wrong seemed like such pathetic little concepts. All he knew for certain was that he didn't want that brief moment to end—he wanted to stay there on the banks of Lake Geneva forever, as her body enveloped him and her long legs suddenly wrapped around his waist, as he lifted her up into the air and then set her down, as the two of them rolled back and forth in the snow, interlocked, as his hands slid down to the clasps of her jeans, as her lips pressed against his neck, as a feral gasp escaped her throat—and finally, he did stop himself before he moved past the point of no return. Finally, he pushed back from her, rising quickly to his feet.

"I'm sorry," he gasped. "I can't."

She looked up at him, confused, tempting, wanting, the steam from the snow still rising off her flesh—a swirl of heat and passion vanishing upward into the pitch-black night. He shook his head, angry at himself.

"I'm sorry. Really, I have to go."

And he turned, quickly heading back toward the hotel.

A kiss, he told himself, it was only a kiss, albeit passionate, but in that moment, damn it, it had seemed like so much more.

Chapter 33

Out of the frying pan and into the fire . . .

By two in the morning the girls were coming by so fast that it was like a moving montage of barely covered body parts: long, stockinged legs; heaving breasts spilling out of demi-bras and tight bustiers; rounded, apple-shaped asses split by leather and lace thongs; and high spiky heels everywhere, from one end of the long carpeted stage that ran through the center of the ballroom to the other. As the girls circulated through the massive hall, they were doing their best to gyrate to the music blaring from the overhead speakers, but it was obvious from the way they were built that none of these girls were dancers—and that, of course, was the point. This wasn't a strip club—it was the main ball-room of the Four Seasons of Houston. These girls—all seventy of them—were too tall and too beautiful to be anything other than professional models. And the crowd of drunken, hooting men who crowded around either side of the raised stage, gawking at the never-ending parade streaming by—each and every girl garbed in the skimpiest lingerie ever to grace the great state of Texas—weren't the white trash customers you'd expect to see, chugging

Budweiser and sticking dollars down G-strings, but brokers in suits and ties, drinking champagne from crystal flutes.

"I can't believe we didn't think of this sooner," one of the suits crowed into David's ear as he stood in the crowd a few feet from the stage. "This is killer, man. Fucking killer."

David faked a grin as a stunning Asian in thigh-highs and a lacy French maid outfit sashayed by, eliciting more shouts and applause from the surrounding men.

"When you said you guys had arranged a fashion show," David shouted back, "I should have guessed it would be something like this."

The suit laughed, clapping a hand against David's shoulder. Jason Cohen was in his early thirties—like most of the crowd—but his young, tan face and wide, athletic shoulders made him look a good five years younger. David had spoken to Cohen many times on the phone, but this was their first real face-to-face meeting. Although David didn't know Cohen well, he should have guessed from the way the young broker had grinned at him in the limo when he'd first picked David up at the airport that they hadn't been heading to some quiet restaurant. Even when the limo had pulled up to the majestic Four Seasons on Lamar Street in the heart of the city's sparkling, modern financial district, David should have figured that Cohen and his buddies had something crazy in mind.

David glanced past Cohen to the crowd of brokers on either side of the high-class flesh parade. There were maybe sixty or seventy young men in the hall; together, they made up most of the heavy hitters in the Houston broker community—a special breed that David had come to know in his short time at the Merc. Mostly young, almost entirely male, the brokers were the middlemen between the oil giants and the traders on the floor; you couldn't have an exchange without the brokers—they were a necessary, if sometimes overlooked, part of the oil supply-and-demand equation. Each one of these men salivating at the sight of the lingerie models represented millions of dollars in potential daily trades.

"Let's see the meatheads in New York pull something like this off," Cohen said, jerking a thumb toward the far end of the stage, where ten more models waited their turn to show their stuff. "We had to bring in girls from as far away as Dallas to fill out the roster. Probably cost close to a hundred grand—spread out, of course, between the lot of us. Now that's what I call a good use of an expense account."

David whistled under his breath. *The eighties were alive and well in Houston, that was for sure.* Even after the debacle of Enron, the brokers—mostly independents with relationships with the exchanges as well as the big oil companies and the major energy-playing banks—lived like the bankers of a different era. Strip clubs, ten-thousand-dollar steak dinners, parties in lavish VIP suites, jaunts to Vegas—the broker lifestyle was unsparingly decadent. The lingerie show at the Four Seasons was pretty elaborate, but David had been hearing stories about broker blowouts like this from Vitzi and the other traders since his first week on the Merc. David remembered one such story, involving Cohen and his buddies, that had taken place a couple of years earlier. A hurricane had swept up the Texas coast and was heading right toward Houston. Rather than close up shop like many of the other businesses in the city, the brokers had caravanned by private jet to the only city that could properly handle both their business needs and their excessive partying needs—Las Vegas. Fifty of them had holed up in the Venetian Resort, racking up record bar tabs at every strip club and dance hall in the City of Sin. *What was a little fashion show compared to that?*

David turned his attention back to the stage, where a pair of decidedly Texan blondes in matching white satin baby dolls were gliding by, to the full appreciation of Cohen and the rest of the crowd. Part of him wanted to get the hell out of there, not because he didn't enjoy the view—he was a guy, after all—but because, after the previous night in Geneva, the last thing he needed was more weight on his already heavy conscience.

For the past twelve hours, David had been flagellating himself for his foolish loss of control. He'd regretted the thing the minute he'd gotten back to his hotel room, and he'd immediately called Serena, not to confess—although in the end the moment had only gone as far as an extremely passionate kiss, a confession would have been sheer suicide, even if it had been the right thing to do—but to quickly wipe away the memory of Jasmine and their roll in the snow. David knew the incident was something he'd probably have to face later on as his relationship with Serena deepened, but for the moment he just wanted to forget it ever happened. The second he'd gotten Serena on the phone and heard her voice, he had known that she was the one he loved. He didn't intend to throw that love away because of a stupid moment of weakness.

The rationalization didn't make the guilt go away, but at least it kept him focused on what was important: Serena, his job, and his new dream of a Dubai exchange. And the truth was, the sultry display in front of him was actually more business than pleasure—even if Serena probably wouldn't have seen it that way. The fashion show at the Four Seasons was actually the perfect setting for what David had come to Houston to do: get Jason Cohen and the rest of the Houston broker community excited about Dubai.

With that one goal in mind, David moved in close to Cohen next to the stage, and while the girls streamed by in ever-decreasing strips of silk, leather, and lace, he began to regale the young broker with the same lurid stories he'd relayed to Vitzi on the Merc trading floor.

As he spoke, he could see the sparks going off behind Cohen's eyes. Because unlike with the conservative board of the Merc, the darker, crazier side of Dubai was what was going to sell the Middle Eastern exchange to the brokers. These young guns didn't want to hear about property taxes and the future of energy; they wanted to hear about Russian girls, money, and booze. To sell them Dubai, David needed to sell them on lifestyle—because to them, that's what mattered most.

By the time the last half-naked model was making her way down the makeshift catwalk, Cohen's attention was entirely on David and Dubai, not skimpy lingerie.

"Sounds pretty amazing," he was saying, and a few of the other brokers had gathered closer to listen in. "But don't let all this fool you: we love to live good lives, and we love to have fun, but if there's an opportunity to make money, that's what really matters. So don't just tell me about the clubs, beaches, and bikinis. Tell me I can make some fucking money."

David grinned back at him.

"More than you can imagine."

"And the Arabs are gonna let this happen? They're gonna let you trade oil in the middle of the fucking desert?"

It was really just a play on the question that had come up again and again—would sharia law make room for an oil exchange in an Islamic world? Even though David still didn't know the answer for sure—Khaled, who had flown straight to New York instead of joining him in Houston, had only hinted that sharia law was something they'd deal with when the time was right—he nodded his head.

"The sheik of Dubai has set up a free zone. Everything and anything goes in the free zone."

It was an exaggeration, but it seemed to work. Cohen clapped his hands together.

"Let's get a junket together, brother. Check this out for ourselves. How long's that flight again?"

"Fourteen hours from New York. But there's a quicker way to experience Dubai for yourself."

David grinned as he pulled an envelope out from his inside jacket pocket. It was something Khaled had given him before they left Geneva. He handed the envelope to the young broker, who eagerly tore at the clasp, revealing a fancy invitation, written in gold-embossed calligraphy. A few of the other brokers looked over Cohen's shoulder as he read the invite to himself. Then Cohen looked up, waving the envelope in the air.

"A party in New York, thrown by an airline? You've got to be kidding."

David shook his head. He had asked Khaled the exact same question when Khaled first gave him the invite to pass on to the brokers. But Khaled had just laughed at the question. It wasn't just any airline—it was Emirates Air. Wholly owned and operated by the ruling family of Dubai. Which meant that the party in New York was a party being thrown by the emir of Dubai himself.

"Trust me," David said in response.

Cohen shrugged, glancing at the other brokers nearby, who seemed game. New York was a hell of a lot closer than the Middle East. As Cohen and the rest turned back to the models, who were now gathered, naked shoulder to naked shoulder, lined up for their final bow, David took a deep breath.

He hoped Khaled understood what was really at stake with the party thrown by Emirates Air. David hadn't just invited the brokers—he'd also already invited Vitzi and the other young traders. And he'd gone one step further: along with Vitzi, he'd invited Reston and a handful of the more energetic and freethinking board members.

David knew it was a bold move, but after the roadblock they'd encountered with Hatfield in London and the question that had been brought up in Geneva, he was convinced the time had come to be bold. They needed to leap forward. With that in mind, tomorrow morning he was heading back to New York.

Sooner or later he was going to have to face the board once again—and Gallo—head on.

Chapter 34

FEBRUARY 5, 2003

Suddenly there was darkness.

David held his breath as a hush came over the throng of revelers, and his hand tightened against Serena's. He shivered from the cold marble pillar against his back, and even though he was a good ten feet behind the crowd that stretched all the way from the raised stage at the far end of the great hall to the edge of the polished-marble dance floor, he could feel the expectant energy rising up from them. Part of him wanted to grab Khaled, who was standing just a few feet away on the other side of the marble pillar and demand to know what was going to happen next. But the other part of him understood that the party was already in full swing, their plan a train filled to capacity and moving at top speed down the tracks; at this point it was clearly out of his and Khaled's hands.

David had never been inside Cipriani's before, but he'd certainly heard of the place many times growing up. Located in the old Bowery building in Midtown, the restaurant and elegant party hall was a true aristocratic landmark and a customary setting for New York's high-class function scene. The interior of the

1920s building, decorated in the style of an Italian Renaissance masterpiece, was awe-inspiring; a living canvas with sixty-five-foot ceilings, massive crystal chandeliers, and towering marble pillars.

At the moment, the masterpiece was also wall-to-wall moderately inebriated men and women, pressed together in a great mass of evening suits, tiny black dresses, tuxedos, and gowns.

Right before the lights had gone out, David had spotted his own crowd of invitees, in prime positions right up near the stage. Reston and Mendelson were standing in a group with eight other board members. The particular members David had gotten Reston to bring along with him were a good representation of the more freethinking elements at the Merc, and they also happened to be symbolic of the board as a whole: four of them were Italian, four were Jewish, and none had ever been to Europe, let alone the Middle East. At least they had all dressed for the occasion: most were in Armani, and even Mendelson had acquiesced to Reston's begging and put on a pair of loosely laced moccasins.

Vitzi, Brunetti, and Rosa were a few yards from the board. At David's request, Vitzi had also brought a crowd of fifteen of the more popular traders along with them. David didn't recognize any of Gallo's team—they were harder to spot without their zebra jackets—but he assumed there might be one or two in the mix. The traders had been moving fast since they arrived at Cipriani's; now they were intermixed with a group of tall, striking Australian girls, most likely flight attendants invited by the airline.

Another few yards from the traders were the brokers. Cohen had brought twelve of his colleagues with him—there were probably two private jets waiting for them on the tarmac at La Guardia. Like the traders, the brokers were surrounded by women, but these weren't flight attendants—they were assuredly models who had been brought in by the high-priced party planners to spruce up the scene.

The rest of the crowd was incredibly upscale, mostly businessmen and their wives and mistresses; David also saw that there were more than a few Arabs in the crowd, and he assumed that Emirates Air had used frequent-passenger lists to fill out its invites. When David and Serena first arrived, Khaled had introduced them to a handful of the airline's executives, and David had been impressed by their polite confidence and by the fact that they already seemed to have been swept up by the idea of the energy exchange in Dubai. Then again, it would mean big business for the airline—in a way, this party was almost as important to them as it was to David and Khaled.

And so far the party had been a moderate success. The music had been good, the food spectacular, and the alcohol free-flowing. Then, quite abruptly, the lights had gone out—plunging the great hall into pure darkness. Now the entire crowd was facing the stage in anticipation. And David was squeezing his girl-friend's hand so hard she was using her nails to defend herself.

As he quietly apologized, loosening his grip, a spotlight suddenly erupted in the center of the stage. In the middle of the circle of yellow light stood a woman in Arabic robes. Her face was entirely covered by a veil, and she was standing behind a microphone.

She leaned forward and started singing. At least David thought she was singing; to his American ears, it seemed like she was just wailing away in Arabic.

David's stomach convulsed, and he looked at Serena. *Christ.* Serena looked back at him, helplessly. Then he turned and threw a glance toward Khaled, but his Arab friend was just staring straight ahead.

David turned back to the stage. He could feel the crowd starting to fidget, and the wailing was just getting louder and louder, heading toward an ear-shattering crescendo—

And then suddenly the woman reached up and yanked off her veil. She shook out her long, flowing blond hair and then tore off her robes. Underneath she was wearing a sparkling gold bikini. As the crowd roared, another spotlight exploded onto the stage—and there, standing at a second microphone, was the legendary crooner Tom Jones, surrounded by ten writhing girls in skimpy gold outfits.

As David's eyes widened and Serena clapped her hands, Tom Jones launched into a high-octane concert while the girls in gold outfits danced elaborately for the crowd. It was, in a word, amazing.

Grinning ear to ear, David crept away from Serena and sidled next to Khaled. He could see Reston and the board—and they were applauding at the stage like school kids. Vitzi and the traders had cameras out and were snapping pictures, and the brokers were howling like it was New Year's Eve.

"I think we're in good shape here," David whispered. "They seem to be enjoying themselves. At the very least, we've definitely stoked their curiosity about Dubai."

Khaled smiled back at him.

"Maybe they'll realize that at least part of the Middle East is in the midst of a prime-time makeover. It's a step forward. We're getting closer, David."

David nodded, looking back toward Serena, who was dancing to the beat of the concert. She smiled in his direction and offered a little wave toward Khaled. The minute she'd met the young Arab—at a lunch David arranged that had included Reston as well—she'd fallen in platonic love with him. And she'd been amazingly forgiving about David's absence over the past few months. That hadn't helped the guilt David still felt about Jasmine, but it had made it much easier for him to feel cautiously pleased with what they'd accomplished so far.

Though they'd initially struck out with Hatfield, they had the curiosity of the European energy community working for them. They had Reston and a few of the board members at least open to the idea of partnering with Dubai. And they probably had the brokers on board.

"Now it's time we solved what we've been putting off," Khaled whispered, and David realized immediately what he was talking about. One more piece in the puzzle—second only to the little task of getting the Merc board to finalize everything and accept Dubai officially as a partner—was the issue of sharia law. David wasn't sure how that issue would be solved—but he had a feeling it involved another plane trip.

"Now we go to Saudi Arabia?" he asked.

But Khaled shook his head. David looked at him, confused, as Tom Jones belted out a song about love, and the dancers undulated across the stage.

"I thought the Saudis make the decisions about sharia law."

"That's correct. But getting an audience with the religious leaders for a business deal like this isn't that simple. The sheiks—including my uncle—have to be very careful to stay behind the scenes with something as explosive as this; the Arab street is always watching. On this issue, we're on our own. But there's a man who can help us. A consultant of sorts."

David turned to watch as Jones danced with one of the scantily clad girls. What was Khaled talking about? *A consultant with an inside track to Saudi religious leaders?*

"Is this consultant here in New York?"

"Not exactly," Khaled answered. "He can be very difficult to find, actually. But I've made a few calls to some of my uncle's associates, and I did manage to locate him."

David didn't like the expression on Khaled's face.

"Where?" David asked.

Khaled only smiled in response.

Chapter 35

Two days before his twenty-sixth birthday, David made a life-altering discovery: there was no cocktail more dangerous than the combination of jetlag and frustration. With thoughts blurred by a sixteen-hour flight, jet lag amplified by a thirteen-hour time-zone difference, and a heavy dose of seemingly insurmountable aggravation, you were bound to do something stupid, if not downright suicidal. After all, you weren't thinking right to begin with, and then some fucking asshole pushed you that extra step, and suddenly there you were—hanging from the edge of a third-story balcony by your fingertips, trying to reach a fire escape five feet below with the points of your brand-new Ferragamo shoes.

David grunted with effort as his extended arms struggled against his weight. He could see the deserted alley that ran past the Beijing Grand Hyatt three stories beneath him, and he knew that if he missed the fire escape, his skull was going to make quite a mess on the unforgiving cement sidewalk. More than that, his apparent suicide—because what else could you call it when a young man, locked in a lavish, four-star hotel room from the outside, toppled to his death from a partially enclosed third-floor balcony—would cause one hell of an international incident. He doubted that Khaled—who was watching his efforts, wide-eyed, from a matching balcony one floor above—would have been able to explain the situation to their minders, or to the international press, or, for that matter, to David's mother, who would most likely cause an all-out war over the incident. But then, the death-defying stunt hadn't been Khaled's idea. David had only him-self—and his jet lag–tinged frustration—to blame.

They certainly didn't teach you this at Harvard Business School. David strained his body a few more inches toward the lip of the fire escape. The air was warm outside, and he could feel the sweat building beneath his Oxford shirt and tailored slacks. He knew that if anyone—say, a bellboy or someone from the kitchen staff—had wandered into the hotel's back alley at that moment and looked up, David would have had a lot of explaining to do to the official Chinese minders who were no doubt still gathered somewhere on the other side of his locked hotel door. He didn't know if they'd arrest him or simply haul him right back to the airport for depor-tation—but either way, he and Khaled would return to the U.S. empty-handed. That was something David simply could not allow.

He certainly hadn't expected his last-minute trip to Beijing to go like this. When Khaled had finally told him the truth—that the "consultant" who could help them arrange a meeting with the Saudi religious leaders was in China's capital city on some unrelated business—David had actually been thrilled by the idea of the trip. He'd always wanted to see China, and even though he and Khaled would be there for only one night, he'd hoped to get a chance to be a pure tourist, at least for a few hours. But from the minute they'd landed at Beijing International Airport, David had realized that things were not going to go as planned.

AT FIRST GLANCE, the old woman had seemed innocuous enough.

David had spotted her first, as he'd stepped out of the jetway. She'd been easy to locate, because of the sign she held high above her head, as if she were the leader of some bizarre, septuage-narian cheerleading squad: DAVID RUSSO. KHALED ABDUL-AZIZ. CHINA WELCOMES YOU.

"It's not a silver BMW, but it's not bad," David had whis-pered to Khaled as they approached her. The woman had been all smiles and compliments as they exchanged bows. David had been expecting a translator and a driver, which Khaled's people had arranged; a den mother seemed twice as good. As the ami-able Ms. Chen had led them through the airport, she explained, in fairly good English, that she would act as both their translator and their tour guide.

"Many wonderful things to see in our city," she had clucked. "You will have wonderful time in Beijing."

Of course, David and Khaled hadn't budgeted much time for sightseeing, but it was a nice thought anyway. As they had fin-ished passing through customs and were about to step out into the main terminal of the airport, Khaled explained their time crunch to Ms. Chen.

"Actually, we need to head straight to our meeting. Maybe we'll have time for a more leisurely tour on our next visit."

And that's when things had turned; the smiling and amiable Ms. Chen was suddenly all frowns.

"I'm sorry, this is not possible. Unfortunately, due to a state holiday celebration, we must head directly to your hotel. Your business will have to wait until tomorrow."

And before David or Khaled could respond, the old woman had gestured with her hands—and four uniformed police officers had suddenly appeared, two on each side. Stone-faced but not menacing, the men had wordlessly escorted them—David and Khaled too shocked to even respond—to a waiting limousine. It wasn't until they were enclosed in the backseat of the car that David had finally found his voice.

"What holiday? What are you talking about? Ms. Chen, our papers are in order, and we've got an important meeting—"

"No meeting. Not possible. I am sorry."

It had taken another twenty minutes of intense questioning before David finally squeezed out of her the real reason for the police escort—and the "holiday" that prevented them from moving freely. In truth, there was no state celebration. The government regulatory agency for which Ms. Chen worked had been asked to keep tight control over David and Khaled—and the request hadn't come from Beijing but from David's own bosses at the Merc. Someone, it seemed, had made a phone call to a high-up official in the Chinese government to "warn" the Chinese about two "known" agitators who were on their way to the Chinese capital.

"This is ludicrous," David had countered, his face turning red. But Khaled had quieted him with a look—and he had understood. They could only get themselves in more trouble by arguing with this woman. She wasn't the one making the decisions. Obviously, someone had taken great pains to screw with their plans.

Once secured and alone in his hotel room at the Grand Hyatt—the four armed police officers and Ms. Chen outside in the hall—David had immediately called Reston, and although the Texan didn't know for sure, he had agreed with David that Gallo was probably to blame. David had no idea how Gallo had known about the Beijing trip—but then again, the man had hired someone to take photos of David and Serena in front of a Gucci store on Fifth Avenue. Adding that to their confrontation in the boardroom, David could not afford to underestimate the Don's abilities—or his enthusiasm.

Reston had been certain that he could work out the situation—but it would take at least until the next day. The problem was that Khaled's "consultant" would have left Beijing by then, and God only knew when or where they'd be able to track him down next. According to Khaled, the man was beyond enigmatic; he was a third-world legend, a Nigerian Arab known in circles throughout the developing world only as "the Fat Man." For some reason nobody quite understood, the Fat Man—really a mercenary who offered his services to the highest bidders—was the quickest connection to the Saudi religious leaders when it came to matters of business; over the past ten years, he had somehow built up extreme goodwill through numerous successful projects in Saudi Arabia and around the region. Although it all sounded very James Bond, Khaled had explained that the evening's meeting with the Fat Man in the lobby of the Commander Beijing was their best and most efficient means of getting to the Saudis in a favorable way.

Irony of ironies, instead of the lobby of the Commander, David had been separated from Khaled and locked in a third-floor hotel suite in the Grand Hyatt—which, it turned out, was a mere four blocks away. But it might as well have been a continent between the two hotels: there was no way past the minders outside in the hallway, and there was no way to reschedule the meeting either. The Fat Man was going to slip out of their grasp.

Unbelievably frustrated, but resigned to failure, David had stepped out onto the balcony to at least try to get a glimpse of the city he wasn't going to get to see. Then he had heard Khaled's voice from upstairs and realized that their two hotel rooms, though on different floors, were close enough for them to communicate. At some point while they were discussing their plight, David had shifted his attention to the street below and noticed the fire escape winding downward.

Of course, Khaled had tried to talk him out of it—but David had only grinned up at him.

Now, MINUTES LATER, David was regretting his bravado. The drop onto the fire escape was a good five feet, and if his shoes slipped when he hit the metal grating—well, he didn't want to think about it. For the first time in his life, he wished he had chosen gymnastics over football, baseball, and crew. But he wasn't a gymnast, he was an American in a suit and tie trying to make a business meeting.

Welcome to the wonderful world of oil.

Without another thought, he swung himself full force toward the fire escape and let go of the balcony. There was a sickening moment of weightlessness—and then his shoes touched metal and he came crashing down on the extended platform. The entire fire escape shook beneath him, but somehow he managed to regain his balance before he toppled forward toward the street.

He gave Khaled a quick thumbs-up and then clambered down the escape, taking the metal rungs as quietly as possible. There was another five-foot drop from the last metal rung to the sidewalk, which he took in a controlled fall. He landed with one foot in a three-inch-deep puddle, sending up a fountain of grimy water—and then he was moving forward down the alley at full speed, away from the hotel.

The alley opened into a wide, three-lane street with low, boxy gray buildings on either side. David spun on his heels to get his bearings; he had memorized a map of the area during the flight from New York, as they had known they'd be on a tight schedule to get to the meeting with the Fat Man a mere hour after they arrived. Of course, David hadn't factored in climbing out of his hotel window—but he'd always been a pretty good improviser.

David glanced at his watch as he jogged to the next corner; it was after 10:00 P.M., which partially explained how deserted the street seemed to be. David assumed that the demonstration—and the resulting crackdown—that the minders had mentioned also had something to do with the emptiness of the sidewalks and the fact that there were only a few cars whizzing by, but he tried not to dwell on the thought. Getting caught in a Chinese "crackdown" might not be the best thing for his résumé.

He took the next corner and saw that he was now in the heart of the city's financial district. Glass and steel buildings rose up on either side, but there was no doubt that he was in a foreign city: all of the signs and billboards were in Chinese, and even the McDonald's across the street was covered in Chinese lettering. He quickly moved to the next corner—and there, at the end of the next block, was the Commander Beijing. From the outside, it looked more like a glorified Holiday Inn, but it was modern, with a rounded driveway encircling a huge, well-lit fountain.

David wiped the sweat from his forehead and straightened his suit jacket as he calmly strolled down the driveway; the uniformed Chinese bellhops outside bowed at him respectfully, and he smiled back. Then he passed through the hotel's glass revolving doors and into a well-air-conditioned lobby.

The lobby was nice, if a little kitschy. The walls were done up in wood tones, and the carpets were lush and green. There were high California palm trees spaced all around the room, and yet another fountain along the far wall, spitting backlit water up toward the spherical ceiling.

There were a few Americans and Europeans sitting in wicker chairs and cushioned love seats strewn about the lobby, as well as a handful of Chinese businessmen—but even so, David had no problem quickly identifying his quarry.

James Bond or not, the Fat Man lived up to his nom de plume. At least three hundred pounds, he was stretched out across a wicker couch, nursing a glass of red wine. His skin was coal black, and his rolls of fat were covered by brightly colored African robes. He seemed to be smiling as David approached, and he raised the glass of wine in his thick, grublike fingers.

"You're early, my young friend," the man said in a heavy Arabic accident.

"I took a shortcut," David said, trying to control his breathing. The Fat Man looked to be about forty, but it was almost impossible to read his expression; his eyes and mouth were fighting a losing battle with the gravity-worn topography of his obese face.

"Where is your Arab colleague? I thought there were going to be two of you."

David shrugged as he pulled a nearby wicker chair over to the couch.

"He got detained. But I'm ready and authorized to give you whatever you need."

The Fat Man looked him over. Then he slouched forward, the rolls of fat beneath his drooping, hangdog face rippling like oil from a desert well.

"I don't like surprises. I was expecting two, now there's one. Why should I believe that you have the authority that you say?"

David eyed the man for a moment, then reached into his pocket and removed a sealed envelope. Although Khaled hadn't expected the two of them to be separated in China, he'd given David the envelope before they'd boarded the flight to Beijing. When David had asked what was inside, Khaled simply shrugged: "On this trip, we are both representatives of the emir; I assure you, the seal on that envelope opens more doors in this part of the world than your American passport and your Mercantile Exchange ID."

Obviously, from the look on the Fat Man's face as he ran his thick fingers over the wax royal seal on the back of the envelope—imprinted with the names of two sheiks—Khaled had been correct. He handed the envelope back to David, unopened, and showed his wide palms.

"So tell me about this exchange of yours," he said, grinning once again. Yes, he was a mercenary—and the seal on that envelope guaranteed that David and Khaled could match any price he desired. Now it was just a matter of convincing him that he could get them what they needed in return. Without further niceties, David launched into his practiced—tried-and-true—pitch about the Dubai energy exchange.

From that moment on, David was no longer in some ratty hotel in Beijing; he was five years in the future, on the morning of the first ringing of that trading floor bell—the bell that was going to change the future of the Middle East, and with it the future of the world.

David wasn't going to stop talking until the Fat Man saw that same morning, heard that same bell, and imagined that same beautiful future. And after that, David didn't care if he got caught in some government crackdown in the streets outside or got collared trying to sneak back into his hotel—because at that moment nothing else mattered to him. The Fat Man was the key to understanding sharia law, and sharia law was the next step in their journey.

David hadn't come this far to let a little international incident get in his way.

Chapter 36

If the villains in a James Bond movie had been anywhere near as expedient as the Fat Man, good old Bond would never have lived past the opening credits. A bare twenty-four hours after David had managed to sneak, unnoticed, past his Chinese government minders—who, along with Ms. Chen, were watching a soccer match on a portable TV instead of watching the locked hotel-suite door of an American "agitator"—and into his room at the Grand Hyatt, Khaled had gotten the phone call from the Saudi embassy in New York. Not only had David and Khaled been granted a meeting with the two highest-ranked Saudi religious officials in New York—but the meeting was going to take place in just a few short hours. That meant there would be no chance for Gallo to pull any more of his shit—on the off possibility that he'd somehow figured out what David was up to in Beijing—or for anything else to get in their way. At the very least, they would be getting a fair hearing on the issue of sharia law.

David had half-hoped the meeting would take place at the Royal Embassy of Saudi Arabia in Washington, D.C., itself—he could only imagine what level of majesty he'd find inside the three-story stone building steps from the White House—but instead he'd had to settle for a visit to the Saudi consulate building on Second Avenue in New York. The consulate, it turned out, looked pretty much like every other building east of Fifth in Midtown—except for the security post out front, complete with X-ray detectors staffed by armed members of the New York National Guard.

David and Khaled had quickly been ushered past the security by a young Arabic man in a dark blue suit, then led through a quiet marble lobby to a mirrored elevator. Four stories higher, they'd been met by another young man in a similar suit, who'd taken them to another lobby, this one carpeted, with pictures of Saudi Arabian cities on the walls and two framed portraits of King Fahd. A third young man had collected them in the second lobby and led them through a pair of double wooden doors into a well-appointed office—fifteen-foot ceilings, expensive-looking Oriental carpeting, and lavish tapestries on three of four walls. There was a desk on one end of the rectangular office, facing a sitting area, complete with elegant Italian couches, a low wooden coffee table, and a pair of high leather-backed chairs. Both chairs were occupied by elderly Arab men in robes—presumably the Saudi religious leaders—who rose the minute David and Khaled entered the room.

David didn't know whether to bow, shake hands, or simply drop to his knees. Khaled had explained to him that these two men were extremely high up in the hierarchy of Saudi religious academia; both were leading scholars at the premier religious university in the Saudi capital, with the ear of the ruling family. Though this meeting itself was unofficial and would never be spoken of in the press or in any other public forum, it was David and Khaled's one shot at getting the necessary, implicit approval from the Saudi religious establishment to go forward with the Dubai exchange. Without these men, and their good graces, David and Khaled's attempt at an exchange would basically unravel in the face of the eight-hundred-pound gorilla that was the Saudi empire; even the threat of a religious edict against the exchange would render it null and void. In short, these two scholarly men held all the cards, so David followed Khaled's lead: a little bow followed by a handshake for each of the men, then a third little bow of respect toward another portrait of King Fahd that hung on the wall behind the Italian couch. Then one of the robed Saudis made a gesture at the young man who'd brought them in, and he quickly scurried around the desk to collect a silver tea set that had already been prepared for the meeting. The young man offered the tray to David and Khaled, who each took a steaming cup.

Once he was seated next to Khaled on the couch, David did his best not to blush, fidget, or turn away as the two elderly Saudis both looked him over. When they finally turned their attention to Khaled, David exhaled, relieved that at the very least they hadn't thrown him out of the room. Though he couldn't be sure exactly how old the two men were, from the depth of their wrinkles and the mass of concentric circles around their eyes, they had to be well into their eighties. Certainly, they were important men; it was obvious from their robes, which seemed to have been spun out of the finest silk, and from their wizened features, which seemed to emanate nobility in a way David had never seen before. Something about the taller of the two men reminded him a little of Giovanni; one day, when he was old enough, Giovanni would sit with that same, high-shouldered bearing—the look of a man who had earned his respect, not a man who had been born into it. David had no idea what sort of lives these two religious leaders had lived, or how they had gotten to this place, but he knew, instinctively, that they deserved his respect.

For the next three hours, David gave them that respect—and little else, considering that the entire meeting took place in Arabic, Khaled only paused to translate the few times that the two religious leaders nodded in David's direction, and by his fourth cup of tea David was spending much of his energy trying to keep his fingers from trembling too noticeably from the caffeine.

From the few snippets of the conversation that Khaled gave him, he understood that the main issue the two elderly men were discussing had to do with derivatives. It seemed that the main problem with the idea of a Dubai exchange was the implication of certain tenets of Islamic law that derivatives were essentially *haraam*—prohibited. Under a strict interpretation of the Koran, the concept of interest was not allowed. And the trading of all derivatives—be they gold futures, stock options, or oil contracts—had an unavoidable component of interest.

As the two religious men dug into this issue, the questions they asked Khaled seemed to grow more heated; at one point one of the men even rose halfway out of his seat, jabbing a wrinkled finger in Khaled's direction as he made a point in thick, furious Arabic. But Khaled remained perfectly calm, bowing as he seemed to agree with the scholar—then quietly explaining why, even so, the exchange should be permitted. David caught a few terms in his response that helped him understand the gist of Khaled's argument—even before Khaled whispered a translation to him.

Basically, Khaled argued, Dubai's emirate had indeed instituted free zones where such interest was allowed, in practice. The two religious men countered, again somewhat heatedly, that the Dubai exchange would incorporate trading policies that would extend well beyond the free zones: as people flocked to trade oil from all over, derivatives would essentially be traded out of Dubai from one end of the world to the other. But Khaled, undeterred, explained that this process was more like the arbitrage that went on in the souks of the Arab street than the interest-bearing strategies forbidden by sharia law.

While David listened to the two robed men arguing with Khaled and then with one another, he was amazed at how technical their discussion seemed to be; this wasn't some question of kosher foods or holiday ritual—this was an argument about a complicated financial instrument. And yet, the two old men didn't seem to have any problem discussing the subject. Likewise, Khaled never backed down from their questioning, no matter how inquisitive and strident they became. He remained calm, collected, respectful—but forceful as well. He wasn't going to give up, and David could see that Khaled's persistence impressed the two scholars almost as much as his arguments. And it was also obvious that the two men had already done much research into the questions they asked, because most of Khaled's answers did not seem to come as surprises to them. Obviously, the Fat Man had done his job—for which he'd been highly compensated by Khaled's people—by communicating the issue in great detail to the two old men, and now they were deliberating on the subject as if it were no different, or more secular, than a question about feeding pork to a starving man.

By the end of three hours, David was literally on the edge of his seat. It wasn't simply the caffeine that had his feet bouncing beneath the coffee table—it was the idea that these two men were about to make the decision that would change the Dubai exchange from an idea into a reality—or would stop David and Khaled dead in their tracks. Although Khaled was still calm and collected, David could see he was beginning to tire. The sheer intensity of the questioning from the two religious men was beginning to take its toll—when suddenly, without warning, the two men stopped speaking entirely and rose, as one, from their seats. Before Khaled or David could move from the couch, the two Arabs moved away from the seating area and headed straight toward the door. David started to rise after them, but Khaled grabbed his arm and pulled him back down.

"They leave first," he said simply. "We wait, out of respect."

David nodded, swallowing back his nerves. When the two men were out of the room, he turned to Khaled.

"What happened? Did they say yes or no?"

"Neither." Khaled's expression was unreadable. There was sweat on his brow, which he wiped at with the sleeve of his jacket.

"Neither? What the hell does that mean? Don't tell me we need to find another Fat Man. I'm not climbing out of any more hotel windows."

Khaled straightened his lapels, quietly finished his tea, then finally rose from the couch. Then he smiled, and David could see the excited relief in his eyes.

"No more hotel windows, David. Tomorrow I am heading back to Dubai. If your board agrees, in two weeks we will break ground on the Dubai exchange."

David gasped at him. Suddenly he understood. It was exactly like it had been with the board at the Merc: the Saudis weren't going to say yes, and they weren't going to say no—and it was only the second part of the equation that mattered.

They hadn't said no. Which meant that the Dubai exchange wasn't *haraam*. It wasn't forbidden.

David grinned, and before Khaled could escape, he gave the Arab kid his second Russo hug.

"This is it, isn't it? We're almost there."

"If you don't get off me, they're going to arrest both of us for improper behavior."

As Khaled separated himself from David's grip, David realized that his cell phone was going off in his pocket. He retrieved the phone as they headed out of the office and back into the consulate lobby.

He didn't recognize the number, but he was in such a good mood that he answered anyway. To his surprise, he definitely recognized the voice.

"David, guess what? I'm in New York."

The French accent tugged at an area much lower than his heart, and he nearly dropped the phone.

"Jasmine?"

Khaled looked at him, and David could see the warning in his friend's eyes. He had told Khaled about the night in Geneva, and Khaled hadn't judged him on his momentary lapse of control—but Khaled hadn't wanted to hear the details either. That sort of lack of control wasn't something a lifelong Muslim truly understood.

"Yes, it's me," Jasmine said. "I'm at the Mandarin New York. One night only. And I'd love to see you."

David swallowed, heat rising in his cheeks. Then a sudden thought hit him. He hadn't given Jasmine his cell phone number. He was hotheaded, but he wasn't that stupid.

Had she looked him up on some hotel guest list? He didn't remember ever putting his cell phone number down on any registration form, but then again, Khaled had made all the arrangements; maybe Khaled had listed David's cell as a contact number when he'd booked the rooms?

David realized he was being foolish. Even if Jasmine hadn't found his number on a hotel form, plenty of people had his cell phone number—one call to the Merc, and she could have gotten it from Harriet. Or she could have called his home in Staten Island—which was listed—and simply asked his mom. There were a dozen ways she could have tracked him down. The question wasn't really how—it was why. And why now? Considering how well things were going, this was a distraction—and a complication—he certainly didn't need.

An image of her flat naked stomach, arched against the snow, flickered behind his eyes. Then he quickly shook his head.

"This is kind of a bad time," he said into the phone as he followed Khaled toward the elevator that led out of the consulate. "And I'm about to step into an elevator—"

"David, just come by the hotel and see me. One drink. And I promise, there's plenty of Toblerone in the minibar."

Khaled was already in the elevator. David knew he needed to hang up the phone. He needed to forget about her high cheekbones and incredible curves—

"I won't twist your arm," she said finally. "It's okay. I just thought it might be fun to see you. But if you're too busy, I understand."

And just like that, David felt himself saying the words: "I'll be there in ten minutes. But I can't stay long."

Then he was in the elevator, the connection was lost, and Khaled was looking at him like he was the biggest fucking infidel in the Western world.

Sadly, for once, David couldn't disagree.

Chapter 37

In a perfect world, David would have come to his senses the minute the icy, early-evening breeze hit his face when he and Khaled stepped out of the Saudi consulate and onto Second Avenue. But in reality, David didn't reach for his cell phone until his cab was past Fifty-seventh Street, just a few short blocks away from the Mandarin, and he didn't dial the number that had shown up when Jasmine first called for a good five minutes after that. In fact, the cab was pulling to a stop in front of the luxury hotel—uniformed doormen swarming like the flying monkeys from *The Wizard of Oz*—when David finally waved at the driver to keep on going, destination unknown, as he held the cell phone to his ear.

Jasmine answered on the third ring. She sounded a little out of breath, bringing up more memories of Geneva, but David was determined to do the right thing. He wasn't sure what had made him change his mind—but now all he could think about was Serena and the future he hoped to one day have with her. A dalliance in Switzerland was one thing, but a full-out affair simply wasn't in his personality.

"I'm sorry," he said into the phone. "Something came up."

Jasmine seemed to understand.

"Okay, David. Maybe next time."

The taxi driver was looking at him, and David just gave him another wave. *Keep on going, man, anywhere but here.*

"The thing is, Jasmine—"

"Not necessary. You don't build expectations out of a roll in the snow. But it's a small world we live in, David. Maybe we'll run into each other again."

With that, she hung up, and David lowered the phone, exhaling. He looked out through the cab window. It was dark now, a little after seven-thirty, and the lights from the traffic and the storefronts on either side blended into strips of flashing color. More than anything, he felt—relieved.

"You want to go somewhere in particular?"

The driver was looking at him through the Plexiglas divider. David was about to give him his address when the phone in his hand started vibrating. He glanced down and saw the text message as it appeared across the display.

Need to see you, asap. Trading floor. Twenty minutes. Nick.

The phone number was unlisted, which was a little strange considering that David had Reston's BlackBerry number imprinted in his cerebral cortex by now. But things were now moving quickly with the Dubai exchange, and since David and Reston hadn't spoken since Beijing, it wasn't surprising that some sort of brushfire had obviously popped up. Maybe Gallo was making some noise—or maybe it had nothing to do with Dubai at all. Reston's text had asked David to meet him on the trading floor. Maybe it had something to do with automation, Reston's other pet project. In many ways, automating the trading floor was an even bigger firestorm waiting to happen than Dubai. Gallo and his kind would survive the Middle East, but Microsoft was another monster altogether.

While he gave the taxi driver the Merc's address, David grinned at the thought of Gallo going up against Bill Gates. He then shot a text back to Reston's BlackBerry, and a second text to Serena, explaining that he was going to be late, again. Reston didn't respond, but Serena came back almost immediately with a sad face, followed by two happy faces, one with a tongue sticking out. David grinned at the icons.

He'd try to put out whatever fire Reston was fighting as fast as possible so he could get home to his girl and add a few more happy faces to the mix.

IT WAS EIGHT-FIFTEEN by the time David passed through the security post in the lobby of the Merc, flashing his ID badge to the skeletal after-hours staff—consisting of four uniformed, armed guards and an elderly supervisor with a clipboard—and letting the twin X-ray machines bombard his cellular structure to their hearts' content. Once he was in the elevator, rising up through the building, he took another look at his BlackBerry, but there was still no response from Reston. Obviously, the Texan was using a different phone tonight. Maybe Reston had lost his BlackBerry again; David remembered a hellish afternoon during his second month at the Merc when he'd had to track down a phone Reston left on an airplane. A Harvard degree meant even less in the infuriating catacombs of JFK than it did in the halls of the Merc.

David shrugged, putting his phone back into his pocket. He'd find out what Reston wanted soon enough. He tried not to let his creative mind invent potential disasters as he waited for the elevator to reach the trading floor. Sadly, it was a losing battle: by the time the doors finally slid open, David was half-expecting to find the floor crawling with poisonous snakes.

Instead, the dimly lit, cavernous room seemed completely deserted; as David stepped away from the elevator, the only sound came from his own shoes against the freshly polished floor. Obviously, the cleaning crews had already come and gone. The snowfall of paper tickets that usually filled the various trading pits had been swept away, and the computer screens and telephone banks were all dormant, the monitors wiped clean and the last traces of eight hundred sweaty Italians and Jews vacuumed out of the ether. In fact, the only light in the room came from a few hundred seemingly coordinated screen savers and the digital readouts on the big board up above. Closing prices blinked out into the relative darkness, bathing the larger pits that were closer to the board in an eerie, reddish glow.

David took a few more steps into the room, then squinted across the trading floor.

"Nick?"

His voice echoed between the warren of computer banks and through the deserted pits. David had never been on the trading floor after-hours before, and even though it was only 8:00 P.M., it may as well have been the middle of the night. Strange that he'd somehow beaten Reston to the floor; maybe the Texan was still up in his office, or on his way down. David was about to head back to the elevator when he heard a sound coming from somewhere on the other side of the cavernous room. A cough maybe, or someone clearing his throat. David rolled his eyes and started forward again. Reston had chosen a strange time to play games with him. Maybe the Texan had just gotten back from Little Tijuana's and was planning some tequila-fueled practical joke.

"Come on, Nick," David called across the dark room. "I rushed all the way over here. What the hell is so important?"

He reached the first bank of computers and phones and cut left, paralleling the largest trading pit, trying to follow the cough back to its source. He was surprised at how narrow the alleys between the trading posts were; he'd never really wandered through the warrens of the different trading positions before. He was now strolling through a real maze of high-tech equipment and shoulder-high partitions stretching all the way around the hundred-foot crude pit. As he went, he had to be careful not to trip over the rubber cables and spaghetti-like extension cords that criss-crossed the tiles beneath his feet. No wonder Reston and Giovanni were always talking about automation, this place was a freaking mess—

David's thoughts were interrupted as a flash of motion flickered by his peripheral vision. He stopped, squinting over the partition to his immediate right. There, maybe twenty yards away, on the other side of the circular, sunken trading floor, someone was dodging in and out of the natural gas cubicles. David couldn't be sure, but it looked like the man was wearing a trading jacket; still, he was too far away for David to see any of the jacket's details.

"Nick, what the fuck?" David shouted across the floor at him. "This isn't funny."

Again no answer. David paused, wondering what the hell he should do. He wasn't going to chase his drunk boss all over the trading floor. Then he felt a buzz in his pocket and realized his BlackBerry was going off again. He angrily retrieved it and glared down at the display.

To his surprise, the text wasn't from Reston. It was from Khaled.

Get out. Now.

David's eyes widened. *What the fuck?* Before he could respond, he suddenly saw another flash of motion, this time from straight ahead, at the end of the long alleyway of computers and telephones. Someone was moving toward him. It was too dark to make out any of the man's features—but from his size and catlike gait, he could see it definitely wasn't Nick Reston. And this time David had a clear view of the man's trading jacket: black and white stripes, like a zebra.

David swallowed, blinking hard. He watched as the man moved toward him. What the hell were a couple of Gallo's traders doing on the trading floor after 8:00 P.M.? And why hadn't they responded when he'd shouted Reston's name?

David realized that his BlackBerry was still vibrating, a metallic earthquake against his palm. He glanced down at the display. Khaled again:

David. Get out. Now!

Christ.

David stumbled backward a few steps, breathing hard. The man in the zebra jacket was moving faster now, striding straight toward him. David didn't know what the hell was going on—but he didn't like it. He had no idea how Khaled knew where he was. And he didn't know what the hell Gallo's traders were doing on the trading floor after-hours. But he sure as hell wasn't going to stick around to find out.

David took one more step backward, then swung around on his heels—

And there, just a few feet in front of him, blocking the aisle, was a third man in a zebra-striped jacket. The man was big, maybe six-three, with spiky brown hair and acne scars on both cheeks. David didn't recognize the man's face—but he was pretty sure he wasn't a trader. At least, David had never seen him before, and the jacket's sleeves barely went past his elbows.

David froze, his heart racing in his chest. If the man wasn't a trader, what was he doing on the trading floor? And what did he want with David?

David decided he didn't want to find out. He could hear footsteps from behind him, getting closer. He had only a second to react. So he did the only thing he could think of.

He lowered his shoulder and barreled forward. The big man stepped back, obviously surprised by the sudden charge—and the heel of the man's right foot caught on one of the extension cords. He stumbled and David crashed by him, shoes churning against the hard floor. David felt a hand grab at his arm, but he was moving too fast. A second later, he was sprinting through the maze of computers. He didn't know if the zebra jackets were behind him—but he didn't care. He could see the elevator now, and the doors were already halfway ajar. His adrenaline spiked, and he lunged at the opening—

And nearly slammed headlong into a huge man on his way out. David caught himself, skidding to a stop in time to see two more men step out of the elevator behind the first. David stared up at the huge man in front—and saw that he was wearing a janitor's uniform. His massive muscles bulged beneath the light blue material.

"Excuse me, sir. We're here to clean the carpets."

The man's accent sounded Arabic or Pakistani, David couldn't be sure. At the moment, he didn't care. He rushed around the three janitors and into the elevator. He jabbed his finger at the buttons—he wasn't even sure what floor, he was just punching whichever buttons were closest. It wasn't until the doors had slid shut and he had collapsed back against the elevator's wall that a sudden, strange thought hit him like a fist to the face.

There weren't any carpets on the trading floor.

Chapter 38

Twenty minutes later, when David stepped through the entrance of the Starbucks two blocks from his apartment in Midtown and took a deep breath that filled his nostrils with the overwhelming scent of Colombia-by-way-of-Seattle coffee, his panic finally started to subside. As he moved deeper into the Starbucks, eliciting a familiar nod from the Goth chick behind the counter, he let the dim lighting and soft, canned mood music calm his frayed nerves. He navigated past the few customers who were indulging their caffeine-junkie needs and took his customary table in the back corner of the café.

Once seated, he forced his body to relax—his fingers laced together on the table in front of him—and tried to order his thoughts. Maybe his mind truly had been playing tricks on him. Maybe he had misinterpreted the entire incident. Maybe he had been mistaken: perhaps the man in the zebra jacket had actually been one of Gallo's traders, just one David had never met before. Sure, the guy's jacket didn't fit, and he had tried to grab David's arm—but only after David had nearly decked the fucker with his shoulder.

And even though Reston had finally responded when David

was in the cab on the way to the Starbucks, saying that he'd never sent the original text, at worst, that only meant that someone had been playing a practical joke on David. Vitzi, Mendelson, hell, Gallo—David wouldn't have put it past any of them. That didn't mean he had truly been in danger on the trading floor. The idea that the three men had been there to harm him in some way, perhaps to derail the Dubai project once and for all—David shook his head. That was ludicrous. Making a call to Beijing to fuck up his travel plans was one thing; hiring men to hurt him was quite another. Even the Don wouldn't go that far—would he?

Then again, none of these thoughts explained Khaled's text message—which was why David was in the Starbucks in Midtown rather that on his way back to the safety of his apartment, where he could get Serena's more grounded opinion on the terrifying incident. David had tried calling Khaled from the cab, right after he'd spoken to Reston, but Khaled had refused to talk over the phone and insisted that David head directly to the Starbucks. It had seemed a bizarre request considering that Khaled was supposedly already on his way back to Dubai. But David had finally acquiesced, given no other choice.

David was about to try Khaled's phone again when he felt a cold breeze wash across the Starbucks. A kid had just entered and was moving quickly across the café. Right toward David's table.

The kid was tall and gangly, maybe sixteen at the most, and obviously Arab. He was wearing jeans and a pullover, with the hood low over his forehead. Still, he didn't look menacing. He looked like—a kid.

He reached David's table and pulled a piece of folded paper out of his pocket. He dropped the paper on the table, then turned to walk away. David held up a hand.

"Wait a minute. What is this?"

The kid glanced back over his shoulder.

"Encryption," he said quietly, in a heavy accent that David couldn't quite place. "You dial those numbers before you make a call that you don't want anyone else to hear."

"Hold on," David started, looking at the piece of paper. "What the hell do I need an encryption code for—"

But the kid was already moving back through the Starbucks, toward the door. David considered going after him—but then decided it wasn't worth the effort. The sixteen-year-old kid wasn't going to tell him anything. That kid wasn't the one with the answers.

David quickly pulled his phone out of his pocket and carefully dialed the six-digit number that was written on the folded piece of paper. Then he dialed the rest, from memory, and waited for Khaled's voice.

"David, sorry about this cloak-and-dagger business. But since we're so close, I decided we can't be too careful—"

"Khaled, what the hell is going on? How did you know I was on the trading floor?"

There was a brief pause on the other end of the line.

"Trading floor? What are you talking about?"

David stared at the phone.

"Don't fuck with me, Khaled. You just sent me two text messages. 'Get out now'? Does that ring a bell?"

Khaled laughed. "Yes, I know, I'm not daft. Last time I saw you, you were on your way to do something ridiculously stupid. At the time, I had decided it wasn't my place to interfere. Three hours into my flight and I thought better of it. Look, this may be a cultural thing, but Serena is a wonderful girl. To ruin what you have, for a one-night stand—"

David closed his eyes, leaning back in his seat. *Of course.* Khaled was talking about Jasmine. When David left Khaled at the Saudi consulate, he had been on his way to the Mandarin Oriental. Khaled had indeed texted him—"Get out. Now"—but he hadn't been talking about the men in the zebra jackets. He hadn't been trying to save David's life—he had been trying to save David's relationship.

David shook his head. He felt like a total idiot. Maybe it really had all been in his head. He'd misinterpreted Khaled's texts. They had added an imagined sense of peril to an already tense situation. Throw in a fake text from a fake Reston and add a trio of janitors who obviously hadn't been long on the job, and you had one hell of a major mind-fuck.

"Are you okay?" Khaled asked. For the first time, David heard the throb of a jet engine in the background. It certainly didn't sound commercial.

"Yeah, I'm fine. I think I just spooked myself pretty bad, though. Hey, are you on a private jet?"

"Yes. Now that we've got the Saudis' okay, and the Europeans, brokers, and traders on board, my ministry has jumped us up to a real priority. David, it's time to get your board to give us final approval."

David rubbed his hand through his hair. His pulse was finally slowing to the point where he could really think. That evening's excitement—real or imagined—aside, was he really ready to try to get the board to finalize the exchange? If he went up in front of them again demanding a yes or no, it could go either way. And a no would be the end of the road.

"I don't know. Maybe a little more time—"

"David, we don't have any more time. The emir wants to move forward. He wants a decision in the next two weeks."

David watched the Goth girl at the counter working the latte machine. He shook his head. He needed to be sure of the board's feelings before he made them take that final vote. He needed them to feel the same way he did—that the Dubai exchange had to happen, that it was important, that it was an incredible opportunity.

Simply, he needed to make them feel the same way he had felt when he had seen the promise of Dubai for the first time. He needed them to experience that same sense of excitement.

And just like that, it dawned on him.

He knew exactly what he and Khaled needed to do.

Chapter 39

Wow, you're really not much for that lived-in look, are you?"

David turned away from the window just in time to watch Harriet come through the open doorway of his office. She had a computer printout in one hand, a cup of coffee in the other, and she was smiling like it was the first time she'd seen him in a month—even though for the past six days they'd been as close as twins, working ten-hour days to get everything just right. Still, it *was* the first time they'd been together in David's office: they'd been using the nearby conference room for the job, because they needed the space and also because David's office wasn't equipped with a teleconferencing system. It had almost been like Khaled was right there along with them, culling through the lists of board members, editing the invitations, putting together the itineraries, making sure every detail was perfect.

"You've never heard of minimalism?" David shot back.

Harriet just rolled her eyes. She was right: his office looked pretty much exactly as it had the day Giovanni and Reston gave it to him: oversized desk, hardwood floors, an empty bookshelf, and little else. Not even a dying plant or a photograph of him and

Serena on a ski slope—nothing but walls, wood floorboards, and windows. Still, Harriet should have cut him some slack. Aside from the past week, David had spent more of his four months as vice president of strategy traveling around the world with Khaled than he had in this office.

While they'd worked in the conference room, David had done his best to describe his travels to Harriet, but she'd just listened politely, obviously more interested in the few details he gave her about the momentary travails of his love life than in the stories of far-off places. Even when he'd tried to describe Dubai, she'd basically turned off—because the truth was, as David had realized a week ago in Starbucks, there was no substitute for the experience of actually going there.

And that, David had also realized, was exactly what he and Khaled needed to make happen. They needed for the board—or a large majority of the board—to see Dubai for themselves. If David could get those Italians and Jews onto an airplane, he felt certain he could win them over to the exchange. In their minds, the Middle East was a place of war and destitution; the minute they saw Dubai, they'd realize how far off base they were.

Of course, simply inviting the board to Dubai would never work. David himself had only gone to Dubai in the first place because Reston had pawned the initial invitation off on him. To get the board on an airplane to the Middle East, David and Khaled needed to come up with something too seductive to pass up.

It was Khaled who had finally come up with the perfect inducement. And once he'd cleared the details with the emir's people—who had jumped at the chance to show Dubai off to a new group of skeptical Americans—David and Harriet had gone to work on the invitations. They'd embarked on the project entirely in secret; not even Reston had known what they were up to in the conference room. David couldn't risk Gallo—or anyone else he couldn't entirely trust—finding out what he was up to. Not until he was ready to take things public.

Twenty-four hours ago, the invitations had finally gone out.

One for each board member—including Reston—and one extra, for the Don himself. In David's opinion, the invites were a work of pure art. Khaled's people had spared no expense. They'd hired the best calligrapher in New York and printed the entire thing in swirling fourteen-carat gold. David had spent so much time hovering over Harriet's shoulder as she checked and rechecked the lettering that he could still see the golden words whenever he closed his eyes:

His Highness Sheik Maktoum bin Rashid Al Maktoum, Ruler of Dubai, cordially invites you to be his personal guest at the Dubai World Cup, the world's richest horse race. All first-class accommodations and travel included.

As David watched Harriet cross his office, printout in hand, David once again mentally congratulated Khaled for his brilliance; in fact, his Arabic friend was more of a genius than even he had realized.

The Dubai World Cup—now just one week away, hosted by the emir at the spectacular Nad Al Sheba Race Course—was the world's biggest money horse race. The Merc Exchange, at its heart, was basically the world's most profitable casino. If there was one thing that men who gambled for a living loved, it was a good horse race. If anything was going to get these guys to Dubai, it was a personal invite to the Dubai World Cup.

"Here you go," Harriet said as she handed him the computer printout. "All the RSVPs are in and accounted for."

David was almost afraid to look at the paper in his hands. He had spent the entire morning pacing back and forth in his office, biting his nails at the thought of this moment. The only distraction had been a quick phone call from Vitzi, down on the trading floor, inviting him out for a night of unrelated celebration; as it turned out, Vitzi had just made a killing in crude in the first fifteen minutes after the opening bell—nearly half a million dollars in sheer profit. A few of the meatheads were going to party at some club in the Flatiron District, and they'd demanded that David come along.

David hadn't known if he'd be in any mood to celebrate, but he couldn't turn Vitzi down; after all, he'd worked hard to get the traders to accept him as one of their own. One more night out with the gang wasn't going to kill him.

Then again, as he finally got up the nerve to scan the computer printout, running his eyes down the long list of board members' names, maybe by the end of the day he'd have already killed himself.

His chest fell as he scanned the list a second time; nope, he'd seen right: out of all thirty board members, only three had check marks by their names. *Christ.*

"I guess that's that," David said grimly. *All that work. For nothing.*

Harriet just laughed at him.

"David, I put check marks next to the board members who turned the invite *down.*"

David looked up from the printout. Harriet grinned at him.

Holy shit.

The board was going to Dubai.

Chapter 40

Ten A.M.

The scorching desert sun already high in the cloudless sky.

Somewhere in the sand, a scorpion crawled through the mind-numbing heat. Inch by inch, the insect made its way forward—a strange little symphony of churning claws and outstretched pinchers, the coordinated effort of a prehistoric brain and nervous system a million years beyond their expiration date. A brain so small, the scorpion did not notice as the sand gave way to hard, black pavement. A nervous system so primitive, the scorpion could not detect the hawk plunging out of the sky directly up above, talons raised for the kill.

Nor would the scorpion ever know how at the very last minute the hawk aborted its dive, with a twist of its magnificent wings, as it suddenly caught sight of the fleet of fifteen silver BMW limousines hurtling down the deserted highway at ninety miles per hour. How one minute the scorpion was there, crawling across the asphalt, and the next minute it was gone, in a blast of revving engines and steaming hot rubber.

Inside the lead BMW, David Russo was having a hell of a time pouring the champagne. Managing three crystal chutes with one hand while uncorking a bottle of Dom with the other was difficult enough, but attempting the feat at ninety miles per hour, while the limo's tires squealed beneath him—each curve in the paved highway tilting his entire world—was nearly impossible. After three attempts, David finally gave up. Truth be told, the champagne was just overkill. The expressions on Nick Reston's and Alex Mendelson's faces—when they weren't smashed up against the tinted windows, watching the desert flash by—said it all.

From the moment Reston, Mendelson, and the twenty-eight board members who'd accompanied David on the journey halfway around the world stepped out of the jetway at the Dubai International Airport and first caught sight of the line of fifty white-robed Arabs waiting to collect them and their bags, they'd all fallen into a near-catatonic silence—but when they'd been ushered outside, just in time to watch the fleet of fifteen silver BMW limousines pull into the receiving circle, they'd erupted in exclamations of pure amazement. Certainly, the first-class cabin of Emirates Air had prepared the board for a luxurious arrival, but none of them—not even David—could have predicted that the emir's personal fleet would be waiting to take them into the city.

Now the desert was screaming by on either side of David's lead BMW limo, and Reston and Mendelson were pinned to those windows in anticipation. David could only assume that the rest of the board members, split up between the other cars in the caravan, were reacting with the same sense of wonder. Even Gallo—alone in the last car, by his own choice—would have had to agree: so far, the experience that was Dubai almost defied description.

David grinned to himself as the BMW tilted thirty degrees— the tires skidding over another high curve—and then the city appeared before them in all its glistening glory.

"My God," Reston said.

David knew exactly what Reston was feeling. David looked

from the Texan to Mendelson and saw the same childlike expression flash across the older man's wide face.

"Wait until we get closer," David said. "It only gets bigger as you get closer."

"What the hell is this place?" Mendelson asked. "And why isn't it on the news every day?"

David shrugged, grinning even harder. If Mendelson was even mildly bothered that he was in an Arab country—in a sheik's car, no less—he certainly wasn't showing it. He seemed completely swept up by the excitement of their arrival—and really, they hadn't even actually *arrived* yet.

According to Khaled, the BMWs were just the beginning. Over the next few hours the board members were going to get a full tour of the city. They were going to see everything: the massive shopping malls, the indoor ski slope, the magnificent zoo, the world-renowned indoor sports complex, the under-construction Palm and World Islands—and of course, the financial center, the free zone where the Dubai exchange would be located. When they were done with the tour, they were going to be checked in to two floors of the Emirates Tower, where David had stayed on his last visit—each member in his own lavishly appointed two-floor suite. The board would have full run of the city—with everything paid for by the emir himself—until the cars came to collect them once again for the short trip over to the racetrack.

"It's amazing," Reston continued as the BMW accelerated again, settling in for the last few miles sprinting into the heart of the City of Gold. "Look at all the fucking cranes. It's like a scene out of *Star Wars*."

David nodded. It really was like watching a Hollywood movie unfold in front of your eyes. So far his plan was working perfectly—and it was only ten A.M. If all continued to go well, by midafternoon—when the board arrived at the racetrack ten miles outside of the city—David and Khaled would be palpably close to fulfilling the dream that had driven them for the past four months. And if the horse race itself lived up to Khaled's description, there was no way the board was going to turn its back on Dubai.

The BMWs were impressive, the city itself spectacular—but from what Khaled had told David, the Dubai World Cup was really going to blow the board members' minds.

THE ENTIRE OPEN-AIR stadium shook as fifty thousand people leapt to their feet and a great roar rose up into the bright afternoon sky. Down below, the horses were a blur of flesh and muscle; nostrils flared, long legs churning, the tiny jockeys bent impossibly forward against the horses' great, undulating backs, the details of who was first and second and third lost in a minor tornado of chalk, red dirt, and sweat. But David didn't really care about the horses, even though he was up on his feet and shouting with the rest of the crowd, the adrenaline racing through his veins, his arms pumping wildly into the air.

The view from the emir's royal viewing box—uncovered, regally carpeted, and extended twenty rows up above the circular track—was unmatched. The twenty-eight board members—plus Gallo, David, and Khaled—were spread out across four rows of cushioned seats, but not a one of them was still seated. They were all like David—alive and on fire with the heat of the crowd, the spectacle of the event. To call it a horse race did not do the Dubai World Cup justice; it was a true happening, a lavish affair down to the dress of the crowd—jackets and ties for the men, expensive gowns for the women—and the beauty of the stadium itself, a marble and gold complex that would have thrilled even the most jaded Caesar of Rome.

"This is unreal!" one of the board members shouted from the row in front of David.

"This is Dubai," Khaled responded, from David's right. Khaled was the only Arab in the royal box with them—the emir himself had chosen to watch the event from somewhere nearer to the track, since a pair of his own horses were in the competition—and

Khaled had been more than a good host during the first few hours of the event, enduring the ribald conversational style of the ex-traders, their profanity-laden vocabularies, and their common use of cultural stereotypes. But as the excitement of the race multi-plied toward the current crescendo, Khaled seemed to have been swept up right along with them. His usually serene expression had cracked wide open, and now he was smiling as wildly as David, so enraptured with the moment that he hadn't noticed the two bodyguards of the emir until they had reached the velvet rope that separated the royal box from the rest of the stadium. Without a word of explanation, the bodyguards gestured toward the board members to follow.

The next thing David knew, the whole lot of them were being led down the stone steps that bisected the stands—and right out onto the field. Before he could even compute what was going on, he was standing in the winner's circle shoulder to shoulder with all twenty-eight board members, Khaled, Gallo, the emir's royal family, and, a few feet away, flanked by his attendants, the emir himself.

From the field, the roar was deafening. Flashbulbs were going off like firecrackers, the crowd's applause echoing off the marble, stone, and gold like thunder, and the horses whinny-ing and pawing at the grass in the background. David just took it all in—the stadium, the audience, the emir. Then his atten-tion moved to the board members' faces. Every one of them was flushed and smiling, caught up in the moment. Even Gallo, near the back of the crowd, had a look of amusement on his gnarled old face. Reston and Mendelson were right up next to the emir, sandwiched between two of the oversized bodyguards, posing for pictures, grinning like they'd both just won the World Cup themselves.

David turned back to the crowd and let the applause of fifty thousand people wash over him. The way he felt inside, they might as well have been clapping for him instead of a horse, con-gratulating him for what he'd achieved. Italians, Jews, Arabs, all joined together—the beginning of something truly new.

David was certain it was a moment that every board member, and Gallo, would remember for the rest of his life.

BACK AT THE HOTEL, the celebration continued out on the stone patio that encircled the massive, temperature-controlled swimming pool. The pool area was like an oasis: clear blue water surrounded by potted palm trees, oversized umbrellas, reclining deck chairs, a well-stocked juice bar, and an outdoor Mediterranean restaurant nearby, some high-class place with "Mosaic" in its name and an actual tiled mosaic for a floor. In fact, it was the Middle East's largest mosaic, according to Khaled, who hadn't returned with them from the race, opting instead to accompany the royal family to a private affair in the nearby Burj Al Arab. The Emirate Tower pool was brightly lit both from below and above, despite the long shadow cast by the early evening sun as it crossed behind the massive tower. From David's vantage, lying back against a deck chair with a mango juice in one hand and a towel in the other, it was easy to believe that the great hotel and office tower was indeed the tallest building in the Middle East—Europe as well, for that matter—and the third-tallest hotel in the world.

A much lower shadow interrupted David's thoughts, and he moved his attention from the tower to Mendelson and Reston, who were suddenly standing over him, fancy juice drinks in their hands, grins on their faces. For the first time, they weren't acting like David's superiors; they were acting like his friends, and it was a great feeling. Likewise, the other board members who were lounging nearby, on deck chairs and in the pool and over at the outdoor restaurant, had all been treating David the same way all afternoon, ever since they'd returned to the hotel from the race-track. David hadn't been this popular since high school—and he was loving every minute of it.

"Maybe they'll elect you sheik," Reston joked as he took a seat on a chair next to David's. "Get you some nice robes, let you run the Merc in New York and the one here at the same time. I'd be happy to stay by the pool and soak up the sun for a few years."

"You know the desert sun's not good for you," Mendelson joked back, sitting next to Reston on the lounge chair. "Shrivels you up in no time. Look what it did to him."

Mendelson gestured over his shoulder, and David strained his neck just in time to lock eyes with Gallo, who was sitting by himself under an umbrella on the far side of the pool. Gallo waved his ever-present cigar, and David grimaced; he'd kind of hoped to avoid running into Gallo until they were all back in New York and the board had actually put the vote on record—but maybe this was as good a time as any to get this over with.

"Whoops," Reston said, realizing that Mendelson's joke had just put David in Gallo's path. "Looks like the shriveled Don has got you in his sights."

David sighed.

"I guess it's time to go kiss his ring again, eh?"

Reston grinned.

"Better you than me, Harvard boy."

David took his time making his way across the patio, shaking hands with board members as he went. As he approached, he noticed that Gallo had actually combed his hair for the first time since they'd met and was still wearing his jacket and tie from the horse race as he sprawled out on the deck chair. Thankfully, the jacket wasn't zebra-striped; it was gray and sallow, almost the same color as the man's wrinkled face.

"You think this changes anything?" Gallo started right in as David finally reached his side. "You got 'em all hot and bothered out here in the sand, and you think now you're running the show?"

Despite Gallo's bravado, David could see it in his pitted eyes as the old trader lay there on the deck chair: Gallo knew that the Dubai exchange was a done deal. He could make a stink all he wanted, but the board was going to vote in David's favor. There was nothing Gallo could do to change that.

David looked right at him. He decided it was finally time to tell the man what he really thought.

"Fuck you, Mr. Gallo."

For a brief moment, it looked like Gallo was about to swallow his cigar. Then he coughed, took the cigar out of his mouth, and shook his head. When he looked up at David again, he was smiling.

"Okay, congratulations, kid. I underestimated you."

But it was obvious from the way he said the words that he wasn't really conceding anything. After all, this was still the same guy who had confronted David in a butcher's shop and shown him pictures taken surreptitiously of him and his girlfriend. This was the same bastard who had filled David's hospital room with enemas after David had nearly died during his first board meeting.

Gallo wasn't going to stand in the way of the Dubai exchange—but he was still the Don. Still, David didn't care. He was finished kissing the man's ring.

"Yeah, well, it happens. I hope you enjoy the rest of your trip. And try to stay out of the sun. You look like hell."

David started back across the patio toward Reston and the other board members. He'd made it less than five feet before Gallo called out after him.

"You just watch your back," the old man said.

David continued walking as Gallo added, almost under his breath:

"Because you know I'll be watching, kid. I'm always watching."

Chapter 41

Eight hours later—and at thirty thousand feet—David's celebration was still in full swing. He wasn't sure which of the board members had smuggled the six bottles of Dom into the Emirates Air first-class cabin, but Reston was doing the pouring, Mendelson was strolling up and down the aisles handing out the glasses, and David certainly wasn't complaining. Even though there was still a vote to be taken and a whole lot of practical negotiations to go, David knew that the tide was moving in his favor. The board members had been charmed by Dubai, and they wouldn't have any reason to stand in the way of a Dubai exchange that would inevitably make them all a lot of money and raise the profile of the Merc. The traders, for their part, would have to see that their little monopoly in Lower Manhattan needed to open itself up to globalization, and this was the first step in a new way of looking at the commerce of oil. The Dubai exchange wouldn't be competing with them, since it would focus on a different form of oil contract; instead, it would be a region-uniting complement that would raise energy currency to a whole new level.

David was so pleased with himself—and so swept up in the

moment—that it wasn't until he stood up out of his seat to match Reston's toast that he noticed something suddenly unnerving. He was halfway out of his first-class mini-compartment, his glass raised in front of him, when his eyes swept past Reston and Mendelson to what appeared to be an empty seat at the back of the first-class cabin.

David was certain that the cabin had been full on the flight over from New York. He started to count off faces in his mind— and realized, with a start, which one of his travel companions was missing. In that instant, his feeling of victory suddenly dissipated, and a cold fear rose in his stomach. He didn't know what the empty seat really meant, but he was certain it was more than significant.

For whatever reason, Dominick Gallo was not on board.

He had stayed behind in Dubai.

IT DIDN'T TAKE long for David to realize what had happened.

He had just passed through customs at JFK and was walking heavily behind Reston and Mendelson through the international terminal when he noticed the group of six board members about ten feet ahead of him. He couldn't be sure which of the men had first noticed the bank of TVs hanging from the ceiling above the gate waiting area, but by the time David sidled up next to Reston behind them, they had all gone dead silent, watching what was unfolding on the screens above.

It took David less than a second to see that the televisions were all set to the CNN Financial Network. Since they were still in the Emirates Air section of the terminal, David had no trouble figuring out why.

The scene on the TV screens seemed to be live—or at least recorded very recently. David immediately recognized the two sheiks, Maktoum and Muhammed, standing together on a raised platform in front of the newly christened financial center where the Dubai exchange would one day break ground. But the two sheiks did not hold David's attention for very long. Because standing right next to them, beaming up at the cameras with an expression of painfully uncharacteristic delight, stood Dominick Gallo. Though the sound was turned off on the television sets, a ticker running along the bottom of the screen told David everything he needed to know.

"Dominick Gallo, philanthropist, energy specialist, and the leading trader at the New York Mercantile Exchange, is partnering with the emir of Dubai to launch the first-ever energy exchange in the Middle East," David summarized, his voice dull in his own ears. "And he's personally bringing over a team of his traders to be the first to work the floor."

Reston put a hand on David's shoulder.

"That fucker. Well, look at the bright side, kid. This means the traders aren't going to stand in the board's way. You got your exchange."

David closed his eyes, his mind racing as he listened to the other board members mumbling angrily to each other beneath the TV screens. Reston was right: David and Khaled *had* succeeded. The Dubai exchange would one day be a reality. Gallo had known that it was a battle he couldn't win, so he had found another way: he had adapted and stolen the board's thunder by announcing it first. But did that really change anything? David had still done something important. In the end, that was what really mattered—wasn't it?

David opened his eyes and looked back up at the television screens. The camera focused in on the sheiks, then panned back to Gallo. And for a brief second it seemed like Gallo was looking straight down at David.

In that second, all David saw was a dark little butcher shop in Brooklyn reflected in the ancient trader's deep-set eyes.

Chapter 42

Even during takeoff, the hundred-million-dollar jet's twin Rolls Royce engines were whisper-quiet, more a whir than a roar. Khaled closed his eyes, letting the acceleration and the angle of the cabin push his body deep into the reclined leather seat, as he tried to picture the shiny, rocketlike airplane cutting upward through the atmosphere—a futuristic, winged machine thrusting away from an equally futuristic City of Gold, carrying him where the cranes and the skyscrapers could never reach.

Then he opened his eyes, turned toward the circular window to his right, and watched as the city receded, just as he'd imagined it in his mind—shrinking but still fabulous, glistening even until the very last skyscraper vanished from his view behind a thick soup of clouds.

Khaled smiled, warmed by the sight of the city, his thoughts finally turning to David and to what they had, together, achieved.

After the horse race, Khaled had spent twenty minutes with the emir, discussing the Dubai Mercantile Exchange. He had been surprised when his discussion was interrupted by Gallo—but he had understood, almost instinctively, that it was really just a sign of how fully he and David had indeed succeeded. He hoped David understood as well; with Gallo acquiescing and the board of the Merc firmly in support of the project, there was nothing to stand in their way. It would take a few years to complete the construction of the building and to hire the right staff to run the place—but it was now an inevitability. *The emir did not start projects he could not finish.* And when the Dubai Mercantile Exchange finally opened—when that soccer stadium in the sand showed the world what the Middle East was really capable of— Khaled could only guess what might come next. The future, for once, seemed wide open.

Khaled turned away from the window as the jet banked to the right, charting a course toward the Mediterranean. The sudden motion took him by surprise, and he had to move quickly to keep the two manila envelopes on his lap from slipping down to the carpeted floor. As the plane leveled off at its new altitude—just above the tops of the clouds, racing forward through bright blue sky—Khaled lifted the two envelopes and turned them over, one at a time, in his brown hands.

Both envelopes were sealed, and had been since Ali Agha handed them to Khaled two days ago in his office at the Ministry of Finance. Khaled decided it was finally time to see what they contained.

He chose between the two at random and went to work on the first envelope's seal. It came apart easily, and Khaled carefully removed a pair of five-by-seven black-and-white photographs. The first photo was grainy, but still quite easy to make out. It had a time-code in one corner, and it showed three unidentified men heading into the Mercantile Exchange building in Lower Manhattan. The three men were wearing zebra-striped jackets.

Khaled turned his attention to the second black-and-white photo. This one was a little less grainy, as if the photographer had finally gained control of his lens. The second photo also had a time-code in one corner—and clearly showed David Russo heading into the Mercantile Exchange building, not five minutes behind the three zebra-jacketed men.

Khaled knew who had taken the photos, and why. Ali Agha had reacted quickly, calling Khaled the minute he'd snapped the shots, saving the evidence for later. Khaled was glad Agha had acted on his instincts. If Agha hadn't been there—Khaled shrugged to himself. There was no way to contemplate a past that hadn't happened.

Mysteries within mysteries—what was real, and what was imagined? The three men in the photo were dressed as traders. It was unlikely that traders would congregate on the trading floor after-hours, but not unheard of. It was unlikely, but not impossible, that they would happen to be on the trading floor the same evening David had mysteriously arrived—also after-hours.

Khaled would never know for certain—but in the end, did it really matter? No doubt, David's enemies had gone a lot further to try to stop him than either Khaled or the young American would ever know. But still David and Khaled had succeeded— and those very enemies were now reluctant allies. It was assuredly out of any of their hands. The Dubai exchange was a living, breathing part of the City of Gold.

Without another thought, Khaled leaned forward and opened a compartment attached to the table in front of his seat. From inside, there emerged a quiet whirring of mechanical gears. His uncle's private jet wasn't just one of the most luxurious and fastest airplanes in existence—it was also a sort of moving office, outfitted with all the necessities that that implied. Computer terminals with online access along one wall. Flat-screen TVs with satellite receivers hanging from the ceiling. And a paper shredder, embedded in the table in front of Khaled, always charged and ready to receive.

Khaled took the two photos and fed them one at a time into the shredder. As he did so, his thoughts drifted to the next few days, then beyond, to his immediate future. First, he'd spend at least a week on his uncle's yacht, relaxing. After that, he wasn't really sure. Maybe he'd return to Dubai, back to his job with the Ministry of Finance. Or perhaps he'd ask his uncle to send him somewhere else. There were still so many parts of the world he wanted to see. He was certain there were more projects to be contemplated—more ways to continue making a difference, repaying his debts. His father had never been a man who felt comfortable staying in one place for very long; Khaled wondered if it was indeed a heritable trait.

As the jet continued to soar through the sky, Khaled finished with the two photographs and the paper shredder and reached for the second manila envelope. The second seal also came open easily, and Khaled removed yet another stack of photographs—five to be exact. Unlike the first set, these photos were in surprisingly good focus—especially considering that they had been taken from quite a distance and in the middle of the night.

Khaled leafed through the stack, his expression darkening.

Ali Agha hadn't taken these pictures; he had stolen them from the desk of a man who worked in the same building as David. Khaled paused over the least graphic of the set.

The photo had been taken from the side, by way of a telephoto lens. The two subjects were clearly visible—in fact, the shot was so clean that Khaled could make out every inch of bare skin, and it took him less than a second to identify the people in the photo: David Russo and the girl named Jasmine, intertwined in the snow on the banks of Lake Geneva.

That such a photo existed was disturbing enough, but to Khaled there was something even more bothersome about the shot. It wasn't just professionally done—it was so perfect that it almost seemed staged. *As if the photographer had known exactly where to be—and when.*

Khaled stared at the photo for a full beat, then finally shrugged his shoulders. All in the past, he repeated to himself. Did it do any good to dwell on mysteries that no longer mattered?

As the jet banked one more time, then settled into a comfortable cruising altitude, Khaled took the second stack of photographs and carefully fed them, one at a time, into the shredder.

EPILOGUE

The minute David stepped out of the taxicab and onto the sidewalk that ran past the brand-new, ten-story, black glass office building on Fifty-second between Park and Madison, he knew something wasn't right. It was more than just a feeling: the thought had been building since he'd received the text from Reston's BlackBerry—this time confirmed and reconfirmed—telling him to meet the Texan at the unknown address and to bring a notepad with him. And now that he'd arrived, a little after noon on a brisk April Tuesday, he could see that his premonition had been correct. It was obvious from the way Reston was smiling at him as he stood in front of the glass revolving doors that led into the building. And it was doubly obvious from the fact that Reston had not informed David that it wasn't going to be just the two of them—that in fact Reston would not be alone in front of the revolving doors. Anthony Giovanni was standing right next to him, dressed in a perfectly tailored three-piece suit, hands outstretched as he watched David approach from the curb.

"And there he is, the man of the hour. Looks like our boy's all grown up, Nicky."

David laughed as he reached the two men, exchanging Italian hugs and Wall Street handshakes.

"So you pulled it off," Giovanni continued. "Nicky tells me the board was unanimous. Even Gallo put his claw mark in the ballot box. Not that it was any surprise—considering he'd already announced the project to the world media. But even so, quite an accomplishment, kid. A Merc exchange in Dubai. That's gotta be a cause for celebration."

David grinned. In truth, he was still recovering from the extended dinner and drinks session from the night before. Serena had surprised him by reserving a private room at one of their favorite Italian restaurants for the affair and inviting not only Vitzi and the gang but also—throwing David for a real loop—his mom and dad from Staten Island. Seeing his dad there enjoying the evening like everyone else had been a wonderful experience for David. It almost made him forget that Gallo had stolen the lion's share of the credit for the work he and Khaled had done. And when his dad had told him that he intended to go to Dubai with David when the exchange opened in a few years' time—to see firsthand what his son had accomplished—it had been beyond moving. The idea of his dad being able to get on a plane, to visit the Middle East—that would be the greatest gift David could imagine.

"Would have loved to have seen you guys there last night," David said, back in the present. "Serena said she tried to get you both to come—"

"We were a little busy," Reston interrupted, jerking his thumb toward the black glass office building behind him. "Working out a few minor details."

David raised his eyebrows. He looked from Reston to Giovanni, then back to the Texan.

"Don't tell me. You're leaving the Merc too?"

Reston smiled.

"David, Anthony and I just leased the top two floors of this building. We're going into business together. We're starting a company—pooling what we know about oil and the contacts we've developed. We've raised a nice chunk of working capital, and now we're going to change the world of energy, one step at a time."

David's eyes widened. Reston and Giovanni in private business together. Reston seemed purposefully vague about the nature of their company, but David had no doubt that together the two men certainly could change the world of energy. David wasn't sure what Reston meant by "a nice chunk of working capital," but he was fascinated just the same.

"And I suppose you want me to come work for you?"

Giovanni reached out and put a hand on David's shoulder.

"No, kid. We want you to be our partner."

David opened his mouth, but no words came out. He was twenty-six years old. He simply didn't know what to say. Reston winked at him as Giovanni moved past the Texan and disappeared through the glass revolving doors. David finally found his voice as he glanced down at the object in his own hands.

"So what's the notepad for?"

Reston grinned.

"What do you think it's for? To take notes, Harvard boy. You might be a partner, but that doesn't make you an equal. Write and walk, kid, that's how you learn in this business."

With that, Reston turned and followed Giovanni through the revolving glass doors, leaving David alone on the sidewalk— notebook in hand.

FIFTY YARDS AWAY and four stories up, a figure dressed entirely in black crouched low behind a partially obscured plate-glass window. The figure watched through a telescopic lens as David Russo tucked his notebook under his arm, stepped into the revolving door, and disappeared into the office building across the street.

When Russo was gone, the figure leaned back from the window—and for an instant a reflection flashed across the sheer glass pane. Though the lighting was bad and the figure was moving, for the briefest of seconds the image in the window was remarkably clear:

A woman, a high-powered camera, and a swirl of jet-black hair.

AFTERWORD
by John D'Agostino

Walking into the New York Mercantile Exchange for the first time was an exhilarating experience. Immortalized in the movie *Trading Places*, the sounds and energy are unmatched on Wall Street—or anywhere else in the world. While U.S. business may be run in the quiet halls of investment banks, when you walk onto the floor of the exchange, you just can't help feeling that this is where the action is. Screaming men and women move millions of gallons of virtual crude oil from one place to another and back again. At the end of each day, when the pits are empty, the place is eerily quiet, and the floor is littered with torn trading tickets, a single, lonely LED panel displays one of the most important numbers in the global economy—the closing price of crude oil on the NYMEX.

Even a casual observer of the trading floor, after a few moments acclimating to what seems like overwhelming chaos, begins to sense an incredibly well-orchestrated dance. Whether credit for this should be given to the traders themselves or to the chaos theory that explains the harmony of motion exhibited by ants is up to debate. What's undeniable is that when you sit and watch the floor for any length of time, you start to understand why Wall Street rules the universe.

There's a saying that an MBA and two bucks will get you a bus ticket. At the exchange, it's worth even less. The floor is the realm of the self-made man—a place where education, race, gender, and religion all take a backseat to one's ability to buy low and sell high more often than the reverse. What's a Harvard MBA against the wisdom that comes from making or losing a BMW in five seconds? It was hard not to feel I had wasted my tuition money when a young trader summed up the esoteric topic of risk management in the best way I have ever heard by quoting Mike Tyson: "Everybody has a plan until they get punched in the face."

A grizzled veteran, seeing me stare at the floor like a deer in the headlights, summed it all up when he whispered to me, "It's the best business in the world—if you can figure out a way to stay in it."

THE LEADERSHIP OF Dubai showed incredible perspicacity in pushing ahead with the project of creating the Dubai Mercantile Exchange. While the region is known for its excess, the DME represents a progressive move leagues ahead of any seven-star hotel or indoor ski slope. Exchanges are the essence of capitalism. To take the essence of capitalism, drop it into the Middle East, and begin pricing *crude oil* using free-market principles is quite simply visionary.

In the context of Wall Street and Dubai, this deal was not a large one. Massive, multibillion-dollar buyouts and development projects seemed to be the norm in Dubai—and certainly no major investment bank in New York would have gotten excited over the numbers we were negotiating over. Yet somehow everyone intuitively understood that this project's importance for the region and—though it's hard to say without sounding grandiose—*the world* was significant.

I've stayed in close contact with the phenomenal teams that took over where I left off. As the launch date draws closer, a very predictable split has emerged between the geographies/ entities that are supporting the project and those that are ambivalent or even hostile. A few large investment banks with energy trading arms have taken a predictably antagonistic attitude toward the exchange. I understand why. Price transparency is good for all—but bad for some. Specifically, it's bad for those who have made very good livings off the lack of transparent pricing.

Without a *clear* and *accessible* reference price, intermediaries are in a powerful position to profit. Let's say you live in a place where it is impossible to buy or import olive oil, but there is a plentiful local supply of corn oil. Let's also assume that these are the only types of oil that exist. The producers and buyers of that corn oil won't be exactly sure how to price the product. They can use the price of olive oil in another land as a reference. That is a *clear* price. But it's not *accessible,* since the olive oil cannot be imported. So if you are lucky enough to establish yourself as the intermediary—helping sellers find buyers and vice versa—you can constantly work to maximize the value of your spread by convincing sellers that the price should be slightly lower and convincing buyers of the opposite.

Without a clear and accessible reference, intermediaries can have a virtual information *monopoly*—even better pricing information than the market principals (producers and consumers) themselves. Some of the groups have spent years building relationships in the Middle East sour crude market. A few of them made the same protest when the NYMEX began trading crude oil. I don't begrudge them resistance to something that will fundamentally change how they do business in the region. However, all good things must come to an end.

Over the last two years, the public markets began to appreciate the exchange business model. Numerous buyouts, consolidations, and public offerings with earnings multiples similar to those of high-tech growth companies blew through the NASDAQ and NYSE. Some saw a bubble, though it's important to remember that exchanges are by their nature a limited pool of entities. Despite the attractiveness of the sector, no amount of venture capital money can guarantee the success of a start-up exchange.

IN LATE 2006, the NYMEX gave in to overwhelming market pressure and launched side-by-side trading—effectively pitting the open-outcry traders against the screen and setting up the final fight over which trading methodology would prevail. While most industry pundits seemed smugly confident that the speed and efficiency of electronic trading would render the pit traders extinct in months—and they are probably right—at the time of this book's publication the final outcome has yet to be determined.

Correspondingly, in the last few years the public markets have "discovered" everything we knew about commodities exchanges. Incredible exchange IPOs with fantastic multiples and Google-like stock trajectories seem to be happening every day. NYMEX's initial public offering was the most successful of the previous *six years*. The New York Board of Trade sold for $1.3 billion—a high-tech company multiple being applied to forward earnings. Suddenly, it is so obvious. Who wouldn't want to invest in the entity that makes money whether prices go up or down, whether traders go broke or make money? Who wouldn't want to own "the house"?

The public market may grant large rewards—but it also has strong demands. Exchanges that moved at their own pace for 125 years have suddenly found themselves staring down the barrel of the Jim Cramer crowd, with demands for aggressive growth into markets, scalability, and emphasis on the bottom line. Open-outcry was the low-hanging fruit. High-cost, not so scalable, antiquated, and prone to ridicule—those crazy traders and brokers running around the floor in their colored jackets just didn't *feel* right in the new, modern world of the exchange.

But for those of us who saw them in their heyday, the move to electronic trading is bittersweet. I left Harvard Business School loaded for bear with a copy of Milton Friedman under my arm. I believed in truth, justice, and corporate efficiency. Yes, electronic trading is more efficient—at least, for plain-vanilla front-month contracts—but there is a reason the design for the spoon hasn't changed since the day of the caveman. It works.

The changing of the guard will, and should, happen. Computers have more horsepower, make fewer mistakes, and are morally incorruptible—but when it comes to recognizing nonlinear patterns amid volumes of constantly changing data with numerous and sometimes *emotional* variables, humans are still competitive. There's a reason it took so long for a machine to beat Kasporov—and chess is a more mathematically *solvable* game than energy trading.

If you don't agree, please try to write an algorithm to predict the downward or upward movement in natural gas prices resulting from a pipeline explosion in Louisiana, or the reaction of oil prices to a picture of the president holding hands with the Saudi oil minister. Energy is one of the few things we trade with *constant demand*. You can stop buying jewelry when gold prices get too high, you can stop buying Google stock when it hits six hundred dollars . . . but it's hard to stop driving to work and watching TV. Until we trade elements, air (carbon credits), and water, nothing like it exists.

The DME is scheduled to trade its first contract in the second quarter of 2007. No one can predict whether the market will flourish or founder. It's likely that, despite the fanfare, the contract will struggle in the early days as participants test out the liquidity. That is natural. Unlike some recent first-day successes, this is a brand-new contract, with little carryover from existing liquid markets.

On November 14, 2006, the Sultanate of Oman adopted the historic policy of allowing its crude oil to be priced using the daily settlement of the Oman sour crude contract at the DME. Around the same time, Oman decided to purchase an equal share of the DME, making NYMEX, Dubai, and Oman partners. Oman was, from the beginning, the wild card. Without its support, the DME is a soccer field with players but no ball. Its commitment is a tremendous boost to the probability of the DME's long-term success.

Both Dubai and NYMEX have a history of getting things right. If they get this one right, they will have made history.

John D'Agostino
New York City
January 2007

ACKNOWLEDGMENTS

Many thanks to Mauro DiPreta, Lisa Gallagher, and Jennifer Schulkind for helping me make this book my best one yet. Once again, I am also indebted to David Vigliano, Mike Harriot, and Matthew Snyder, the best team of agents any writer could ever hope for. Enormous thanks also to Dana Brunetti and Kevin Spacey, and my entire family at Triggerstreet, who continue to make my life much more exciting than I ever expected it to be.

As always, I am incredibly grateful to my parents, brothers, and their families for their constant support. And to my incredible family in Boston—Tonya, Bugsy, and yes, that damn bird too—I couldn't do what I do without you. I truly believe I'm the luckiest guy I know.